John Carroll

Sceptical sociology

ROUTLEDGE & KEGAN PAUL
London, Boston and Henley

First published in 1980
by Routledge & Kegan Paul Ltd
39 Store Street, London WC1E 7DD,
9 Park Street, Boston, Mass. 02108 USA and
Broadway House, Newtown Road,
Henley-on-Thames, Oxon RG9 1EN
Set in 10/12 Sabon by
Oxprint, Oxford
and printed in Great Britain by
Page Bros (Norwich) Ltd
Norwich and London

British Library Cataloguing in Publication Data

Carroll, John, b. 1944

Sceptical sociology.
1. Sociology
I. Title
301   HM51

ISBN 0 7100 0587 3

Dedicated to Ormond College (University of Melbourne)
and its Master (1959–79), Dr J. D. McCaughey

Contents

Preface

This book is a collection of essays, written to a theme. In addition to all the usual vanities and obsessions that drive people to write books I have been stirred by the belief that sociology since 1918 has tended to make the world as dull as it is at its worst, and this tendency needs reversing. My second animating belief is that sociology lost contact with the great metaphysical questions that elevate men's lives, that precipitate crisis and that underlie feelings of success or failure – Tolstoy's questions of how to live and what to do. From there I have tried to develop a sceptical sociology. The first essay spells out the programme and the following ten attempt to put it into practice. The twelfth essay apologizes.

For their various contributions I am indebted to Lynne Cooke, Anthony Giddens, Alvin Gouldner, Agnes Heller, David Hickman, Bobbie Lederman, Graham Lederman, Robert Manne, Elizabeth Pittman, and above all to Freya Headlam. Many ideas sprang from conversations with Charlotte Zinn von Zinnenberg.

Acknowledgments

Several of these essays have appeared in journals. The author and publishers would like to thank the following: the editor of *Quadrant* for permission to reprint 'Shopping World: the palace of modern consumption', 'Automobile culture and citizenship' and 'The sceptic turns consumer: an outline of Australian culture'; the editor of *Theory and Society* for permission to reprint 'In spite of intellectuals'; the editor of the *Journal of Philosophy of Education* for permission to reprint 'Authority and the teacher'.

1 Sceptical sociology

Preamble

In a word, human life is more governed by fortune than by reason; is to be regarded more as a dull pastime than a serious occupation; and is more influenced by particular humour, than by general principles. Shall we engage ourselves in it with passion and anxiety? It is not worthy of so much concern. Shall we be indifferent about what happens? We lose all the pleasure of the game by our phlegm and carelessness. While we are reasoning concerning life, life is gone; and death, though perhaps they receive him differently, yet treats alike the fool and the philosopher. To reduce life to exact rule and method is commonly a painful, oft a fruitless occupation: And is it not also a proof, that we overvalue the prize for which we contend? Even to reason so carefully concerning it, and to fix with accuracy its just idea, would be overvaluing it, were it not that, to some tempers, this occupation is one of the most amusing in which life could possibly be employed.

David Hume, 'The Sceptic'

It may well be late in the day in our civilization, but not in one of its late developers, our discipline, sociology. While many, with reason, regard that discipline as retarded, and therefore to be closed down and forgotten, there are grounds for reserving judgment a little longer. By and large sociology has, since 1918, taken false paths, or in cases in which it has shown more promise, not advanced very far. Nevertheless, our present offers avenues of endeavour to sociology, worthy enough to justify another enquiry into the mistakes of the past, and another attempt to establish a more fortunate method.

One of the marks of a decadent civilization is that it likes to indulge in introspection, to know where it is, and where it has come from, without much hope about where it is going or indeed much expectation that understanding that future might in any way improve things. Like an ageing person it focuses with mounting absorption on the process of its own decay. There is an important role here, in the heart of the reminiscing, for sociology, but not the type of sociology that has littered bookshops since the 1960s, and catered to the opposite, utopian craving.

Sociology has behaved rather like a parvenu, who has made money, due to some flair for the historical moment, and wanting to be valued by those of more cultivated taste, invests in the wrong things. His lack of background, his innate hostility to the authority of those by whom he wishes to be recognized, leads him into squandering large reserves of energy on fruitless activity. The three investments that have carried him astray are science, idealism, and social relevance. They have made him uninteresting, except in the minds of other parvenus, who, when true to type, are blind to all but the glitter of their own tinsel. (The social usefulness of business parvenus, whose dynamism boosts the society's economic product, has no equivalent in the cases of their academic counterparts.) Either garish or drab, this sociology's truths have not been piquant enough for our decadent civilization, which, at its best, craves for stimulation of a delicate type.

The three temptations that sociology fell for combined to ensure that it would produce so little of use as far as knowledge is concerned, and so many fiascos in application to real social problems, that we should now be glad to ditch them. We sociologists have managed to add another layer of fat to bureaucracies already wheezing with corpulence, by selling governments, councils, and even business corporations the line that our presence is indispensable. But we could not advise one person how best to organize one day in his life; somehow we thought that we should be better at masterminding abstract utopias for concrete masses. And what has sociology contributed to Western knowledge since its classics, since Tocqueville and Durkheim showed the positive role of constraint, since Marx explored some of the ways in which man is a social product, and since Weber demonstrated some of the dynamic links between ideas, personality, conduct and institutions! Where contributions to social theory have been made in recent times it has been by intellectuals on or beyond the margins of academic sociology

(Hannah Arendt, Philip Rieff, Clifford Geertz). Incidentally, the shrewdest of sociology's prophets, Tocqueville, was aloof from all three temptations.

Enough has been done since the classics for us to realize that our science is disastrously compromised, our idealism is either spent or so battered that its remaining output is intellectual incoherence, and our relevance has proved a flop. What is left for us to do, indeed what is demanded of us if we can still take ourselves seriously, is to take a cool, clear look at what we are, what we have done, and what we might be capable of, a look to be taken once the simplifications of the scientific eye, the glamorizations of the idealistic eye, and the guilt of the activist eye have, like cataracts, been removed. Our mood should be one of sanguine scepticism, our first aim to go back to first principles and spell out what constitutes human nature. And in our pursuit of the psychological disposition of Western man, and in our later sorties into personal, cultural and historical questions, we should not expect too much of our knowledge, remembering that our minds are feeble in the face of Goliath reality, and that doubt and wit lead one further away from falsehood than do dogma and piety. Which is not to mock all seriousness, but to ensure that the intellectual's traditional inclination towards righteous indignation in defence of his certitudes is put off-balance. The classical sceptics asserted the impossibility of knowledge; they rejected all dogmatisms; they suspended their judgment. Timon's goal was imperturbability of mind. This is extreme: what I am urging is a dose of the sceptic potion. Later sceptics modified their perspective into a general one of doubt, believing that experience provides the sole phenomena on which reason may operate.

Thus we might educate. Thus we might help our civilization to bow out with dignity. A sanguine scepticism will shed youthful idealism, and other commitments that are absurd at our time of life, and given our failing vitality; it will narrow the gap between what we believe and what we are. Just as some lives work, and some relationships are viable, and in many different ways, there is a manner of living well in each phase of life, and at each point on the arc of civilization. For us intellectuals today, the way is that of cool-headed realism, and the moral integrity available to one slightly distanced from his passions, but not so distanced that the flame has no warmth. We have a task, not an exciting one, but one that might bring some gratification. We may clown, but extravagance is no longer in us,

and we hanker, if there is any sense of vocation left, for understanding and for grace. Our decadence is highlighted in the delight
we take in piercing pretences, a frivolous activity in earlier times, but
for us central to our self-respect. Of course, what I am proposing is
an ideal in itself – but I hope the appropriate ideal, and one watched
by us sceptics for any hints of it starting to make a fool of itself.

There is no time to lose. Late in the day, we are somewhat in the
position of the ageing Casanova, who retains his passion for young
ladies, but finds his resources ravaged by time, and each new
conquest requiring even higher expenditures of craft and guile, of
energy. Before exhaustion catches up with us, and our goals lose
their seductiveness, we must act, not lusting high, rather settling for
the girl down the street. We could carry out a series of modest
projects with some distinction, and in putting them together arrive at
a quite impressive work. In any case, the grand works, the total
theories, the Olympian tracts, are deservedly out of fashion, and
should be left for the moths.

I am writing a kind of manifesto. As in all decadent times, there are
moments when the failing organism kicks out, finds a new lease of
life, and gaily believes that it has regained its old virility. Thus the
West in the 1960s experienced a decade of strident calls for revolution, of this and that. Manifestos were swarming, and were listened
to. What they seem to have served to quicken, however, is the end,
setting more dogs at the heels of the few productive forces that
remain in the society. Manifestos were the order of the day. Mine is
an anti-ideological manifesto, seeking to be cautious in its pieties,
airing its puzzlement at that quaint ambition, 'to revolutionize
society'. It is un-radical to the point of trying to expose the
illusoriness of the 'critical intellectual', he who stands back from
society, and works against its grain. Society is many-grained, and
those who take pride in their independence of judgment are following one grain whose path happens to diverge from some others; they
are of the same wood. An intellectual, like anyone, fits into the given
grains. Thus, in a time of manifestos, I write a manifesto, and such is
my wont. And the grain I wish to highlight is the one that I believe,
given the state of the wood, will show us off to best advantage, and
provide us sociologists with a sense of something still worth doing.
(It might be whispered that those who have something worth doing,
go ahead, without wasting time justifying themselves. Would that
still were true – in any case, part of my point is that we have entered a

period in which our worthy causes will feed off their own narcissism, and appear effete in their social consequences. One of our challenges is to make such self-indulgence dignified.)

Our time is dull enough. Oskar Kokoschka said just before his death that in his ninety years he had lived through many periods, but he had never known one as empty as the present. Sociology, as the intellectual fad of the period, has kept scrupulously to the tone demanded – tedium. In its barbaric jargon, in its legalistic syntax, in its statistical tables, in its obsession with the humdrum, it has made society as dull as it is at its worst. Indeed, sociology has exercised some skill in separating the yolk of contemporary man's egg, and poking around in the white. Such is a commonplace today about our discipline amongst all intellectuals apart from sociologists themselves. The last insult is that the better newspapers and television stations usually do a better job at interpreting the contemporary social world than do departments of academic sociologists. It is time for sociology to wake up, or give up the ghost altogether; time to kick its creaking skeleton, oil its brittle sinews, and see if it cannot discover a little to laugh at, a little to blush at, in our world.

1 Scepticism's classics

If we are to live thoughtfully we need the help of a past, and maybe several pasts. We need the cautioning image of a failed past, commanding us what not to do. We need equally an image of a virtuous past, or at least one that was similar enough to provide exemplary figures of some relevance, a past that we can scrutinize for clues about how to act, which turns to take, which passions to encourage, from which we can learn the likely consequences of different responses to a not too dissimilar reality. For this worthy past I think we should look to the English eighteenth century. It is attractive for its model political institutions, its growing affluence, and for its rather neglected brilliance in the field of social theory, and in particular of theorizing about its own change.

Eighteenth-century England is relevant in that, like our own time, it followed a century of dynamic moralistic Puritanism; it had to cope with living in the wake of a long period of ascetic idealism, of religious ferment, of radical social changes, and of violent wars. In that wake it experienced growing prosperity and growing disenchantment, and made some progress in working out how to live with weak commitments in a tepid, secular present. The best minds of the time proposed a sanguine scepticism rather than a remissive flight from authority into pleasure – they saw the futility of the latter course. The dominant political figure of the earlier part of the century, Sir Robert Walpole, said of himself: 'I am no saint, no Spartan, no reformer.' In our century, the reaction of sociology to the boredom that seems an inevitable companion of peaceful affluence has been to show outrage at the lurking aimlessness of suburban life, and to rush into glamorizing the denser humanity to be found in cow-sheds and amongst the urban poor. Our eighteenth-century forefathers demonstrated that this escapist utopianism was not the only way; in their sceptical realism they made some progress in coming to grips with the forces that were moving them.

A further reason for choosing eighteenth-century England is that sociology has been hypnotized by the industrial revolution and the French revolution – its best work has reacted to one or both of these two phenomena. We are now far enough beyond both of them to try a more independent line. But to find mentors whose work is not somehow pinned to their root ideas, to their ideals, we have, by and large, to go back to the time before their advent.

Of course, the eighteenth century was different. It experienced the heady youth of *laissez-faire* capitalism; we know the dinosaurian stumblings of welfare capitalism. Our secular pessimism is confirmed by our economies. The eighteenth century was more confident about itself. Christianity remained a force, and cultural relativism had not emerged to qualify the pride men took in their achievements. And it was a tougher time; failure was easy, and not cushioned by welfare; consequently it was a more serious time, as indicated by its reading habits. For a decadent culture to be sceptical rather than remiss requires a high level of seriousness, a fact that casts doubt upon taking eighteenth-century England as our analogy. But, doubt or not, it is the best analogy we have.

The eighteenth century in England saw a continuation of the cultural brilliance of the seventeenth. Two of its leading intellectual figures select themselves as exemplary fathers for a sceptical sociology: Samuel Johnson and David Hume. A number of their contemporaries also contributed to a sceptical view of the human condition, the more notable being, allowing a slight stretching of the dates, Jonathan Swift, Alexander Pope, Oliver Goldsmith, Adam

Smith, and Edmund Burke. They all either lived before, or remained untouched by, the spirit of Romanticism, whose star rose into ascendancy through the latter half of the century.

Although Samuel Johnson was a devout Christian, the bulk of his writings and sayings are assertively secular. His outlook on life was influenced by a pursuit of understanding rather than faith or revelation. His interest was in expressing the truth about social life, which he did in a judicially sceptical manner. In his fable on the varieties of human life, *Rasselas*, he portrays a prince and princess who grow up in a kingdom of perfect harmony. They become restless for adventure and change, and escape to experience the real world. They travel, visiting a variety of men who appear to be happy, a rich man, a powerful prince, a wise man, an astronomer, a hermit, a group of young revellers. All are portrayed as the best and most successful of their type, but none turn out to be happy. 'We are long before we are convinced that happiness is never to be found, and each believes it possessed by others, to keep alive the hope of obtaining it for himself.' Through these adventures Johnson makes his own comments on a range of situations, for example on the advantages of marrying young, of marrying old, of not marrying at all:

Such is the common process of marriage. A youth and a maiden meeting by chance, or brought together by artifice, exchange glances, reciprocate civilities, go home, and dream of one another. Having little to divert attention, or diversify thought, they find themselves uneasy when they are apart, and therefore conclude that they shall be happy together. They marry, and discover what nothing but voluntary blindness had before concealed; they wear out life in altercations, and charge nature with cruelty. . . .
[Better then marry late, experienced, but . . .] when the desultory levity of youth has settled into regularity, it is soon succeeded by pride ashamed to yield, or obstinacy delighting to contend. And even though mutual esteem produces mutual desire to please, time itself, as it modifies unchangeably the external mien, determines likewise the direction of the passions, and gives an inflexible rigidity to the manners. Long customs are not easily broken: he that attempts to change the course of his own life, very often labours in vain; and how shall we do that for others which we are seldom able to do for ourselves?

Many, including Johnson himself, had noted that *Rasselas* shared similarities with Voltaire's *Candide*, published in the same year, 1759. But the latter illustrates little more than the extremity of evil that can be met in the world, and the absurdity of Leibnizian optimism, which it does at repetitive length. Johnson's classic, on the other hand, discourses on a wide spectrum of human experience, and does so with wit, colour, and a cheerfully sceptical penetration.

Johnson's strength in comparison with Voltaire, a strength that makes him 'modern', or rather 'universal', is linked to the fact that unlike his contemporary *philosophes* he did not make an ideal of reason. Consequently he was not distracted from the manifold ambivalences of life by visions of human progress, of man emancipated from superstition into the sublime heavens of science and intellect. One of Johnson's biographers, John Wain, writes of him:

> as an individual, [he] was highly independent and unbiddable. He did not fit smoothly into any system. Intellectually, on the other hand, he approved of systems. Free of any starry-eyed notion of the natural goodness of man, he insisted on the need to keep up the outward forms and conventions that act as some check on man's natural lawlessness because he felt its power in his own anarchic impulses. . . .
>
> Johnson's premise, on the contrary [to that of the average intellectual who argues for a world in which *he* will get what he wants, who when he is ill at ease with his family, wants to abolish all families], is that the world must arrange itself in a way that suits the majority of its inhabitants and gives them a chance to live decent, peaceable, and useful lives; and that he, and people like him, will then take their chance of happiness within that order.

Johnson preferred a society that preserved distinctions of rank, on the grounds that such distinctions cut out 'a perpetual struggle for precedence', and therefore created no squabbling and envy – a view later to be elaborated by Tocqueville and Nietzsche. At the same time he was noted for his compassion, his acts of personal generosity towards the poor, his temperamentally egalitarian nature.

Johnson's *Rasselas*, with Pope's *Essay on Man*, provides modern scepticism with a strong literary basis. Scepticism's philosophical basis was laid contemporaneously by David Hume.

Hume developed first a sceptical epistemology, insisting that human reason can never reach absolutely certain conclusions. The problem of induction – of how we must doubt even that the sun will rise tomorrow – in the terms he framed it, has still not been superseded by philosophers (see Karl Popper, *Objective Knowledge*, 1972). Hume uses his theory of knowledge to build a system for understanding human action: starting from an analysis of human nature, of passions, of innate habits of mind, he creates a model of human motivation which he then applies to the range of human behaviour from the intimate through to the political. Thus he is the only intellectual apart from Freud to have investigated society from the standpoint of a complex model of individual psychology. What results is not a colourless and futile abstraction, but a range of observations of social life that are striking for their integration of an urbane sceptical wisdom with an analytical rigour that keeps constantly in mind the first principles of human nature. For example, Hume on the origins of religion:

> The anxious concern for happiness, the dread of future misery, the terror of death, the thirst of revenge, the appetite for food and other necessaries [create hopes and, more significantly, arouse fears, and so] men scrutinize, with a trembling curiosity, the course of future causes, and examine the various and contrary events of human life. And in this disordered scene, with eyes still more disordered and astonished, they see the first obscure traces of divinity.

In politics it was Hume, even before Montesquieu published his *Laws*, who spelt out the theory implicit in the liberal political institutions that were developing in England. As Lewis Namier summed it up, he valued the checks and controls, the 'mutual watchfulness and jealousy' which the British mixed form of government demanded from all concerned. He cherished a constitution that safeguarded the rights and freedoms of citizens, when 'in almost every other nation of Europe' public liberty was 'extremely on the decline'. Hume saw that the bulk of mankind preferred to be governed by authority rather than reason, but argued that both authority and liberty were essential to civil society, and that the leading political task was to establish a balance between them.

Hume lived sanguinely with himself and his beliefs. He did not shy away from the scepticism of his philosophy, which allowed no superstitions, and which gave his understandings at best merely probable validity. Like Johnson he did not make a God out of reason, nor out of progress through enlightenment. Indeed, he doubted that the liberation from superstition was either continuous or inevitable. He recognized the almost total domination of passion over intellect in human life: one of his characters comments on the rationalist arrogance, 'What peculiar privilege has this little agitation of the brain which we call thought, that we must make it the model of the whole universe.' He saw human history mainly in terms of cycles. And it seems to have been his benign disposition that made him unusually independent of the climate of opinion of his own time, and free from the mixture of vanity and resentment that renders intellectuals with an interest in society so vulnerable to ideals, which then cloud their perceptions of the realities of life. Hume's scepticism was cheerful and uncomplaining; it sought to understand men as they live.

Adam Smith unwittingly contributed to the sceptical tradition, most conspicuously by the psychological foundation he gave to his economic treatise, *The Wealth of Nations* (1776), the first systematic account of economic life ever written. *The Wealth of Nations* is a work of great optimism, giving theoretical account of the industrial revolution as it happened, spelling out principles of manufacture and trade; it served, much as Machiavelli's *Prince* did for late Renaissance politics, to lay out the guidelines for success. Smith derived his principles from the leading assumption that man's nature is egoistic. As he put it in a famous passage:

> It is not from the benevolence of the butcher, the brewer, or the baker, that we expect our dinner, but from their regard to their own interest. We address ourselves, not to their humanity, but to their self-love; and never talk to them of our own necessities, but of their advantages.

He reinforced his egoist assumption with an anticipation of evolutionary theory: institutions develop by a principle of the elimination of the less effective. However, in one key regard Smith moved away from Hume and towards Rousseau: he argued that economic life does not require external checks and balances, for an 'invisible hand' operates behind the scenes ensuring a harmony of egoisms and protecting the social good. This is an absurd and utopian notion.

Modern sociology, and some of modern economics, have tended to neglect Smith's emphases, preferring the utopian view that egoism drives only a degraded form of social life, and competition an evil economic system. However, there seems to be a change in economics, as western nations experience unforeseen constraints on their affluence; growing interest in the work of F. A. Hayek is indicative of this. Hayek professes Smith as his mentor, and opposes the centralist, welfare-conducive theory of Keynes. History is now teaching that to fail to sufficiently reward the productive elements in the economy leads to over-all inefficiencies, and a smaller cake from which everyone can eat. Sociology, unfortunately, is not so tied to the material consequences of its doctrines as they work themselves through in the everyday world, and will prove slower in adjusting to the failing legitimacy of the Rousseauist ideal. A sceptical sociology, having as one of its tasks the hastening of utopianism's demise, will have frequent recourse to Adam Smith's self-interest premise.

For their contribution to political theory, and in particular for the clarity with which they derive their precepts from observations of how men behave in political life, I would include Edmund Burke and James Madison in my list of eighteenth-century British contributors to scepticism (although Madison was an American, it was English political practice, and English political theory, with the exception of the work of Montesquieu, an Anglophile himself, which influenced him). Burke, in his life in politics, and in his writings, developed Hume's perspective. He wrote of his ideal practice:

> By a slow but well-sustained progress, the effect of each step is watched; the good or ill success of the first, gives light to us in the second; and so, from light to light, we are conducted with safety through the whole series. . . . We compensate, we reconcile, we balance.

Madison, in his contributions to *The Federalist Papers*, developed the theory of checks and balances in defence of the practice that was established in America. He argued that the aim of every political constitution ought to be:

> first to obtain for rulers men who possess most wisdom to discern, and most virtue to pursue, the common good of the society; and in the next place, to take the most effectual precautions for keeping them virtuous whilst they continue to hold their public trust.

He was aware that it will not always be the case that the most virtuous men hold power; and one should plan accordingly. His sober realism is a worthy reminder in a time that has its share of mediocre elites. (Madison, like most eighteenth-century political philosophers, was influenced by the example of classical Rome. It should also be noted here that the discussion of scepticism has been restricted to that perspective's *modern* classics.)

2 The influence of Rousseau

Something went drastically wrong late in the eighteenth century. At a fork in the political road, Europe inexplicably took the wrong direction. English liberal philosophy and English political institutions, which had been the envy of the world for a hundred years, were suddenly forgotten, and a new movement began that would in the end infect those English ways themselves, that would corrupt the urbane, sceptical rationality of Johnson and Hume into the facile, mechanical rationality of utilitarianism. More specifically the balance of authority and liberty would be disrupted by the weakening of the conservative check, emphasizing hierarchy and tradition, caution and the virtue of the common law. Burke's call that a man 'should approach to the faults of the State as to the wounds of a father, with pious awe and trembling solicitude' was silenced. Without the conservative check the liberal-rationalist tendency, that brought many advances to nineteenth-century British politics (for example a civil service that began to take some account of merit in its recruiting), would go too far, on the one hand reducing politics to administration, on the other sacrificing the ideal of liberty to that of the welfare state.

A celebrated sequence of events that took place in the third quarter of the eighteenth century serves us well as a parable. In 1765 Jean-Jacques Rousseau, exiled in Switzerland, needed somewhere else to take refuge. David Hume invited him to England. In fact Hume conducted Rousseau from Paris to London, where he immediately devoted himself to finding accommodation for the famous French philosopher. After Rousseau had declined several possibilities, a satisfactory place in the country was found. Hume also interceded with the king to get Rousseau a royal pension, and was again successful. However, Rousseau inexplicably declined the pension, and wrote a letter to Hume on 10 July 1766, accusing him of a series of treacheries – spying on him, collaborating with Voltaire and his other enemies, participating in a hoax letter from Frederick the Great of Prussia mocking Rousseau. Rousseau later came to the view that Hume's invitation had been a trap to keep him in England, so that the manuscript of his *Confessions* would never reach publishers. In his *Confessions*, he defied Hume to publish any account of the affair without 'enormous falsifications'.

Hume was known for his benevolence, his gaiety of spirit, his sanguine lack of malice; the French called him 'le bon David'. Adam Smith wrote of him: 'Upon the whole, I have always considered him, both in his lifetime and since his death, as approaching as nearly to the idea of a perfectly wise and virtuous man, as perhaps the nature of human frailty will permit.' Of Rousseau, Dr Johnson had commented, and before the turn against Hume had occurred: 'I think him one of the worst of men; a rascal, who ought to be hunted out of society, as he has been.' Hume was at first very angry, calling Rousseau a 'most atrocious villain' and a vulgar liar (amongst other things, he had affected poverty, hence the king's pension, whereas the royalties from his books kept him pretty well off). But when Hume realized that Rousseau was in fact mad, his anger turned to pity, and he again supported a pension for him. Moreover, when he heard that his ungrateful guest was making for France, he wrote to Turgot there asking that endeavours be made to give him protection.

In 1766 who would have thought that if the next two hundred years were to bear the profound mark of one of the two great philosophers, it would be Rousseau, that the view of human nature espoused by this self-obsessed paranoic would dominate the future course of European political thought and action? Rousseau was the intellectual father of revolution, the seminal articulator of its credo. It was he who gave dignity to the *people*, who elevated the most common of citizens into a sacred entity with virtues potentially superior to those of any magistrate or king. And for Rousseau it was the potential that was all-important. It was his formulation of the innate goodness of man, the famous dictum that 'man was born free', and his further conclusion that human nature could be transformed, that history could make a fresh start; it was these radical postulates that set the political tide that carried, with minor cross-currents, the next two centuries. It was Rousseau who created the totalitarian belief that the people has a 'general will', and more, that this will, this universal perspective, embodies all social good. Those who were blind to the will were to be made virtuous, forced to be free. The new man will transcend petty private interests, he will shine forth with the will of all; his every enthusiasm will be for the common good, and pave the way towards the purely organic, perfectly harmonious society. Rousseau further consolidated his position as the intellectual father of revolution by alternating in his ultimate enthusiasm between a primitivist return to nature, the anarchist dream of the free and noble savage, and at the other extreme, a new Spartan era of strict discipline, a highly normative dictatorship of the people.

Thus it was Rousseau who mounted in effect the riposte against liberal democracy, at the moment of both its emergence in eighteenth-century British parliamentary democracy, and its theoretical zenith, in Hume's social and political philosophy. He carried attention away from its more realistic accounting for the moral ambivalence of human nature, the fickleness of human passion and judgment, and the precariousness of the balance of liberty and authority in an open society, the only society in which the individual has a crucial measure of freedom from the coercions of politics. And with his 'I know only what I feel' he not only renounced rational politics but gave to such an erratic disposition as his own a dignity superior to that of a David Hume. Rousseau would politicize the whole of life; he replied to liberalism with the great mystical abstractions, 'the people', 'universal harmony', 'pure virtue', and 'total freedom'. Rousseau was the antithesis of Hume: out of paranoid fears of what *is* he devoted himself to what *ought to be*, dealing with an uncomfortable reality by attacking it from the standpoint of alternating extremes. He thereby led a troupe of Westerners into the realm of fantasy, insensitive to the networks of hierarchies, distances, privacies, and thoughtfulness itself, which protect society from the slide into totalitarianism.

It might well be asked, what is the relevance of the evolution of political ideas and practices to a discussion of the intellectual discipline, sociology? The simple answer is that sociology's texts have always been coloured by political ideology. This is in part inevitable. Sociology cannot begin without taking a position on the nature of man, and on the general manner in which he is influenced by social forces. Thus from the outset there is a social ought lurking behind the scenes; a sociological interest brings with it one form of moral orientation or another. Moreover, when sociology is being written the ought will inevitably be present, at the least in the form of implications for reform. Hobbes and Rousseau are directly relevant to sociology; Marx is one of its classical writers; in Britain the influence of Fabian welfare socialism has dominated the mainstream of twentieth-century sociology.

In arguing for a sceptical sociology there are two precepts, drawn from Weber, that are pertinent at this point. First, minimize the political content, contain the 'ought' as well as possible, be as 'objective' as possible: in short make the pursuit of the 'what is' the overriding aim. Second, as some political content will inevitably remain, demoralize this, by examining the performance of that ideology when applied in practice: in short become aware of its social consequences. In this way the idealistic element is also minimized, constantly under the check of reality. Thus, to compare Hume and Rousseau is in part to compare the political systems that best embody their philosophies, that operate most closely according to their assumptions about human nature.

1918, the year that saw the end of the World War that brought the last curtain down on aristocratic, imperial Europe, may be taken as a marker in the history of sociology. The major nineteenth-century figures, Tocqueville and Marx, were long dead; Durkheim died in 1917; in 1918 Weber delivered his great lectures 'Politics as a Vocation' and 'Science as a Vocation' – two years later he too was dead. Since 1918 sociology's record has been dismal. I think this is in no small part due to the fact of it having chosen Rousseau, with very few exceptions, such as Pareto who finished publishing his last work, the *Treatise*, in 1923 (it lies virtually unread today). Moreover, it is both fronts of Rousseau's revolt against the present that have been extensively employed, on the one hand extolling the virtues of a return to nature and a noble, simple life, on the other, proclaiming the Spartan dictatorship of the people, and their general will.

First, the back-to-nature exponents. Between the wars American sociology was dominated by the Chicago School. The research of Park and Wirth on urbanism and the city stimulated a wide range of studies, all working under the assumption that the growing urban centres corrupted the true virtues to be found in rural and small-town America. This resentment against modernism and the great metropolis was exactly that of Rousseau, hankering for community life, where everyone knew each other, where everyone worked the land or was an artisan, and where the pace of life was governed by the seasons, the crops, and the speed of a carthorse. Industrialization, enforcing a division of labour, and producing the mobility and anonymity of the modern city, had smothered the innate goodness of man living in simple surroundings. The Americans got their Rousseauist ideal from, on the one hand, Thoreau and Emerson, and, on the other, Tönnies, and in a more ambivalent way, Simmel. These same values were expressed by the young Marx in his writings on 'alienation', his *1844 Manuscripts*, which themselves became a seminal text for a new generation of sociologists following the middle 1960s. A variation of the same theme is to be found in another genre of sociology, which finds virtue in traditional working-class enclaves in large cities, where, it is argued, the humanity of the small community survives. There is justification for worrying about the impact of the modern metropolis on its individual inhabitants: however, an idealistic nostalgia for the golden age of the rural village must blinker any attempt to understand the strains of urban society.

Second, the Spartan revolutionaries. Although the figure of Marx, as embodied in his later works, and the Rousseauist utopian element in his historical model, is a major influence on this group, many of them were more reformist than revolutionary. Belonging here are the Fabians, in particular the Webbs with their Bersteinian form of evolutionary socialism, and British welfare sociology, which the Webbs pioneered. What is advocated is an enlightened state, intuiting the real will of the people, holding the reins of political and economic power to the exclusion of self-interested individuals. R. H. Tawney belongs to this group; and Karl Mannheim joined it after he moved to London. A similar ideology, but without such readily placeable mentors, has been influential in American mainstream sociology since the 1930s, as witnessed in studies of immigration, of the family, of poverty, and most obviously, of social stratification. In Germany, the Frankfurt School carried the banner of the Spartan revolutionary, although its predilection for hermeneutics, and for Freud as a fortifier to Marx, has minimized its political relevance, except in providing an ideology for extremist students.

Since 1960, various syntheses of the two strands of Rousseau have emerged, especially in sociology's most potentially innovative centre, the United States. In the popular field of deviancy studies, and in allied areas like mental illness, the dominant perspective of 'labelling theory' has blamed an evil society for imposing its repressive definitions on the weak and underprivileged. The virtues of simple humanity have been read into the lives of those on the margins of productive social activity, and extolled, with the suggestion that there would be no more labelling in an enlightened, less capitalistic and individualistic society. A similar bias towards the back-to-nature Rousseau, but with traces of the revolutionary, has governed that wide range of interests summed up as 'symbolic interaction', or later 'ethnomethodology'. Here an emphasis on describing face-to-face contact, on the subjective nuances of individuals interacting, reflects a desire to reach the simple things that tie people to each other, and get away from the more abstract and impersonal historical and psychological forces that underpin social life – and which form the classical framework of sociology. This move to discover the openness of direct human contact would have been justified if it had been done well: in practice, however, it appeared as another idealistic simplification. Finally, stratification studies have always indicated a tendency towards the second, Spartan revolutionary side of Rousseau; recently they have grafted on ideals of noble simplicity, of society without alienation, as spelt out by the early Marx.

There has been sociology since 1918 that has moved independently of Rousseau, but remarkably little. The theory of Talcott Parsons, influential for a decade in the 1950s and 1960s, provided a utilitarian model which could be used, as it was, by researchers of various moral persuasions. In another corner, a quantitative-empiricist tradition has been strong in sociology through the period in question; theoretically feeble, it has borrowed hypotheses from various sources, and not exclusively Rousseauist ones.

It may be retorted that I have unfairly exaggerated the particular influence of Rousseau. I have not sought to get into a detailed intellectual history of who precisely read Rousseau and when. That would require a book in itself, and probably would not prove productive for my purpose here. I do wish to assert that Rousseau's work, directly as read, and indirectly as passed down and developed through succeeding generations, has been decisively influential. To take one example: the Fabians seem to have drawn their socialist idealism from Owen rather than Rousseau. However, Owen himself probably read Rousseau; he certainly read Godwin whose work bears a strong Rousseauist imprint; and he would have been receptive to the Rousseauist current in the intellectual air during the formative period of his thinking.

Above all, I am taking Rousseau as the representative of one tradition in social theory, for the obvious reason that he more than anyone else founded this tradition, that he most clearly spelt out its root ideals, and that his was the dominant intellectual influence over the sequence of events, the French revolution, that has stood as this tradition's leading symbol of social possibility. At the same time it remains true that Rousseau was a great philosopher, that his work is subtle and many-sided, and that he cannot be held personally too responsible for the way history chose to magnify one only of those sides.

3 Theory

Classical works of sociology, like great works of literature or art, reveal important things about the human condition that had not been seen before. Moreover, they do this with a technique, with a sense for what can and cannot be said, for the range of problems created by their interpretative thrust, with a depth, or a range, or both, that means that later works will never entirely supersede them. These are feats of intelligence, of disciplined interpretation, that cannot be encompassed. There are also scintillating fragments; and they have their place, rather like the minor but indispensable performers in a theatre troupe.

The laying bare of social life is *theory*. It takes a set of particulars and in being mindful of them, in living with the tension of concentrating on them in their formless, chaotic state, it places them.
. This placement is a process of making intelligible, of finding a pattern of common features, causes, and functions. This making intelligible means at its highest that life is breathed into inchoate matter. The Greek root of *theory* meant 'viewing', as a spectator does. Theory is thus a bringing into sight, and a gaining an image of.

The Greek *theoria* had religious origins, and carried with it the sense of ecstatic revelation. Its Orphic mood was of passionate and sympathetic contemplation. The Pythagoreans were the first to intellectualize it, to turn it into metaphysics, by changing the object of its viewing from God to truth. Theory is to do with the disclosing of the essential, and in this it has not changed. Disclosing the essential is not describing literally the petty and routine course of everyday life. It is rather the getting behind that everyday life to reflect it in terms of the metaphysical questions of how to live and what to do, or alternatively the questions of where we are and where we might be going. Everyday life is interesting only in the way it challenges individuals to make something more of it than passively accepting its routines as a way of filling time. Theory has the task of laying bare the way in which individuals take up those challenges, or cope with the sense of failure at having relinquished their hopes in favour of the humdrum. Without its metaphysical core theory loses its power of revealing, loses its compelling mythic force, and declines into mundane hypotheses. Mundane hypotheses are means of ordering the inchoate mass of the empirical; but they operate at little distance from that mass. Without the distancing of metaphysical concerns there can not exist the tension between the other-worldly and the this-worldly, or empirical, that gives theory both its pungency and its ability to select what is significant. The mundane hypotheses of atheoretical work have no means for deciphering what is significant and what is trivial, except in the lowest utilitarian terms of material welfare, of what might improve an individual or a nation's level of consumption. One outstanding piece of post-1918 social theory in this mode of illuminating everyday life is Hannah Arendt's *The Human Condition* (1958); moreover, this work tackles head-on the Humean challenge of getting at the roots of human nature.

I have mentioned the first of theory's two tasks, to get behind everyday life and illuminate it. Individuals experience their lives as a series of significant moments or episodes, whether traumatic or joyful, separated by periods of everyday routine. In many cases the number of significant or memorable events is small, but the long stretches of routine may bring their own mild pleasures. Theory's second task is to focus on the moments of significance, and disclose their meaning. In the domain of individual biography, Freud was the exemplar of theory in this mode; he was interested only in decisive moments, moments of trauma, of breakdown, moments of vivid psychological pull, turning points. We perceive social action, whether viewed historically or in terms of its contemporary functions, in the same manner. The exemplary work of theory in this area is Max Weber's *The Protestant Ethic and the Spirit of Capitalism*, which selects the key series of events in the formation of modern western society, and works its theory from there.

The example of Weber's *Protestant Ethic* should quell any suspicion that arguing in favour of theory that recovers its origins in passionate revelation argues for sociology becoming a branch of mystical theology. There is no criticism here of the rigorous use of appropriate evidence, nor of taking extreme care to make clear the values that underpin the work in hand. The point is that while technique, or method, is important, so too is the metaphysical yearning that drives all our quests for understanding.

Theory in its early Orphic form served to renew a sense of mystical oneness and collective participation. It remains true that theory should serve to reattach us to our communities and to ourselves. It should serve to heighten both our interest and our respect. It heightens our interest by showing us things that we did not see and are significant. It enlivens our world by bringing into sight things that had lapsed into oblivion, or things to which we had always been oblivious. It inspires. Like Scheherezade it transforms a one-night ritual that ends in death into a thousand nights of wonderful stories, which is life. Theory heightens our respect by reconnecting us with our own metaphysical yearnings, which in turn put us back in contact with nature and the cosmos, in a state of wonder. The mood of genuine theory, whatever it is theorizing on, is beautifully caught by Burke's image of approaching the wounds of a father, with pious awe and trembling solicitude.

A sceptical sociology, like any sociology, or indeed like any of the humanities, must take the form of theory.

4 The two axes of sociology

Picturing sociology as a two-dimensional space defined by Cartesian co-ordinates, then the axes are, in terms of axiomatic propositions:

  x: man is a social product
  y: society is the product of unconscious wishes.

These are the axes that have defined sociological endeavour. They have commonly, and confusedly, been referred to as, respectively, taking society as given and working towards the individual, and taking the individual as given, and working towards society.

To date, work along, or in proximity to, the x-axis has proceeded well, or at least did so before 1918. Marx and Durkheim mapped out the main lines along which the society into which an individual is born, through its culture, through its patterns of family, work, religion, and so on, influences the beliefs and habits, the enthusiasms and anxieties of that individual. Work of this nature has been aided by that of historians, and in particular economic historians, who have plotted the development of the various institutions that are influential in modern Western societies.

Negligible progress has been made in plotting the y-axis. Sociology has been singularly reluctant to approach in any serious manner the problem of human nature, the Humean challenge to get straight to the roots of individual disposition, starting from the question of which habits of mind and body are innate. After 1918 this negligence has been inexcusable, for we have had available for the first time a complex and systematic theory of human motivation – that of Freud. Moreover, the Freudian tradition has made more and more obvious the degree to which society is an objective space into which individuals project their unconscious wishes, and which gets manipulated by those wishes. (Dennis Wrong has argued that sociology needs to take the problem of human nature more seriously – see Part One of his collection of essays titled *Skeptical Sociology* (Heinemann, London, 1976). Incidentally, Wrong's 'skeptical' seems little more than a substitute for 'critical' or 'radical', and is not historically grounded.)

A persuasive psychological theory is a prerequisite for progress in integrating x and y, that is in moving into the centre of the field that ought to be sociology. One of the reasons for failure in this key regard has been sociology's refusal to view the individual as a complex entity governed by biological and psychological forces. Sociology has taken the individual as an empty concept, a *tabula rasa*, defined by society through the process of socialization into roles. There has been little room for work focusing on the individual himself, for he has been defined away. The Freudian specification of the y-axis strengthens the rather flabby proposition that society is the product of its individual members, and, by articulating the psychological mechanism at work, should ensure that the sociological trivialization of the 'individual' does not re-emerge.

5 Know thyself

There will be little progress in interpreting society as the product of the unconscious wishes of its individual members while the sociologist lacks self-understanding. Consequently, I would insist that our students be made fully conversant with the experts on human nature, not just Johnson and Hume, but also La Rochefoucauld, Nietzsche, and above all Freud. And having reached this point, I would save some time by ditching Durkheim, on the grounds that Freud's social theory is no less developed, and it has the unique strength of drawing on a rich individual psychology.

'Know thyself' is the sure antidote to the three temptations that have ruined sociology. It should produce a sense of what constitutes significant knowledge about human behaviour, and a corresponding disdain for the simplifications that the pursuit of science has forced upon the discipline. It should produce a resistance to ideals that have not proved themselves by being lived through. Finally, by suggesting how complicated is an individual, how hostile to change, and how little he controls the changes that do occur, it should produce a severe scepticism about the relevance of sociology to social reform.

It is virtually impossible to turn any of the experts on human nature into authorities for slogans, or programmes for reform (an exception was the weakest side of Nietzsche, represented in some of his political statements, which were naive to an extreme and used later by Nazism). Once the sceptical moral thrust has been understood, the call of the sociological simplifiers, the Rousseaus, becomes shrill. Moreover, the sceptics point out just how much the pursuit of knowledge is a self-rationalization, a means of sublimating personal disquiet, of the sociologist coping with his own nagging metaphysical problems, in short a means of projecting unconscious wishes. George Devereux, working from a psycho-analytical perspective, argues that any human science is at root counter-transference, that is the projection on to the world through his work of the researcher's private psychological needs. Consequently if we are to have any control over our method we must know ourselves, that is, have some sense of which unconscious wishes we are projecting, and why. Devereux's *From Anxiety to Method in the Behavioural Sciences* (1967) should be our basic text on method.

Devereux's 'The analyst does not really interpret the patient's unconscious, but the reverberations of the patient's unconscious in his own' applies equally for sociology. The sociologist gains his insight by interpreting the impact of what he is studying on his own unconscious, whether this be supermarkets, tourists or family life. He can collect evidence in an objective manner, but he can interpret it only subjectively, which means more specifically by coming to understand its impact on himself. The sociologist's lens is his own experience; if he chooses not to put it to good use he is reduced to imitating others, and producing opinion, prejudice or platitude. The same holds for all the human sciences, and indeed for many spheres of creative life. An actor, for example, as Grotowski tells us, must draw on past experience of his own that is analogous to that of the part he is playing, and he must imagine himself back into the emotional climate that it aroused in him, if he is to bring his role to life. 'Know thyself' is thus the first principle of sociological method: it is the means to all knowledge.

The consequences of a sociology that has ignored the classical 'know thyself' command include not only dull books. Equally high on the list is the fact that a proportion of sociology students now leave the university with little reflected experience of either private life or social action. Indeed we seem to be training many of them to repeat the clichés of vogue political ideology. In his impeccably sceptical work, *A Critique of the New Commonplaces* (1966), Jacques Ellul comments that the god 'literacy' has risen unchallenged in the non-Western world, but when that literacy is used solely to read newspapers it is worse than useless. The same might be said about our universities, to the degree that they educate in the easy commonplaces of the time. (It is doubtful whether universities were much better in this regard in the past. However, they had more excuse for confirming orthodoxies than does the particular discipline of sociology, which is predicated on gaining a critically thoughtful distance from social life.)

6 Contra science

The first defence against 'know thyself' has been science, the obsessional drive to turn sociology into an exact science, like Newtonian physics, where everything is certain, and the researcher is perfectly objective in framing his laws – that is, his own personality does not intrude into his work. The fact is that any significant move in understanding human nature, or in developing a sociology from that base, which includes all sociology except for a strictly limited type of economic history, enters a world of formidable complexity, where motivational ambivalence and causal multiplicity are the rule, and where the attaching of precise weights, or probabilities, is unjustified. The science obsession has led the revolt against the manifold difficulty of the sociological universe. Like all obsessional acts its object has been control – to establish contact with the world external to the individual, but in a rigorously managed way. The obsession originates in the researcher himself, and a personal insecurity, a fear about his own unworthiness. It leads him into not wanting to be revealed, therefore not wanting an element of himself to be present in his work, which is public, and may be scrutinized. Although he views his work as 'objective', some fear remains that it may be vulnerable, and he in it; so he further intensifies its scientific rigour. The counter-transference at work here renders the researcher blind to his own intentions, and weaknesses. Lack of self-insight combines with simplification of the social world to make theory impossible. It is a commonplace today that positivist science applied to sociology, in making simplifying assumptions about its material in order to fit it to mathematical formulae, which cannot handle many variables, has produced methodological monstrosities, whose conclusions are trivial. Commonplace or not, the same discredited practice goes on unabashed, as is typical of obsessive action: it is futile, for example, to point out to a lady who feels compelled to scrub her kitchen table every hour that she is overdoing it. (When quantitative sociology has produced work of value it has been in the form of demographic data, on income, population mobility, migration, and so on. Such data in itself is not sociology, but may provide the empirical material with which sociology can *begin* its task of theoretical interpretation.)

Sociology as science has been particularly nervous about theory, for the good reason that once metaphysics enters the arena certitude's cause is lost. Ultimately science cannot choose between different metaphysical systems, however cleverly it may clarify their origins, their biases, and their consequences. So, as the positivists put it, one must stick to 'fact-picturing propositions'. The case of Wittgenstein is instructive here. Wittgenstein, in reinforcing the division between the metaphysical and the factual, argued that the former contained all that really matters in human life, but nothing could be said about it – 'the unsayable alone has genuine value'. Philosophy, in following him, was left with the task of thinking about a trivial, a task it has taken to with great seriousness. A parallel curse dropped on sociology, as a result also of the science temptation; thus theory was banished.

More specifically, the second task of theory, and with it of understanding, was to remember the moments of significance in individual and collective life. It is through significant events, of rare deeds in response to fateful moments, that lives become meaningful – that history is created and individual memory comes to life. But statistics can operate only on large numbers. A quantitative methodology is forced by its own ground rules to deny what is individual and significant: it can measure them only as deviations and find in them no more content than that, that they are exceptions. Sociology, in wedding itself to quantitative methods, has banished from its sight the very events that give human life its meaning and its dignity. Moreover, the first of theory's tasks, the illumination of everyday life, is likewise excluded; it depends, if it is to get colour into its portraits, on gaining access to the enthusiasms and the disappointments, the insecurities and eccentricities, the attachments and the envies, of the people that it studies.

The obsession to be scientific increases respect for the experts – the specialists, the professionals and thereby their formal education and qualifications. It increases the authority of institution at the expense of individual, increases the power of government bureaucracy as the ultimate authority in a society of experts, and fosters the bureaucratization of the university. At every level this process is at odds with forces conducive to true learning.

There needs to be some 'science' in sociology, but science in a spare, cannier mode. At the surface level its commands ought to be to cover the relevant ground, to take account of evidence that is appropriate, and of literature on allied subjects, and to write clearly, economically, and consistently. The sociologist ought to complement his scientific ambition with a literary one, to reveal something novel and significant about what people do. The literary ambition also carries with it a stylistic command, that the work be elegant. (Richard H. Brown, in his book, *A Poetic for Sociology* (Cambridge University Press, 1977), has done a fine job of laying the ground for an integrated literary-scientific sociology.)

In any field it is important not to go too far. Over-farming reduces fertility. One of the vices linked to the passion for the perfect, for the improved line, the more precise statement, and for the more pungent association, all central to our joint scientific-literary ambition, is that this passion readily produces precious work, work that has become so fine in its lines, its shadings, that the shape of its subject is lost. But this is hardly a danger given the current state of sociology.

Authors of ambitious studies in the humanities, worried that their generalities are vulnerable to the attack of more positivistically-inclined colleagues, often include the word 'notes' in their titles. I am not here, however, in placing a warning against even our softer science, arguing for writing 'notes'. Precisely not, for the existence of a 'note' suggests that the real work, the definitive, weighty work, remains to be written. Invariably this is a delusion: notes are written by those with a mandarin bad conscience, who let their hair down for a moment, and wish to protect themselves from attack from some vulgar person not finding them seductive with their hair down, with the disclaimer that the work is not altogether serious, that they didn't have their make-up on. Many nineteenth-century novelists planned to write vast three-volume tomes, and apologized for finishing only the first introductory piece – such was *The Brothers Karamazov*.

As a footnote to this section, it ought in all fairness to be mentioned that Rousseau was not guilty of introducing the science obsession. It was rather Bentham, under the influence of other Frenchmen, enlightened men like Holbach, who sowed the seed that sprouted into utilitarianism. By the time of Saint-Simon and Marx, however, the influence of Rousseau had fused with the science temptation (except in the anarchist tradition, which managed through its history to keep the Rousseauist ideal pretty free from positivist leanings).

7 Contra idealism

The second defence against 'know thyself' is idealism. Freud interpreted idealism as a form of suicide: in adults it serves as a means for denying reality, for building a barrier between unconscious wishes and external reality, for renouncing the sane task of accommodating one to the other, and for preferring to channel wishes away from reality into the invincible safety of ideals – beliefs founded on wishes. This flight from reality makes it difficult for the individual to find gratification, for his perceptions of the normal channels of love and work are gravely distorted. One common result is a politicizing of the personal, fierce proclamation on the virtues of brotherhood by precisely those who have little capacity for it, and who then blame others, and particularly those in authority, for its elusiveness. Idealism is, at its extreme, schizophrenia, representing a complete separation from external reality, complete absorption in internal fantasy.

It is instructive here to look at the phase of individual life most prone to idealism, that of adolescence. A normal element in Western adolescence in recent centuries has been asceticism. Adolescents have been carried away by potent fantasies, extravagant hopes, intense cerebral passions, all of which have little grounding in reality. Indeed, it has often been a part of the passion that it should not be tried out, that it should not be contaminated by experience; the greatest pleasure has been that of indefinitely postponed gratification. One may be attracted to adolescents, may find certain appeal in their naive vitality, but one can hardly find them interesting as personalities. Their starry ideals and Olympian hopes are not yet tested. They have hardly entered the arena in which their various charms and talents, and such aspects of their characters as ambition and perseverance, will tangle with fortune, and in particular with the possibilities of work and intimacy that the time makes available to them. In this arena the challenges are set that most will grapple with the rest of their lives. And here the ideals of adolescence are either abandoned as irrelevant or unworkable, or they are tempered by experience into the enthusiasms that sustain the mature man. It is only ideals in this last sense, with the flesh of living's challenge around them, that are of intellectual interest. And yet, sociology, in choosing Rousseau as its mentor, chose to fixate in the unrealities of adolescence.

To consider one example, the Rousseauist ideal has taken sociologists into the field of *deviancy* with their trumpets blaring out against a society that persecutes those who do not fit. Even a hastily constructed model of human nature, and in particular human ambivalence, would repulse this sally. We all know that most schoolboys get involved at some age in petty crimes like shop-lifting, and sometimes in more serious crimes. They are not 'conforming' to social norms; on the contrary they are practising anarchists. But very few end up as delinquents. A blend of tolerance, indifference, ignorance, and turning a blind eye meets schoolboy crime, unless it becomes excessive or provocatively flagrant. While accepting the influence of such social factors as class, a sceptical sociologist might suspect that there is a need in those who end up 'delinquents' to be caught, to be punished, to be institutionalized and even treated badly by those in authority – thus vindicating the delinquent's view of authority as repressive, and of himself as ruined by external corruption rather than internal, personal deficiency.

Scepticism in our sociology is timely, as an antidote to simple-minded optimism about human nature, to simple-minded hostility to institutions, groups, or collectivities larger than the small rural community, and to the refusal to see malice, competitiveness, resentment, envy, and vanity as anything but the products of a corrupt society. A sociologist armed with Rousseauist ideals is rather like the British Light Brigade charging with their sabres drawn up a valley which they did not know to be dominated by Russian guns. The good-natured urbanity of *Rasselas* must in part derive from Johnson's preference for living in the thick of London life, familiar with the taverns, the poor, the prostitutes, the artists, and the politicians. A robust worldliness is probably the surest antidote to idealism.

Rousseauist idealism has reinforced the anti-individual tendency of modern life. Rousseau's notion of the 'general will', which lies behind any socialized image of man, subordinates the individual to the collectivity, making his life a means to the communal good, and denying his right to differ. Similarly, Marx's central notion of 'alienation' points to freedom as ultimately lying in man's 'species-being', a collective empathy in which 'bourgeois individualism' dissolves. (While Marx also emphasizes the role of work in allowing the individual to realize his higher capacities, following the paradigm of the artist, he does not recognize the private, individualist nature of this type of work, an oversight that permits him to preserve his ideal of the communal species.) Utopian togetherness denies the universal fact that human beings are ultimately alone, and the particular fact that since the Renaissance most of what the West has valued about itself has derived from the emphasis it has placed on the 'individual' as some sort of absolute value. This form of idealism, stressing the importance of social forces, placing the individual merely as a receptor, has typified most of sociology. It has an ideological rationale: the task of reform is simplified if one can argue that one only needs to change institutions if one wants to change individuals. When individuals are viewed it is assumed that they are malleable, and can be changed at will by operant social conditioning. Consequently this brand of idealism carries with it peculiar hostility to any position that gives some ultimate virtue to individuals, that focuses on individuals; its worst enemy is the Freudian position that does all this, and, further, considers that individuals are singularly resistant to change, especially after early childhood. There is thus an ideological reason for sociology having made little progress in interpreting society as the product of unconscious wishes.

Finally, idealism, to take up Freud's linking of it with suicide, precludes thought. Thought is driven by a wrestling with doubt; idealism is the asserting of certainty. In this contrast lies the connection with science. Idealism in looking around for a companion, someone who lives by the same wishes, discovers science; hand in hand the new comrades proceed to fortify their certitudes. Science provides idealism with a perfect alibi, rationalizing its commitments as knowledge, verified by empirical research. Together they turn on theory, as the embodiment of everything that threatens them, calling it superstition, mysticism, or mere speculation. To connect speculation with theory is of course correct, in terms of their common classical etymology. But to reject speculation is to reject the dynamic core of Western thought.

8 Contra relevance

The third defence against 'know thyself' is relevance, action rather than thought. The politically-inclined tend to regard intellectuals as effete, lost in their endless cogitations. And indeed for the intellectual to cross over into the world of action usually requires an overdose of idealism.

In sociology there has been a compromise: stay in the university, yet pretend to be relevant, or even take advisory jobs. But what has a sociologist to contribute on the planning board of, say, a proposed new town? He can advise that some people are more reluctant to move than others; he can warn against impersonal mass living spaces, against lack of recreational facilities – thus he may, like anybody with a modicum of perceptivity, counter some of the worst prejudices of others on the board. But he cannot do any more; he cannot spell out a blueprint for a prosperous, happy community. And the assumption that he can do more, an assumption that he himself often cultivates, puts him around a table with engineers and politicians looking expectantly at him for enlightenment. Unless he is shrewd in this situation he may do more harm than good.

There are limited ways in which sociology may be socially and politically relevant. I am not concerned here with its personal relevance, the fact that it might serve the individual who embraces it as a sublimation, means of coping with certain frustrations, or as a rationalization, or as a celebration of what he has done, or failed to do. To proceed with the question of social relevance I need to amplify the earlier distinction between theory and that type of social inquiry that produces data, such as population statistics. I wish to expand the latter category to include surveys of public opinion, that is quantitative studies of attitudes, which may require a rudiment of theory in setting them up. This expanded category constitutes 'low-grade' sociology: it is virtually atheoretical. What it produces is facts, rather than understanding.

There are cases in which low-grade sociology is useful in the framing of social policy. For example, a body deciding on regulations for the unemployed may benefit from studies on their attitudes to work. Such studies may counter the view that in the main the unemployed are indolent parasites. They will, however, give no impression of the true meaning of *work*, of how deeply its ethic is entwined in the dispositions of individuals, affecting their aspirations, their sense of competence, indeed their whole view of life. The utility of such studies is, in short, extremely limited. Moreover, a significant piece of sociology on work such as Studs Terkel's *Working* (1974) is of very little use to those having to make decisions in specific institutions. Terkel interviews Americans in a wide range of jobs about their work, and through his own rare capacity for selecting responsive individuals and talking to them sensitively he brings to life a vital part of American society, justifying his book's ambitious subtitle, 'An Autobiography of America'. He leaves a vivid general picture of the enduring centrality of work, and the deep sense of failure that most experience because of the nature of their jobs. But, as Hannah Arendt points out, labour is labour, and sugaring the pill will not change its inherent tastelessness. Terkel's study serves to remind us just how much of modern work is in fact unrewarding labour. This recognition would make the men who set up factories or offices, and the union leaders who negotiate with them, more sympathetic to the moral plight of those who labour and hold jobs, but this greater humanity is powerless to change the economic and technological necessities which determine the nature of most modern jobs.

To choose another example, it might be argued that there is a sociology of power and institutions that is useful to those involved in politics and administration. A man arbitrating between unions and management, the argument might continue, will benefit from an understanding of the theory and history of class conflict. There may be some truth to this, but not a great deal. Experience in the situation, of the individuals involved, of the issues and their particular history, of handling committees and meetings is far more important than theoretical background on industrial society, and the behaviour of groups. Moreover, the type of sociology relevant here is again low-grade. Theory-centred sociology on, for example, the rise of capitalism, deals with a complexity of historical and psychological issues that render it of only the most oblique relevance to the arbitration meeting. Indeed, it is more likely to distract the man it interests from the difficult challenge at hand.

There are a few cases in which theory itself might prove relevant. While the humanist ideal of the educated man (aware of his culture and trained in thoughtfulness) as the wisest administrator has been rashly glamorized, and distorted by utilitarians into 'training', it nevertheless carries some weight. Humanist education may well not be relevant in the arbitration court, but there are other areas in which it does have a role, and an important one. For example, at the highest level, when constitutions are being written, or when long-term political policies are being framed, a theoretical bent is essential.

Theory might also be relevant to a social worker dealing with delinquency. Familiarity with such case studies as *The Jack-Roller* (Shaw, 1930) should increase understanding of the sort of pressures that produce delinquency and induce some sympathy for what the symptoms mean. Here theory plays one of its most important roles, in contributing to knowledge about human nature and its many socialized forms. Such theory has some relevance to everyone in their personal lives, and to a few in their public working lives.

The urge to be relevant in sociology has far outstripped what was justified. Recognition of this fact takes me to the crux of my argument, that the exaggerated sense of sociology's own power has brought its own form of distortion to the discipline. The roots of the relevance temptation rise from the same soil as Rousseauist idealism, and they commonly support the same tree. The Rousseauist ideal stresses that the innate goodness of man might be recovered by changing the social institutions that have corrupted it. This ideal carries with it its own exhortation to political action, and recognizes no inherent split between understanding and practice. Consequently those sociologists touched by the Rousseauist spirit have believed that their perception of virtue will cut through the confusions, the prevarications, the complexities of social policy as they see it doggedly set out and acted upon around them.

The union of relevance and idealism produces bad politics. It does not understand with any adequacy the reality on which it is trying to operate, which means that it produces consequences that it never imagined. Moreover, the relevance urge among sociologists has suited the growing habit of governments when under pressure to call an enquiry. Enquiries in which assemblies of experts deliberate at length often serve mainly to defuse the issue, allowing governments to do what they wanted to do in the first place, and with a better conscience. Thus sociology has been used to give a semblance of often illegitimate rationality to public policy, used to convince that consequences are foreseen and will be favourable. This is the first drive of the relevance temptation.

Of greater importance for our discussion is the fact that the union of relevance and idealism reinforces the adolescent fixation in sociology, the preference for idealistic simplifications of reality. It leads not only to bad practice, but turns back on sociology to support bad theory, or more, the rejection of theory. The tendency to simplify has two sources. The first is a practical one. The world of politics, of swaying opinion, of mounting campaigns, of using mass media, requires relatively simple clear-cut formulations of policy. It is difficult to resist the temptation to promise too much, to be over-optimistic about consequences. Thus the very desire to be relevant will bring with it pressures to simplify. Moreover, it is not part of the Rousseauist conscience to worry about long-term consequences; indeed the sceptical caution of a Burke is derided as a rationalization for inactivity.

The second source of this tendency to simplify is historical. The historical origins of the conjunction of relevance and idealism lie with socialism, and in particular, to name the main line, the influence of Rousseau elaborated by Marx. This influence has pushed sociology in a materialist direction, attaching it to Marx's notion of man as the *animal laborans*. (While Marx does make a distinction between labour and 'self-activity', the latter being akin to skilled, vocational work, his historical model portrays a capitalist society in which work is progressively replaced by labour, labour being the source of all productivity. Capitalism transforms into communism when, in part, productivity is high enough to require little labour per man. But there is no specification of what 'self-activity' might mean when the economic base for vocational work has been eliminated.) The view of man defined by his labour, as Hannah Arendt has argued (*The Human Condition*), in effect reinforces the twentieth-century emphasis on consumption rather than use, confuses brute servile labour with skilled work to the detriment of the latter, and degrades by neglect the higher qualities of human life. It hinges on Marx's utopian assumption that the attainment of abundance, the emancipation of man from labour, will release imaginative capacities and make of leisure a paradise. All the historical evidence suggests, however, that it is not in man's nature to handle abundance well, and that in fact man lives best caught in the middle of a tension between abundance and necessity. Arendt points out that it should be all too clear to us today that the *animal laborans* spends his spare time on nothing but consumption. The materialist simplification, dominant in sociology since 1918, has singled out economic differentials, income inequalities, welfare and the lack thereof, as its key interests, to the point that 'art' is studied by and large in terms of the class background of its patrons and consumers. Man reduced to the labourer-consumer is not only man without art, without guile, without wit or charm, without infatuation or jealousy, without tragedy, even without intellect; he is also man stripped of his metaphysical core. It is only natural that a discipline that focuses on animalized man should itself become atheoretical. This focus, with its simplification of the human condition into materialist terms, itself facilitates the relevance drive. As economic science discovered, to be able to argue purely in terms of material variables such as incomes, prices, and profits makes it much easier to formulate precise political programmes, programmes whose backing appears 'scientific'. Alternatively, once the metaphysical is recognized so are multiple moral ambivalencies, and the politics of Dostoevsky's 'great simplifier' loses its sway.

The urge to be relevant in a sociologist suggests a distaste for thought, for the reflective mood, for theory. It assumes a simple relationship between theory and conduct. But, as all sceptics have discovered, knowledge that carries any sting, that moves with enough finesse to catch a new fish, works on experience, and hence surfaces only after the action, after the events are completed, and often quite a while after. It is in the nature of understanding to follow action, but never to catch it. It functions at a different tempo and it emerges at a different time. Knowledge is inimical to relevance; it tends to inhibit action by making painfully apparent how complex and unpredictable are the likely consequences of any significant political move. Accordingly, when relevance sociologists draw on the precepts of others it is almost inevitable that they will choose banalities, and often from that flashiest and most simplistic subspecies, ideals. So what a government gets, by and large, when it hires a sociologist are the commonplaces of the time dressed up in jargon. The sociologist legitimates that government's bad practice, and compromises his own calling.

9 Authority

A central and recurring task that a sceptical sociology must address, whatever specific situations it chooses to work upon, is the problem of authority. 'Authority' has proved a stumbling block, if often a subtle one, to the Rousseauist tradition, which has never progressed beyond the trite Marxist view that reduces authority to power, which is interpreted simply as the physical capacity to coerce, a capacity belonging to the dominant economic class and its political institutions. The poverty of sociology in relation to the issue of authority is complemented today in the West by the mediocrity of elites, spanning the social spectrum from politics to education, a mediocrity that must in part be the result of a Rousseauist temper at work in the general community, nurturing resentment against any authority.

More importantly, a sceptical sociology, in taking Freud as one of its mentors, has to come to grips with the thesis by which his social theory is generated from his more fundamental individual psychology. The thesis is that all individuals at some level long for authority. (Talcott Parsons in his essays on Freud's relevance to sociology emasculates the link by focusing on the 'superego', and treating it as the vehicle for socialization.) The importance of Freud at this point is to ground in a fully-fledged theory of personality Durkheim's assertion that men need external constraint, in the form of norms, to order their potentially chaotic, internal drives and to establish purposes through which to give their lives meaning. His challenge is consequently to work through in all spheres of social life, from the family, to the school, to the office, the role of the individual's unconscious wish for authority, the form that this wish takes, and how the conflict between it and its frequently present opposite, hatred for authority, plays itself out. One of the spheres in which Freud does this himself is that of religion, examining the projection of the father problem on to a patriarchal deity and its worldly institutions (*The Future of an Illusion*).

It is Philip Rieff, in his peerless study *Freud: The Mind of the Moralist*, who points to the importance of the authority theme in Freud's social theory; he counters the simplified view that instability in the individual is due to difficulties in controlling a single unruly instinct, sexuality. Freud postulates a dichotomy between the emotional states of tenderness and sensuality, a dichotomy corresponding to different stages in the development of the infant child. The first form of love is authoritative, and derives from the child's gratitude to his parents, for protecting him, for providing a family circle which is secure and bound by tenderness. A longing for this primary happiness, depending on the subordinate individual being dominated, although benignly, remains throughout life. Sexual love comes second chronologically, in the form of a possessive erotic attachment to the mother. In the pure form of this love, the individual is equal and autonomous. Thenceforth the experience of love, that is of emotional attachment in all its diverse forms, will result from attraction to one type of fusion or another of the authority figure and the sexual object. Gratifying relationships will depend on the successful infusion of sexuality with tenderness.

Intimate relationships, however, constitute only the more obvious type that come under the sway of the longing for authority. An individual's fantasies in relation to authority influence his behaviour in every sphere of social life, and come to influence the groups in which he moves and the institutions in which he works. To give a crude example: a political revolution in a country in which institutions are traditionally authoritarian will, except in extraordinary circumstances, merely produce a replacement set of authoritarian institutions. This is not simply due to some inertia towards change; if people long for authority, of whatever type, they will, through their work and their political responses, make sure they get institutions that satisfy that longing. If it is true, as Max Stirner claimed, that every Prussian carries his gendarme in his breast, then there is little point in reforming the Prussian police force.

The longing for authority plays a positive role in the development of the individual. It is linked with the achievement of emotional tenderness, and it contributes to the achievement of maturity in relation to work – including a range of competence in the public world. For example, the core of a successful education is a benign master-apprentice relationship. It is true for the university, as it is for the school, that a student learns best when he projects on to his teacher the vestments of charismatic authority; he thereby creates a situation in which he is inspired to learn, without the dissipations of rebelliousness or indifference, what his master has to teach him. Of course it is crucial that the teacher be equal to the responsibility. In the process of learning, of the student slowly coming to his own mastery, the apprentice emancipates himself without undue fret from his submissive role, and, all being well, he will never again have a longing for authority of this particular type.

It is of particular importance that sociology come better to grips with 'authority'. There has been virtually no significant work on the subject, Bendix's *Work and Authority in Industry* (1956) being a notable exception. It is the area in which the Rousseauist ideal has been most tangibly corrosive of a real understanding. Moreover, at the general cultural level, authority is the problem of our time: the failure of authority, of past commitments and constraints, of present elites, to maintain levels of communal and individual purpose, is responsible for the remiss state of contemporary Western civilization. Boredom, lethargy, depression, violence, pornography, often selected as the symptoms of current decay, all derive from the failure of authority, externally in important social institutions, internally within the character of the individual himself. (This last assertion is argued at length in my book, *Puritan, Paranoid, Remissive: A Sociology of Modern Culture*, 1977.)

The failure of sociology to address adequately the question of authority is to be further witnessed in a subsidiary neglect, its avoidance of what Nietzsche called the reactive emotions – pity, vengeance, resentment, and envy. Helmut Schoeck, in his comprehensive study, *Envy* (1966), draws on ethnology to argue that envy is universal to the human condition, and, furthermore, that without envy there could be no social group of any size. What is extraordinary, in relation to our discussion here, is that sociological investigation of norms, values, constraints, inequalities and so on can happily proceed without taking any account of this ubiquitous motivating force. Such a neglect is consonant with the Rousseauist refusal to recognize any but virtuous elements as innate to man, and with a certain bad conscience in the socialist movement at its own success having depended to a marked degree on the manipulation of envy. Significant that Schoeck himself should have singled out the date 1920 as the approximate demarcation point, before which there were numerous sociological studies that investigated the effects and the nature of envy, after which there were very few. (Another neglect of the same ilk is of *property*, and its nature, as Alvin Gouldner has noted – *The Coming Crisis of Western Sociology*.)

10 The twentieth-century heritage

Before repeating the call for a retreat to the eighteenth century for mentors for a sceptical sociology, it is incumbent upon us to enquire into whether our own century, which has been noted in many spheres of culture for its championing of the subjective, has not made significant contributions to the study of society as the product of unconscious wishes, that is, apart from the contribution of Freud.

George Simmel, in his meditations on culture, and essays on such subjects as adventure, and the ruin, makes some suggestive comments on the unconscious ties of the individual to his society. But they do not add up to much, and end up dissipated in an over-refined cerebrality which is not tempered by any strong grip on the tissues of human motive. Simmel's work has a cripplingly pre-Freudian outlook. The same is to be said about Vilfredo Pareto.

Marx's seminal contribution was to the other dimension of sociology, illustrating man as a product of the society into which he is born. This contribution has been enlarged by followers, with particular success in such fields as literary criticism. However, there has been only one serious attempt to bridge the gap between this and the other sociological dimension, by the Frankfurt School, which has endeavoured to integrate Freud and Marx. While impressive but rather anarchic aphorisms have been produced by Adorno (*Minima*

Moralia), and an equally impressive epistemology has been produced by Habermas (*Knowledge and Human Interests*), there has been little sociology, apart from research on *The Authoritarian Personality*, which added nothing of substance to Freud.

The new theoretical perspective that has made the strongest claims to transform our understanding of the subjective individual has been phenomenology, a truly twentieth-century phenomenon. But it too has singularly failed to contribute to sociology. Husserl's work, itself a mixture of mandarin abstruseness and simple wisdoms, has produced disciples who are no more than mandarins, or epistemological nihilists, thus defeating the master's leading purpose of reconstituting European rationality. Heidegger's work took him finally, and as its logical outcome, into a realm of poetic mysticism, and the philosopher retired to his hut in the Black Forest, remote from the worldly realities of society. Phenomenology, in the end the most other-worldly of twentieth-century intellectual movements, ended up abandoning the very reality of which it set out to provide a new view. (Sartre, more a borrower than a lender, fled from his earlier phenomenological concern into Marxism.)

Certain sociologists – notably Schutz, Goffman, and Garfinkel – have been described as phenomenologists. It is claimed that through concentrating on the subject and his own perceptions of his reality, the inhuman distance between the 'objective' researcher and his object has been removed. This is the technique of the creative writer; unfortunately the writings of these sociologists do not compare well with the best twentieth-century novels or stories, in their perceptions either of social relations or of individual sensibility. Moreover, in rejecting the disciplines of both academic history and academic psychology, these sociologists have cut themselves off from sociology's strongest roots.

Apart from Freud, there has been one major contribution to our understanding of the impact of the individual on social life, that of Max Weber. His work draws on many examples of the workings of the unconscious wishes of the individual, in religion, in charismatic authority, in the ambitions of politicians, above all in his masterpiece on the relationship between the Protestant ethic, the type of personality it fostered, and the rise of the capitalist economy. This work is still today the major piece of synthesis in sociology, bringing together the two dimensions. Nevertheless, its individual psychology is rudimentary, leaving the field wide open for the importation of the more sophisticated theory of Freud.

11 The story-teller

It is in the form of stories that human life is remembered. Moreover, our capacity for remembering the past is essential to our humanity. Stories are told after the events, often long after. The very process of transforming action into a story gives it a permanency, an immortality, and above all a dignity that it is otherwise denied. That action will come to life again when another man becomes absorbed by the story. Hamlet's dying wish, with which he entreats Horatio, is 'to tell my story'. It is a profound and universal wish, and it carries a much deeper significance than the desire to be understood simply in the sense that the facts are got right. The story will give Hamlet a type of metaphysical vindication, saving him from oblivion, as if by its telling the gods would recognize and witness, rather than forget, what he had been.

History has it written into its name that it should proceed by means of stories. Sociology too is forced to proceed by telling stories, although failure to recognize this has brought a lot of confusion and bad practice. Story-telling is the art of description, of being able to select a sequence of events or an area of conduct and retell it vividly as it was. Sociology is the interpretation of social life, but one cannot interpret without having first described, and, furthermore, the great battles of interpretation are won or lost in the descriptions themselves. The art of story-telling is essential to sociology.

Robert Nisbet has suggested, in his *Sociology as an Art Form*, that the classics of sociology brought to life such types as 'the bourgeois', 'the worker', and 'the bureaucrat', and such scenarios as the 'metropolis'; they did this by developing techniques analogous to those of the portrait and the landscape painter. In fact they were using some of the skills of the story-teller, in choosing particular individuals and scenes that generalize into being somehow typical of the time, and giving insight into it.

There is a special reason for sociology focusing more single-minded on story-telling. The raconteur's vocation has strong inbuilt defences against our worst vices. The truth has been that the more abstract our treatises, the more disenchanting, the more they have reduced social life. Indeed, some of the most influential sociology since 1918 has traded on its incomprehensibility. Stories don't permit too much abstraction. Moreover, if the writer bungles the ending, listeners have the good sense to complain, for stories are close enough to reality for anyone with a moderately fine ear to be able to pick a fake. Stories thus counter idealism, as well as gobbledygook. For the same reason they act as a safeguard against the scientific itch, which attacks even the best bred sociologist as soon as he is off his guard. Finally, there is little danger that anyone, especially in government or business circles, will consider them to be relevant.

But our story-telling must be different. Heidegger referred to Kierkegaard not as a philosopher, but as a philosophical writer. Similarly, what is under discussion here is not sociology in most traditional senses of the term, not literature, but something in between. Samuel Johnson himself defies classification: his *Rasselas* is in part a literary tale, in part an essay in morals, like Pope's *Essay on Man*, which was also a poem. One might refer to sociological writers, but that is long-winded, and, what is more, the purpose of the manifesto is to argue for a new direction for *sociology*.

There are areas of sociology that will not always be amenable to interpretation through stories. Textual exegesis, trade figures, accounts of government legislation, details about the rise of an institution's power, to take four examples, may all play important roles in a sceptical sociology. Nevertheless, sociology has such an embarrassing record for woodenness, for painting a Pinnochio and rail-timetable world, that enforcing for a decade a first commandment to publish only in the genre of the story, must prove salutary. Some classes, one suspects, might be necessary in life-drawing, followed by sessions in instruction in how to get colour into the charcoal cheeks. These would replace our current courses in methodology.

A story-telling sociology should have an excellent future. The history of sociology as a discipline would take a welcome fork in the road. Moreover, the novel and the story as pure art forms seem near the end of their track, if not off it altogether. They have frequently this century sought revitalization from the academy, from such disciplines as history and psychoanalysis. We could try to help them out, by starting to build from our bank of the river. If the bridge actually meets in the middle it might turn out to be a splendid artifact.

We could all take a cue from a medium that still produces work of excellence, the film. In recent years the French have produced three outstanding films set in the period of Nazi occupation. Louis Malle's *Lacombe Lucien* is a beautifully observed portrait of a simple French peasant stumbling into becoming a Nazi, and his reactions to a renegade Jewish family whose cultivated daughter he falls in love with. The film presents a close-up of a circle of individuals in a tense situation, while providing insights, inaccessible to orthodox sociology, into the links between private lives and a large-scale political movement. The second film, Robert Enrico's *The Old Gun*, is notable for its psychological realism, a sustained study of how a man copes with devastating grief. It is a particularly fine study of the working out of strong feelings using the elements of an extremely restricted social situation. Third, there is *The Sorrow and the Pity*, the long social documentary on collaboration and resistance during the occupation.

It is something to have told a good story. Terkel in his excellent book, *Working*, simply tells good stories. The stories are so telling that he does not need to interpret. And can we dismiss the fact that Terkel's background was not in formal sociology, but as a disc-jockey?

12 The sceptic

Those who are drawn to sociology generally have the disposition of moralists, wanting to take their society, shake it, make something better of it. (One ignores those who have slipped into the job-holding role.) The moralists, with the Puritan strong in their disposition, have to face the time in which they live. The culture is remissive: moralistic in its desire to elude controls, and yet generally remiss. These sociologists, having steered past the Scylla of science, idealism, and relevance, the monster of malign moralism, still have to negotiate the Charybdis of remiss decadence. The latter is the more tricky, although weaker, hazard. It calls for skilful navigation. On the one hand, if sociology works at too great a moral distance from the culture, it will neither understand it, nor speak to it. In short, to aim for a serious Puritan sociology, with the values of civic duty, individual responsibility, and private tact underpinning it, would be like setting sails for a wind that doesn't exist – a miscalculation that readily capsizes the boat. On the other hand, sociology sailing close to the wind of the culture has to ensure that it does not itself succumb to the careless, phlegmatic mood of the material it is wooing. The course between this Scylla and Charybdis is peculiarly suited to a sceptic. Scepticism will cut across the moralism, while using its better strain; and in its own ironical moralism it will retain a self-discipline which distances it from the society it scrutinizes. A sceptic is always swinging between a love of seriousness, and a disgust for it. As sociologist, he should address the moralist Scylla with light contempt, and the anarchic Charybdis with troubled intent.

It seems that we are not intending to take ourselves utterly seriously. And this is programmatic. Our theses are stories, and who knows how typical of anything they are? Who knows even how internally consistent they are? We have vague ideas. But only vague, and therefore we need to be ironical, both as a check on claiming too much, and a release for our exasperations at doing so poorly. It would not be a bad idea to make our style ridiculous enough not to be taken dogmatically, and yet not so ridiculous that its content is merely laughed at.

But irony may carry a deeper deceit. We all need order and meaning, sociologists more than others – otherwise why rack our brains so hard trying to find patterns? For our own well-being we *have* to believe in our patterns, and pretty fiercely. The voice of experience tells us we are fools, kidding ourselves, that this is all a game, nothing to do with Truth, all to do with Sanity. We buy this voice off by getting him to play the role of irony, letting him think that he undermines our certitudes. But under the surface we remain fanatics to what we say, and now the trickier to trip up in this desperate hypocrisy.

Yet we are serious. Our doubting is in order to find out what binds and what is true – in short to discover that about which we can and ought to have no doubt. We Westerners have as our exemplars Socrates, the stinging fly, for whom, like his greatest and most devoted son, Plato, the unexamined life was not worth living; and we have Nietzsche, the philosopher with the tuning fork, tapping the ideals of himself and his time to hear how hollow they rang. Our scepticism has two branches. We doubt in order to understand: here our pursuit is the knowledge of truth. We doubt equally in order to become good: to know virtue. Socrates's own scepticism in the pursuit of truth was limited by his reverence for the law, although that law treated him unjustly. In his own case virtue included obedience to the law of his community; but that obedience would not hinder his other pursuit, that of truth. Socrates, like Nietzsche, doubted in order to be sure. We have uncovered a quest for authority, for individual authority.

To complete the summing up of the sceptic's role. Our aspiration in relation to our parentage is to integrate the monumental psychological theory of Freud, with the deflating, judicious scepticism of Johnson, the systematic clarity of Hume, and the gay pungency of Nietzsche. Our root is human nature, and society growing as the product of unconscious wishes. Later we recognize that society works partly under its own laws, and has its own role in the patterning of the unconscious wishes. The problem of authority is uppermost in our minds. We proceed by telling stories. We have our rules, a hybrid scientific-literary code. And we don't expect too much: we shall not overcome, the world will not be shaken by us, nor will individual lives. We represent one type of contemporary narcissist, trying to have some fun, or stay sane, in our own peculiar way, trying to turn our compulsion to control the world through writing about it into a kind of flirtation with ourselves, and, if we are lucky, with some others.

2 The fur hat

Every decent citizen ought to be warned about the fur hat. Just as the reptile species celebrated life with the taipan, the fish with the great white shark, the feline family with the Indian tiger, so *anthropos felix* visited the fur hat on a blithe unsuspecting world.

Fur hats can be encountered on the loose in every one of the five great continents. Their lineage, however, twists out of the past towards us from one primeval forest, fecund with the genes of a Pandoric mutation. And it is that dingy cramped little village on the Danube, that same cradle that rocked Schubert, Freud, Kraus, Wittgenstein, Strauss, Franz Josef, and the Sachertorte into shape, that was responsible, and would accordingly in a just world suffer from the sniffs of our resentment.

Our specimen is female, usually middle-aged, and gets its name from the fact that in Vienna, where malice is no less a way of life than coffee, every woman when she attains a certain age, usually somewhere in her thirties, suddenly awakes one morning with a throbbing passion to purchase a fur hat, which she thereafter wears whenever she slides out of her house in the colder half of the year. In more benign quarters of the globe the major turning point in a person's life is the coming of puberty, or the taking of a spouse, learning to walk, or talk, the losing of a job, or ending it all with rat poison. For our heroines, however, it is this day that transforms their lives, or rather, stands as a symptom of a momentous inner revolution, their Damascus Road. From this day until she finally lies on her death-bed our friend will feel herself naked, ill-at-ease, vacant if she moves in public without the emblem of her ghastly disposition clamped down over her scalp. With her fur hat on, her spirit rises, her eye glints and she gains the courage to have it always both ways – in a bus queue she is the one who does both the pushing and the complaining. And the genuine fur hat, the one of 'by appointment' quality, demands to die in full regalia, the dimming eyes finding their ultimate repose under the bristling shadow of an overhanging pelt.

If one wishes to observe fur hats at play, in their thickest element, as it were, one only needs to visit their favourite hunting ground, the Viennese coffee house. There they gather, usually huddled a pair to a table, leaning towards each other across the cakes, their flushed heavy-jowled, pig-eyed Cardinal faces flesh-to-flesh, mouths twisting, snapping, smacking, leering as they whisper out, drip upon drip, their vitriol. One can tell from the colour of the eye, the curve of the mouth, its speed, the moisture on the lip, and above all from the state of the cake, how many murders are being committed each minute. Only a fur hat's most carefully rehearsed, dramatically orchestrated tale of misery and brutishness can touch the other, the companion, and draw her out of her own monster-infested well of introspection, rescue her from her own hurricane of fantasies.

For a veteran fur hat stories about husband assassination are too tame, men being too easy. The veterans, the professionals of the species, like all serious hunters, are challenged only by encounters with the best of their own kind. For our beasts of prey the choicest tales relate to other fur hats; the most finely wrought spite winds around the closest accomplice. Nothing is more highly valued than betrayal of the closest friend – indeed here is the path to intimacy for a fur hat. Fur hats typically have two intimates, thus permitting them to alternate. A friend is one who is well enough known to be knifed with precision, deftly, so that the most sensitive tissue can be exposed on the table, in full view of the second friend, and dissected with the skill of a Mephistophelean eye surgeon.

Fur hat scene 1

Two fur hats sitting in a coffee house discussing cemeteries over gorgeous cream cakes. A man sits absently between them. One complains that the central cemetery is a long way from her house; she spends a lot of time there, so she is always travelling. The other responds that *she* in fact lives close to the cemetery in which her family has its plot; an excellent plot with a beautiful clear view of the Vienna woods. The first fur hat nods abrupt approval, and quickly seeks to regain her advantage by stating that *she* has the last place in her own family grave. The other asks with surprise, gesturing in the direction of the man: 'What about him, then?' The first, now firmly in the chair, sits up shaking her head and waves a finger as if warning a child against swearing in church. 'No,' she urges with a thin grin, 'he wants to be burnt.' The man smiles to himself and seems to nod his assent. The second fur hat gets a glazed visionary look in her eye, and whispers, almost lecherously, as she sinks her teeth into a large Sachertorte: 'Like a little piggy with the fat glistening, roasting on a spit.' In Vienna death and food are celebrated as if it were 1900 and they were Kaiser and Kaiserin.

Fur hat scene 2

Morning mass, Christmas Day, Stephansdom, Vienna. A fur hat in the front pew chews her gums, lips tight, manic by disposition. She knows the ritual of the service as if it were her own toilet – standing at precisely the right moment, sitting too with a supercilious familiarity, as if she and not the organ were the official prompter. Her first claim on our attention as a potentially interesting member of her species is her manifested belief that when she answers the priest's incantation fractionally before the rest of the congregation God will hear her, single her out for special recognition. So from the outset a lonely, rather harsh and unmelodious 'Gott sei Dank' peals forth from the front pew pitched at the gaunt wooden Christ gazing mournfully down from the high reaches of the Gothic vaulting. It is followed by its echo, the slower, slightly unsynchronized, bass 'Gott sei Dank' of the rest of the congregation. Through the service she consolidates her special relationship, never missing an entry, singing at full blast, praying deeply and reverently down low over her knees. So far, however, we have witnessed but the preparation for her definitive scene, but the practice for the *coup de grâce* – her taking of the Eucharist. Before the priest is quarter way through the wine and bread preliminaries with his assistant, before anyone else has moved from their seat, she has walked forward to a place, as if by formal arrangement with the church, halfway between her seat and the rail at which the communicants will kneel. It is only once her fellow communicants have moved forward, and the first sitting has taken its place, that her intentions become clear. The problem is that not just the chief priest, vested in baroque magnificence, dressed in the authority of this most important rite on this most important day, not he alone will administer the sacrament; he is aided by a subaltern. Now our fur hat is determined that she will not be attended by some bumbling apprentice, little more than a boy. However, on this holiest of holy days, her shrewdness is foiled, for the priest and his assistant are so slow in arranging their gifts that the first sitting is kneeling by the time they indicate from which end of the line each will start. She is further frustrated when, about to take her place for the third sitting, the priest unexpectedly changes direction, forcing her into an awkward reverse trot. By the fifth sitting her agitation is close to panic. Now merely a dozen people remain waiting, and it appears she has dithered her last change to act with some confidence. A properly-dressed elderly couple are well ahead of her heading for the remaining two places in a line that the priest has just commenced – probably his last. Now our fur hat, not one to wither at the finishing post, reins her flustered sinews, and, like a bull at the brink of death, glimpsing red through the flashing steel of the lances of the closing picadors, she charges, crashing past the lady, bayonetting her out of the way with a jab of the elbow, and dives for the centre of the empty space. Gasping, she thrusts her hands high on to the railing in prayer, and raises her triumphant face to meet her God. Later, she turns, and, as if intoxicated with benevolence towards all mankind, she glides back to the front pew.

Fur hat scene 3

A sunny spring day; a queue of cars heading for Switzerland stopped at the Austrian border; a young lady in a floppy straw hat, the hood of her Austrian registered Deux Chevaux down. The car rolls gently, negligently forward into the car in front. A fur hat leaps out, speeds round for a close inspection, raises her head trembling with rage, stares agog at the lady who continues sunning her cheeks, and starts to shout. The lady quietly asks whether there is any damage. The fur hat pauses, straightens herself, glowers, and slowly shakes her head. The lady quietly asks what then the fuss is about. The fur hat opens up again, shouting that the lady might at least get out of her car, that it is a crime to run into someone else's property, that her papers were certainly not in order, and that she should get out immediately and produce her driver's licence. The lady, clearly Viennese herself, used to fur hats, and by now enjoying her dangerous bluff, looks contemptuously down her nose, smiles, and advises the woman to call the police. At this point the fur hat's husband gets out of their car, and wearily walks round to size up the situation. Pleased to have had her attention taken up elsewhere for five minutes, he realizes that his respite is over and he must, as usual, quieten her down. When the young lady finally arrives at the customs she is ordered to get out, and is left to stand helplessly for an hour watching her car ransacked for hidden drugs.

Has anyone ever spotted a fur hat in love? It is not that their hearts are stone. Nor is it that they really disapprove, in spite of all their talk about the rabies, of how those pathetically sentimental creatures, dogs, turn to frothing and raving even more than usual. And one should not take too seriously their favourite maxims, repeated again and again with pinched smiles and knowing nods, such maxims as the following, one of the more ornate: 'the final choice whenever the heart is involved always comes to eating or fasting, the former leading to indigestion and repletion, dreams fading as surely as Leonardo's *Last Supper*, the latter leading to obsession, an endless craving for cake.' The fur hat knows that her maxims are true. But we should not be duped by her assured manner. There is a particular meanness that rises in her whenever she comes across creatures who have been struck by passion, and gives away only too clearly her own lingering hopes. How naive. How un-fur-hat-like. (While I remember, another fur hat maxim: 'Cats, when they are at a loose end, lick themselves.')

Although it is indisputable that nowhere on today's earth can be seen such an assembly of evil faces as in Vienna, and one wonders half in pity, half in righteous indignation, half in apprehension, what woeful history could have conspired this hideous lineage, and although one sees in every second passerby a barely suppressed Nazi awaiting his, or usually her, next cue, or in the far from uncommon crazier cases, the Second Coming, it is equally true that this twilight world is never dull. Nor are the fur hats dulled. They live long, and not for them the fade into decades of vacancy and mumbled inanity. They stalk the streets, stocky furtive personages out of the canvasses of Hieronymus Bosch, or the stories of Franz Kafka (a quasi-Viennese himself), their noses in everything, itching every minute to unleash a stream of comments, advice, moralizations, especially moralizations. To survive in Vienna one needs the alertness of a Jesuit stranded in Mecca; the pleasure comes later.

We are still being too unkind to our specimens. We have said no more in their favour than that the siege mentality is catching, that after a spell in Vienna other cities seem flaccid, their grip loose, their tolerance more like indifference. In fact, the fur hat wins our affection to a small but significant degree for her zest. And her vitality, her prickly longevity, is not utterly the fruit that grows on the tree tended by the vigilant loving hand of malice. While one does not have to be very old to suspect that sustained nastiness is the malt in the beer of human alertness, there are other ingredients. To start with, compare the fur hat, who is an artist, a perfectionist, her work meticulously scrutinized by other professionals ruthlessly guarding their standards, compare her with her British equivalent, nattering over four o'clock tea her monotone account of where her daughter travelled yesterday, and whom she saw, and how nice everything was, countless fact after dreary fact, met by a coterie of nods, mumbles, and grunts among the yellow doughy crumbs.

Fur hats appoint themselves overseers of not only public behaviour, but also of public taste. And they often have taste. Their favourite adjective, 'disgusting', is routinely applied to most persons, to most buildings, to most objects, but above all to that plasticated modernity that the socialist surgeons are transplanting into the fluttering heart of old Vienna, without any sensitivity to the preference of bodies far less fastidious than our sibyls for rejecting foreign tissue.

As the fur hat is a master criminal, she is equally a master psychologist. It is a rare talent. Her eye pierces deep into the softest membrane of the human soul. But her pleasure is more than that of the successful execution of the supremely crafty, sublimely elegant murder. She is almost as merciless in the baring of her own heart. Her talk is coursed with exposures of her latest failure, the flawed pattern of her friendships, her affairs, her marriage, the blighted destiny that has been her life. The milieu is of vigilant, relentless introspection, coughed up, poked at, tinkered with, in the form of savage caricatures of her contacts. The tireless snipping away at others is the public expression of a desperate inward striving for purity and harmony, for a serene passage; the disgust at the slovenliness of the human world is the pressure valve for her fear that she too is not far from the grub. Our fur hat's corroded idealism pours out in irony-soaked, spite-oiled discontent. She licks her wounds with gossip, but aware herself of what she does, that she has, in watching the gossamer hopes of her youth puff away, grown into her talk; she has become her fur hat.

I, for one, prefer a fur hat any day to her American counterpart, powdered, skin-lifted, tinted, rinsed, desperate parody of lost youth, beaming hysterical optimism, crooning on about problems and solutions, as if life *were* an old pop song, tackling the bulging deceit together with sentimentality, her panic insidiously swelling as the weight of reality, of the inescapable, of decay and of death, steadily accumulates and threatens to drop through the bottom of the worn package. That ultra-Viennese, that genteel, cleverly professional fur hat, Freud, admitted to two life-long hates, religion and America, both phenomena being founded on illusion.

Fur hat culture is rich. These ladies and their forebears have made much of the condition of being born with talent and intelligence into a society that provides them little opportunity for a vocation, little outlet of any public kind for their ambition. They have cultivated their gardens of frustration with tender passion, and unwittingly built a tradition that may well have had a formative influence on Viennese high culture, and especially on its great period early this century. Freud, for example, found his inspiration in his indefatigable curiosity about motives, in his life-long obsession with laying bare the human heart, both peculiarly fur hat passions. There possibly is a moral.

However, let us not ourselves become sentimental, about the fur hat, for not only is she dangerous, but such a misanthrope does not hold the future of the West in her hands. Fur hats do not pioneer, they do not build, they do not dream of brave new worlds. They are, to put it mildly, bad for the morale of the species, and should one and all be exiled to their native hunting ground, their spiritual home, Vienna, where they could be left to grow old with their beloved city. The rest of us would occasionally visit the reservation, for entertainment, and also to jog our memories about what a splendid consumptive decadence our civilization is capable of, if left unchecked.

In conclusion, a parting word to you, whoever you are, dear reader. If you have not found this little story amusing then one thing is certain, you yourself are not a fur hat, and therefore should regard our extravagance here as a warning, no more than some advice from a well-meaning friend, a cautionary, a moral, tale. I am sure you have done such in any case. If at the same time you believe that I have merely been relating ills that an Anglo-Saxon takes for granted as being commonplace beyond the shores of that precious stone set in a silver sea, then you are little other than a busybody, and self-deluded at that. Vienna has simply provided a metaphoric convenience. Finally, for the rest, the fur hats themselves, they are splitting their sides.

3 In spite of intellectuals

Just as there are seven deadly sins, or, if one prefers, seven sublime virtues, there have been seven types of intellectuals. Or, at least, when one has reached seven, one has enough to suggest variety, and not too many to bring confusion. At the same time one has confirmed divine order and kept the devil happy, so altogether we are off to a satisfactory start.

Intellectuals are those with a passion for thinking, for ideas, for the abstract. They set out to understand things, to discover the truth, to interpret the world of man and nature for themselves and for their less mindful fellows. They are those of superior intellect. And they teach: they pass on to the young the accumulated knowledge and culture of their tribe. Such is the conventional wisdom about intellectuals. The reality has been somewhat different, presenting a bizarre array of types, in fact quite a pantomime of clowns, mountebanks, lunatics and obsessives. The pursuit of truth has disguised many a pathology. So let us now tug a little at the costumes, the moustaches, and the noses, and see who actually turns up on stage. The seven performers, in their order of appearance, are the mandarin, the engineer, the chess player, the chiliast, the shaman, the Galahad, and the king's fool.

1 The mandarin

The Chinese literati or mandarin evolved from the court astrologer, a figure singled out by his knowledge of the calendar and the stars. He came in time to form a class of public officials with a monopoly on literacy, attached to the belief that learning and scholarship are paths to rational government. Under the influence of the mandarins a literary education became the yardstick of social prestige in China. The literati of the feudal period were called *pou che* – 'living libraries'. Their highest proficiency was in ritualism; they made of the ancient scriptures magical objects. Their influence became so strong that even the rank of a city god depended on the rank of the city's mandarin, adviser to the prince. Max Weber reports the resolution of a violent dispute between an able general and a literary man in the feudal state of Wei, after the latter had been appointed first minister. The literary man, having conceded that the general could better conduct wars and master similar political tasks, urged that it was, however, revolution that threatened the dynasty. The general immediately accepted that the literary man was the better choice.

After Confucius, with his maxim that caution is the better part of valour, an extensive examination system developed in China. There were three major degrees, for the first of which alone ten types of examination were necessary (a system introduced by a parvenu in the Han dynasty). An elaborate hierarchy of schools became necessary. The mandarin ethos finally became so predominant that the first question asked of a stranger in China was, inevitably, how many exams have you passed?

The scholar is an important figure in any society. He keeps the archives; his patience and diligence through long years dwelling on the culture of conduct and its literary representations, of the deeds of the worthy forefathers, keeps alive the past, and makes possible a more sophisticated and self-conscious present. The mandarin is not principally interested in Truth: his passion is rather for the rules, the traditions of his vocation, and for confirming their strict maintenance as ritual. This zealous ritualism has its own social function: it demonstrates to the less ruly majority the virtues of self-discipline, that there are absorptions other than the sensual and immediate, ones that might bring a different and more enduring gratification. The mandarin, moreover, is an exemplar of public service, which is not, of course, to praise his motives.

Mandarins, scribes, priests, and tight ritualism – a strain to make anyone cautious. And indeed the ascetic life puts an individual under acute internal pressures. The valves of sensuality, of the physical, of intoxication and tranquillization, through which other men find release from the strains of the day, are shut off. An ascetic life is conducted under the watch of an Argos conscience, with the source of pleasure shifted upwards to the mind's eye and its witness of performance. Now when, in addition, this conscience belongs to a mandarin, idealizing literature and learning, it lives constantly in the presence of great works, and will, unless it is endowed with unusual native humility, suffer the repeated insult of having to recognize the mediocrity of its ward. Moreover, the fact of spending an entire lifetime with books, with sensitive comments on life, and refined judgments about it, is unnatural and adds further pressure to an already over-strained organism. The safety-valve most likely to open in these circumstances is that of resentment. In fact the mandarin is a paradigm of resentment, as Nietzsche pointed out. He directs resentment against anyone who breaks the mandarin code, who crosses the boundaries between departments or disciplines, who dares to be both mandarin and creative writer in one (the great are bearable only at a distance, remote from extended comparison). The mandarin is typically paranoid, fearing loss of control, fearing the bottomless pit of uncertainty, guarding himself against an eruption of the forces in himself kept back by the halter of his ascetic calling. Mandarins do not fear philistines; they are threatened by their brothers who stretch the rules and thereby put in danger the entire order; the playfulness of these siblings is interpreted as a nihilistic aggression against their own family, fratricide on a mass scale.

At the same time, the mandarin's paranoia serves his calling. Out of exaggerated fears about the consequences of successful attack by critics, he works over his arguments, the weight of his evidence, his qualifications, with fanatical scrupulousness, and consequently produces work of extraordinary thoroughness. The scholarly virtue of rigour is dependent on the mandarin's paranoia-inflated fears of his peers, and his imagining of catastrophic consequences if he fails to keep his thesis intact.

2 The engineer

The man with a passion for thinking that is directed by the goal of making things work better has often been scorned among intellectuals. While he is not dedicated to thought for itself, and does dirty himself in the market-place, he nevertheless belongs to the general species. And his easy reply to his critics is that nobody in fact dedicates himself to ideas for their own sake; the difference is merely that his motives are more social than personal, and, by comparison with the chiliast, who claims to have society at heart, more realistic.

The doyen of engineers was Machiavelli, drawing on his own extensive observations of politics as practised to write principles to be used by princes to retain their power and strengthen their states. (Remembering that the great usually defy simple categorization, I am instructed that the heroes of this exemplary political realist were Moses, Theseus, Romulus, and Cyrus, all wholly or in part mythical.) Lenin, with his ruthless devotion to 'what is to be done', belongs to the engineering species, as does that modern professor-diplomat, Henry Kissinger, oiling the machinery of international relations. There was even something of the engineer in the utopian Plato planning his Republic, although one doubts whether his over-educated princes would have kept their power very long. And, counter Plato, it is important to stress that the engineer when he is a man of political theory, like Edmund Burke, despises idealists, and especially the revolutionary type: 'This sort of people are so taken up with their theories about the rights of man, that they have totally forgotten his nature.'

Next there is that class of eccentrics called inventors. The men who conceived of the stump-jump plough, the safety-pin, the sphygmo-manometer, the steam engine, and chewing-gum had traces of the engineer in their hearts. So did that Puritan scientist who dominated the early years of the Royal Society and the rise of science in England, Robert Boyle. One of his many publications was titled, *That the Goods of Mankind May be Increased by the Naturalist's Insight into Trades*. As he was intensely practical, so was his assistant and friend, Robert Hooke, a natural craftsman who made the apparatus that made the Boyles and Newtons possible.

The economic sphere has its own need for engineers. Taylor with his 'efficiency maximization' and Mayo with his 'human relations' used their streamlining sciences to increase factory productivity. Keynes with his multiplier and his General Theory provided tools that enabled governments for two decades to gain a measure of control over their trade cycles, thus alleviating the miseries of economic depression.

3 The chess player

Some claim that chess was invented by Mandarin Han-sing.

In this circle of intellectuals we witness pure scientists, logicians, theologians, economists, and all those others more attached to the form of a theory, its lines, its links, than what it explains. Thus we lay bare the lust after the self-contained perfectly-constructed system in the work of Aquinas, Spinoza, Gauss, Russell, Ricardo, and contemporary American economic theorists. The same may be detected less obviously, and not necessarily as a leading theme, in the creations of Milton, Raphael, Hume, and Henry James. But the exemplary chess player was Euclid.

The simple, lucid lines of an Euclidean theorem, every element in its place, every element with a precise and explicit function, nothing superfluous, and all movement articulated in one direction, like a long silk dress echoing a dusk breeze, leading to the completion of this perfect system. An archetype of elegance. And the pleasures of constructing it: starting with a few elements and a problem, then sensing the course of the proof, setting it out step by step, each step leading inexorably to the next, confirming the initial intuition, until the puzzle is resolved. Recapturing the delight of the child planning his hide-and-seek strategy, and winning; is it, as Freud suggested, the pleasure of bringing back the mother at will, thus resolving the primal anxiety of separation? Or is it, additionally, Oedipus solving the riddle of the Sphinx, and thus saving himself and Thebes, if only temporarily? That is, is this pleasure of the chess game that of winning time from death, gaining some respite in the sublimity of this finitely-determined abstraction from the infinite darkness of death? The very riddle that Oedipus solved was that of human life, starting in infancy and ending in old age.

All intellectual activity serves as a means for gaining control, for drawing purpose out of chaos. The ultimate control is to will away death, the most real of all realities. There is in the withdrawal of the intellectual into the remote world of spirit an attempt to deny, to stave off this ultimate chaos. The chess game, as Ingmar Bergman perceived, is to spite death. And as much as death is separation from all warmth and nourishment, it stands as the final momentous re-enactment of the child's early experiences of the loss of the mother. Chess is the form of social intercourse most therapeutic for the intellectual as paranoid. The competition is so strictly governed by rules that there is minimum danger of a spasm of rage in a tense moment destroying the game, sending the opponent away hurt, the proceedings irretrievably sundered, as is likely to happen in real life. No, in chess, as in medieval warfare, the knight can move to only two places, and the consequences are accessible to thought. The game gradually tames fantasies of a shock violent attack from the opponent striking an unguarded spot; if he does strike home it is not as a monster, but as a civilized equal, bound by a camaraderie of rules. Such a successful sublimation of violence is the foundation of social harmony, and a rare achievement among that vain, unruly, headstrong breed, intellectuals.

Moreover, working within strictly defined rules to create perfect forms introduces another one of control's consolations. The real world is messy, and those who work in it, engineers, shamans, even mandarins (they test their arguments against the ultimate mess, that of reality's infinitude of facts), have to settle for small gains, minor clarifications. As long as one restricts oneself to forms, to mathematics, perfection is possible. Individual life also is messy; the chess player in playing a peerless game takes his mind off his own imperfections, which he cannot much improve by practice, over which therefore he has little *control*. For a while he can identify with the sublimity of his play. The longing to create perfection is the phoenix longing to be reborn, without original sin, without infirmity, without blemish.

The Sphinx riddle reconstructed: at one end of a vast dark hall, in a niche bathed in cosy light, the virgin and child, at the other end, shadowy in a purple after-glow, a hunched skeleton tottering around, and in the middle, under a spotlight, in sepulchral silence, two men playing at chess. Or to amend an old Chinese tale, cherished by Tolstoy: two men chased by a lion scramble down a well to find a tiger at the bottom snarling up at them; they cling to the one available branch, whose roots they discover are being gnawed away by rats; there they jam a small chess board in the branch's fork and lose themselves in the game, jubilantly.

One last variation. Marcel Duchamp in his 'ready-made' constructions established the tradition of art games that has swamped Western galleries in the recent decades with patterns in paint and toys in chrome and plastic. However, Duchamp himself became disgusted by the context of the masterpiece, which on recognition was immediately interred in the mausolea of culture. Once he had proved that he could paint, he gave up painting; he spent the last thirty years of his life literally playing chess. He gained twice out of the switch. He was able to continue his artistic play, but in a milieu in which there was infinite possibility of challenging variation, and therefore less danger of repetition, of imitation, in short boredom. Moreover, he had escaped the spectre of death, of finding himself forced to lead a ritual that honoured the product and not the process, that was solely concerned with the end, the work, the excretion, and found the man and his trials, the way he built his challenge and executed it, irrelevant. In chess, the play itself is the end; the check-mate merely serves as a cue to set the pieces up anew, or to break for tea. Thereby, chess for Duchamp, unlike art, did not engage in the phony activity of institutionalizing futility, of working to give meaning to the meaningless.

4 The chiliast

In 1096 a small thin man with a long grey beard who never touched meat or wine, travelling barefoot, attracted the masses of over-populated, flood, drought- and famine-ridden, plague threatened north-eastern France and western Germany with his inspired eloquence. It was said that Christ had appeared before him, commissioning him to summon the first crusade. This was Peter the Hermit. He soon had a vast mob swarming after him on militant pilgrimage to recapture the holy city, which Moslems had now held for half a millennium. Jerusalem, symbol of salvation, focus of all hope, was where the disinherited would enter into a paradisiac realm of material and spiritual well-being, where for one thousand years goodness would reign.

Many have come after, especially since that paranoid, bladder-tormented Romantic, Rousseau, reasserted so influentially that men were born free. A second mob with its head turned east, a mob of anarchists, socialists, communists, and fascists has in its various ways set out from its homes, charged here and there, setting on fire much that stood in its way. And all for what? For an idea, loosed on a prevailing wind, by some chiliast intellectual, some pyromaniac Isaiah, disgusted by the sordidness of everyday life, inspired by hope, or rancour, some ascetic spirit ill-attuned to the everyday, wanting to take suffering humanity by the hand.

But without hope our lot *is* no more than one of daily toil and drudgery. The chiliast reminds us that when Pandora opened the box and let evil into the world, hope too was freed. The chiliast lifts us out of our sluggish routines, enchants us with his visions, we mountains that may be moved but usually are not. He scorns all but our innocence. He seeks to make eternal the moment of self-transcendence, the moment of wonder, of rapture, of ecstasy, the idyllic moment of deep and direct communion with man or nature. If only we could loose ourselves from worldly pride, then one day: 'The wolf also shall dwell with the lamb, and the leopard shall lie down with the kid; and the calf and the young lion and the fatling together; and a little child shall lead them.'

The chiliast is of the idealist mould, attached to a vision of social revolution, of the transformation of the imperfect present into a utopian future. The future may come soon, or it may be the reward of an after-life. It may come as the result of human action, or divine determination. The latter distinction is the more interesting for us today, providing the reef on which the political left, the home of the chiliast in modern Western times, has lain foundering since its one Olympian intellectual, Marx, discovered himself stuck fast a century ago. Marx's genius was such that he came to know much about the nature of that reef. But here, where his greatest gift to his followers lay, was precisely where they preferred to look away, and imagine that some tide of history would soon wash them free; the more simple-minded chose to wish the reef away altogether, and imagine themselves scudding purposively towards the dawn. Marx, himself more than a tinker prophet, was too much the sober engineer, the wise fool, and the erudite mandarin, all in one, to take revelation seriously. The mandarin combined with the engineer to study history and discovered a vast momentum of infinitely complicated forces working, as if under its own laws. Some of these laws he laid bare. But while the chiliast in him saw a diabolical tale behind the historical events, a tale that surely ought to have a happy ending, the fool told him that individuals had no role in this process, that all they could really do, if they chose, was to stand back a little and gain some idea of what was happening.

Marx thus found himself back where he had started, with Hegel, and the goddess of wisdom in the form of a night-bird taking flight only after the action. His final picture was of evolution, through the logic of capitalism, until society's own contractions so worked themselves through that the bourgeois phase of the history transformed itself into its utopian sequel, without violence and without revolution. Certainly there were moments when Marx became excited by the activities of some political group or other, but these moments were few and short-lived. His asides about the rubbish dump of history, where all those ultra-chiliastic Jacobins, and many others who imagined themselves on the central stage, would end up, were jokes upon himself. For he had stared into the face of his own Medusa and had the courage to recognize the reality: that if he was chosen to pursue understanding, as he was, then he had to accept the judgment of that understanding, that knowledge has no significant influence over history. ('Knowledge' is meant here as the understanding of the self-conscious and historically-conscious individual; it is distinguished from the more general notion of 'ideas', which have influenced history in such forms as religious convictions or political science.) Forced to choose between history and the millennium for his seductress, Marx opted for the former. History is its own master, except at the trivial margins, and even there the tone of the chirp of Burke's complaining crickets is governed by history and not by any far-seeing consciousness. So Marx retired to the British Museum, close to the Elgin marbles, declined offers to exhort at the barricades and took on full-time the role of mandarin. The old Marx, recognizing 'struggle' as the principle underpinning all life, smiled at the memory of the young man who had so grandly complained that philosophy had merely interpreted, not changed, the world. The intellectual biography of Karl Marx is the sole significant parable for today's left, for it speaks to their impassable stumbling-block, the relation between thought and action.

Marx himself reiterated the diction of both Hegel and Lamartine that those who do not understand the past are doomed to repeat it. And the imitators disgusted him. So, in his own day there were the Herzens, the aristocratic revolutionaries keeping warm their ephemeral lives in exile by producing incendiary pamphlets. There were also the Bakunins, the simple-minded activists, who would race off at the first news of political disturbance, and usually turn up just in time to be locked up with the revolting rabble. And what of the twentieth century's intellectual Marxists? Inevitably, the more sophisticated, in Frankfurt, withdrew into philosophy and devoted themselves either to ironic aphorisms or to vast and prodigiously intelligent treatises on method. The first stage of the retreat is by now well accomplished, the study of the real world fully abandoned in favour of the study of the problems of studying the real world – in short, working out how to begin. (The alternative tactic has been utterly mandarin, the dedication of an intellectual life to establishing whether this observation or that interpretation can be legitimately classed as 'Marxist'.) This is that faggish dead-end that prefers the flirt to the fusion, and indeed does nothing but flirt, or complain about those so vulgar as to think they can fuse without the hermeneutic prolegomena. The contemporary Marxist is faced not only by the eternal and universal fact of the impotence of knowledge in relation to history; he has the additional problem specific to capitalism that, as the Western economic system advances, the power of the individual decreases in every sphere of public life, and the gargantuan network of institutions and habits that pins society becomes the more invulnerable to the agitation of dissenting individuals.

The sole successor worthy of Marx, although he would not have been interested in the honour, was Dostoevsky's fictitious Kirilov. And Kirilov completes the tradition. Kirilov, the clear-headed, was a chiliast who believed that men would be freed only once they had overcome their terror of death. Fear was the root of all evil. Thus the task of the messiah was to make men into gods by demonstrating that they need not be afraid. Kirilov himself would do this, by killing himself, not out of fear, but in order to demonstrate in the only indisputable manner available that he was not afraid. Only likewise could a Marxist (and all higher revolutionaries are Marxist) transcend history, proving that its iron laws are not definitive and that he, the free individual, was independent. But of course Kirilov was not merely fictitious, he was a lunatic.

Chiliasts of the political right have also troubled the West since the Paris mob imagined that it could start history again at Day One, and Napoleon imperially put its hope into practice. However, for the time being at least, Hitler's devastation of half of Europe in his pursuit of the thousand-year *Reich* seems to have proved a cautionary experience. There is sense nevertheless in remembering how suddenly intellectuals, always potentially more in love with the heroic possibilities of their own visions than the nature of the real world and its constraints, preach war; how quickly their weakness for righteous indignation focuses as militant nationalism. Richard Wagner and Thomas Mann, not to mention the galaxy of duller stars, were not alone in their different calls for the Germany army to protect the Fatherland and its superior culture from the creeping plagues of British democracy and French rationalism. Those astutely worldly, those pioneering exposers of the chiliast mentality, Weber and Freud, for moments during the First World War both defended German militarism. More significantly, during the same episode, that intellectual President of the United States, Woodrow Wilson, in 1916 and 1917 used, and was used by, intellectuals who successfully campaigned to change the prevailing opinion of the American people from neutrality towards the war in Europe to military intervention, and who whipped up a crusading mood throughout the country that led to persecution of dissenters as traitors.

The deep yearning for heroic militarism, which has come to be labelled politically rightist, is little different from the alternative chiliast fanaticism that is rarely far beneath the surface amongst the political left. Nadezhda Mandelstam reports her brother claiming that prisons and terror were in fact unnecessary in Soviet Russia, for the intelligentsia had subjugated themselves, by their attachment to the word 'Revolution', which none of them could bear to give up.

There is a warning here against the contemporary trend of narrowing the distance between town and gown. When the intellectual enters the city he has proved likely to lose his head. Like many others, he has been brought up on heroic mythology, and learnt that to be of worth he must undertake ten Herculean labours. More worldly men, tempered on the constraints of physical life, gradually realize that there are labours in the small movements of daily events, that in their midst values can be worked and dignities won. The chiliast intellectual, however, while he hankers to be relevant, is familiar solely with metaphysics; he takes the myth literally and as a result over-dramatizes things, seeking to quicken their pace, to precipitate crises, to cut Gordian knots, to crusade against evils, to declaim against 'the strong and slow boring of hard boards' that forms the real politics of life. He is drawn to the imperial and the monolithic; he is excited by size, and favours centralization. He is better off left in the confines of the monastic university, where his heart is not carried away, and he can coolly reflect on the consequences of things. As La Rochefoucauld put it more cynically: 'Philosophy triumphs with ease over past evils and evils to come; but current evils triumph over it.' The intellectual should not seek to be very relevant, even very useful: his task is not to seduce the youth, but to prepare their minds for whatever challenges they wish to take up when they re-enter the city. The monastery was an institution dedicated to the teaching of piety and humility. Our increasingly *relevant* universities, under the sway of chiliast fashion, are in danger of producing arrogant philistine revolutionaries.

While on the power of myths, a concluding note about that strange political hermaphrodite, Georges Sorel: in the late 1920s the governments of both Soviet Russia and fascist Italy are reputed to have offered to restore his tombstone. Sorel argued that a new myth must be created if decadent Europe were to be regenerated. He proposed the culturally therapeutic value of violence, imagining a berserk proletariat organized into syndicates rampaging through the torpor of bourgeois society, with the effect of wakening it up.

This variety of Romantic chiliasm has little cogency, at least in the relevant case, that of twentieth-century Europe. Neither of the two great wars generated anything that might be generally referred to as a cultural revitalization. Yet even he who knew most about the destructive potential of forces from below, Freud, at times argued for the restorative power of barbarism; and that very astute social commentator, George Orwell, learning nothing from the experience of the First World War, could the next time assert: 'How much rubbish this war will sweep away'. The Sorelian metaphors have kept recurring, and especially in the 1960s.

5 The shaman

The shaman, elected by spirits, descends into the underworld during his initiation. He is tortured by demons, his body is cut into pieces. Finally he is reborn with special powers of communication with the spirits. The initiate is under instruction from masters, but is welcomed as a fully-fledged shaman only if he manages to interpret his pathological crisis as a religious experience, and succeeds in curing himself. Then he is fit to cure others, which he does by using his own madness. Not that the shaman is himself mad; he is not actually possessed by demonic forces. Sickness is the condition in which the soul either wanders, or is captured by demons. When a patient suffers from sickness of the first type, the wandering soul, the shaman constructs a ritual of sympathetic ecstasy in which he dances and chants his diagnosis in a mythic form whose climax is the recapturing of the soul, and the replacing it in the body of the sick person. In the second case, of demonic interference, the shaman undertakes a highly dangerous ecstatic voyage into the underworld.

Like the engineer, the shaman works in the world, or rather enters it during the day from his retreat on its boundaries. Like the chiliast, his success depends on personal charisma, and his vocation is predicated on a belief in the transforming power of knowledge. But his patient is the sick individual, not the sick society.

The rise of science in the West had as one of its effects the standardization of the shaman figure in the form of the medical doctor. An exotic history of oracles, astrologers, Cassandras, Merlins, alchemists, mountebanks, potion and lotion tinkers, blood-letters, and hypnotists has been tamed. It is a commonplace, however, that the modern doctor depends no less than his ancestors on personal charisma: it is faith in him and his science that draws the patient to him. And his science, in spite of its pride in 'objective research', is a maze of arcane lore, whose magical aura is intensified to an awesome level by its technology, its fantasia of chrome-decked machinery, flashing lights, pulsing cathode screens, endless rubber tubes, pumps, bottles, multicoloured pills, microscopic gadgets, needles, operated by teams of surgeons, anaesthetists, nurses, physiotherapists, cardiographers, gynaecologists, who glide in white costumes along gleaming corridors. Indeed, the very objectivity of medical science has become magical.

The doctor, in the period before the concentration this century of populations in the cities, often had a wider role than that of healer. In the provincial Russian towns of Chekhov's stories and plays, for instance, the doctor is often the solitary intellectual. His interest in curing the body leads him out into a range of social problems, the preservation of forests, education, the condition of the poor; it is he, moreover, who poses the metaphysical questions of where from, why, and where to.

The modern doctor who most faithfully continues to practise the ancient techniques of the shaman is, as Lévi-Strauss pointed out in his book *Structural Anthropology*, the psychoanalyst. Freud wrote that the analyst must

> surrender himself to his own unconscious mental activity, in a state of *evenly suspended attention*, to avoid so far as possible reflection and the construction of conscious expectations, not to try to fix anything that he heard particularly in his memory, but by these means to catch the drift of the patient's unconscious with his own unconscious.

This is an 'ecstatic' technique. The analyst sets up a ritual, to which he too must surrender, in order to provide the patient with a secure milieu in which he can relax and release the stream of his most sensitive associations. The analyst now has his material, and, drawing upon his training, his experience, and his gifts as an interpreter, he starts to construct a meaning. But he constructs from within the ritual, with the intimate collaboration of the patient, so that the patient believes that he himself is reconstructing his own story. The drama can advance only when the patient is totally absorbed; when the analyst guides it to its climax, the point of therapeutic release, the breaking of the neurotic bond.

The analyst's own background is often reminiscent of the shaman. He himself has usually suffered from acute psychological pressures, which his training analysis has helped him to overcome. This struggle with himself carries him to a point of control, at which he becomes peculiarly suited to help others with similar difficulties. In Adorno's imagery, the splinter in the eye is one's best magnifying glass.

Freud provides a useful context in which to distinguish the shaman from the chiliast. Freud, in contrast to Marx, focused his interest, his analytical acumen and his therapeutic hopes on individuals. Second, he was thoroughly sceptical about the possibility of rapid and major change. The millennium was a delusion, in any of its many guises. And although the analytic situation bears a shamanistic form, Freud believed in small gains, that his patients might at best learn to live a little better with themselves. Thus, while he did hold that knowledge may change things, it took a lot of knowledge, and a long-lasting, painstakingly constructed and patiently worked ritual, to produce a small change in reality, a slightly less nervous patient.

The most charismatic of all our heroes, Jesus Christ, carried many of the marks of the shaman. He was born obscurely, elected by a long Judaic tradition preparing for the messiah, announced by portents, journeying seers, and John the Baptist; he underwent a pathological crisis in the wilderness, where he fasted for forty days and was tempted by the devil. On his return he began to preach, and to heal all those who had *faith*.

6 The Galahad

Each knight journeys his own way in search of the Holy Grail.

Lancelot, punished for his adultery with Guinevere, sees the Grail only in a dream. The chaste Perceval, and Bohort, with one involuntary lapse from chastity, receive higher revelations. Gawain, who does not seek the help of divine grace, fails utterly. Sir Galahad, the strong and the pure, is alone in devoting himself single-mindedly to the pursuit of the Grail. He, the chosen one, does find it, and looking inside at mysteries barred to human senses, he dies.

The noblest among intellectuals pursue Truth. Truth is their passion, their bride. They are, moreover, the only members of the species to be absolved from the disdain of worldly men, the Sir Lancelots, for Lancelots too, in an amateurish way, through their activity, their 'deeds', pursue Truth. These intellectuals aspire to sainthood, reflecting a pride that deservedly makes them ready targets for malicious gossip. They may retain their elevated status only by ensuring that their lives are scrupulously chaste, and that their universities maintain their monastic heritage.

The most insistent of all our Western hunters after Truth, Plato, provided his own parable of the ambition to emerge into the sun from the gloomy cave of ordinary perception, in which life is interpreted from shadows flickering on a wall. In spite of the pagan imagery, the message is no less lofty than that of the Arthurian legend.

Mystics, alchemists, students wandering across Germany from university to university, troubadours, free spirits, Lutherans seeking union of their God, Illuminati, Romantics devoted to their Blue Flower, Hölderlins, Dostoevskys have one and all been moved by the Galahad spirit. There is probably a trace of the Galahad in all men of literature, philosophy, and science. What characterizes the type is its life motif, that of the ascetic, passionate quest that is tyrannically absorbing. The precise nature of the Truth, not that there usually is any degree of precision, is of little importance. Indeed, all that can be said about this Truth is that it is an ideal, serving as the ultimate goal; and it promises some kind of comprehensive revelation. Everything is in the getting there. No day in the Galahad's life is futile, for each step is a move closer; even wrong turnings provide experience that is useful. There is no comprehension of either absurdity or scepticism.

It is a mystical quest. The Galahad of twentieth-century philosophers, Martin Heidegger, calls his Grail 'Being', the essence, the what-is of things. The knight's task is to think, or rather to theorize, in such a state of serenity that things lay bare their essences.

Heidegger has in mind the Greek '*theorea*', which he interprets as 'reverent observation of the disclosure of what is present'. *Theorea*, a word of Orphic origin, does refer to a state of fervent contemplation, and participation in the sacred rites. There are countless other testimonials that the emotion that many great scientists and thinkers have experienced when deeply immersed in their work is one of awe, a cosmic wonder that carries them out of the constraining shell of their own egos. Belief in an unknown order has been for the scientist the equivalent to the mystic's belief in an unknown God. And he has often alluded to this order as preordained, the work of a divine mathematician, an infinitely complex yet perfectly conceived system underlying all things. In approaching his Grail, the scientist has had one ambition, that of Galahad, to look inside. Einstein wrote:

> What a deep belief in the intelligence of creation and what longing for understanding, even if only of a meagre reflection in the revealed intelligence of this world, must have flourished in Kepler and Newton, enabling them as lonely men to unravel over years of work the mechanism of celestial mechanics.

Einstein also claimed that the serious research scholar was the only deeply religious human being left.

7 The king's fool

King Lear is told by his fool that now he has divided his kingdom and banished his youngest daughter he is a peapod, a circle without its figure, a nothing, for he was not more than he gave away. It is the fool who sees the truth, and strangely enough he is allowed to tell it.

The fool, in his medieval context, whether attached to a court, a household, a tavern, or a brothel, generally had neither social nor physical standing; typically he was deformed, often a dwarf. Like Sophocles's sage, Teiresias, who being old and blind was no longer of the world, he was not in a position in which he might lose his heart, to fantasies of rank or intimacy. Disinterested, he was unlikely to lose his head. In short, he could see the truth impartially.

The fool may not have been kept specifically for his insights; indeed, the last of the French fools was banished by his king, Louis XIV, for impertinence. Nor was his buffoonery valued merely for its fun. It was believed that deformity kept the evil eye turned away, and that abusive raillery transferred misfortune from the abused to the abuser. The fool's costume, the foxtail, coxcomb, eared hood and bells, may have had its origin in pagan sacrificial garments.

The fool exposes in mockery the vanities of man, his artifices, deceptions, and pretensions. He serves as a cultural counter-balance to pride: not the meek Christian alternative that preaches the antithetical virtue, humility, but the sceptical, nihilistic one that challenges man to know himself. In medieval France, the 'feast of fools' at Christmas saw a mock pope and bishop elected from among the paupers, followed by an elaborate parody of ecclesiastical ritual. The most celebrated of Greek fools, Diogenes, stationed in his barrel in the market-place, remained indifferent to the honour of being specially visited by Alexander, who offered him any wish: Diogenes asked merely that the great Hellenizer get out of his sunshine. And the old seventeenth-century Duke, La Rochefoucauld, after a life of active romances, championing ladies in distress, conducting political intrigues (with a knack for backing the wrong side), spent his evenings in a quiet salon in Paris entertaining his friends with his maxims on the manner in which the entirety of human passion is threaded on self-esteem: 'Amour-propre is more clever than the cleverest of worldly men.'

The fools all pursue truth, not Truth. They are sceptics, doubting all ideals: goodness, beauty, progress, knowledge. Their fraternity is ably represented in *Essay on Man* by Alexander Pope, himself a sickly, hunchbacked dwarf, four-and-a-half feet tall:

Behold the child, by Nature's kindly law,
Pleased with a rattle, tickled with a straw:
Some livelier plaything gives his youth delight
A little louder, but as empty quite:
Scarfs, garters, gold, amuse his riper stage,
And beads and prayer-books are the toys of age:
Pleased with this bauble still, as that before;
Till tired he sleeps, and life's poor play is o'er.
Meanwhile opinion gilds with varying rays
Those painted clouds that beautify our days;
Each want of happiness by hope supplied,
And each vacuity of sense by pride:
These build as fast as knowledge can destroy;
In folly's cup still laughs the bubble, joy;

The most perceptive of nineteenth-century fools, Nietzsche, with-drew from his worldly station, his professorship at Basel which he had held for ten years, and, aged thirty-four, began his years of wandering, between Sils Maria, Turin, and Genoa, virtually always alone, with one suitcase, the philosopher with the tuning-fork, whose ambition was to tap the ideals of the time to hear how hollow they sounded. He tapped most insistently at his own three tempta-tions, his own ideals: his desire to be a priest, his moralism, and his compassion. And when he had finished they lay bare on the dissect-ing table, every fibre carefully pinned, so that no origin, no function, no connection, no consequence remained concealed. Nietzsche's life-work was to make a fool of himself. Incidentally, he made much that went on around him also look foolish, apart, that is, from most that passes for human behaviour, which he found unspeakable, less than disgusting. This wandering went on for eleven years before the gay scientist, the creator of Zarathustra's drunken singing, fell apart.

The fool has a darker side. He is never far removed from the devil, the Mephistopheles, whose cynicism carries a mocking edge, who scorns, not out of benign sagacity or an urbane distance from men, but out of a rancorous need to disenchant, to poison the naive joys of those who are still able to play at living. Nevertheless, there is good sense to the words that Goethe put into the mouth of his Mephisto: 'But one must not give one's brains too fierce a racking'.

There have been a few twentieth-century fools, like the Dadaists, Kraus, Beckett, but I prefer to close this section by recalling an old tale told at the expense of intellectuals. The venerable philosopher, Thales, was walking along gazing at the stars, meditating on the secrets of the universe, when he failed to see a well, down which he fell. A pretty peasant girl, looking on, broke into peals of laughter.

Conclusion

Vain, power-hungry, and obsessed by the need to control, so we have observed the disposition of intellectuals, though, surely, not of them alone. Even the most amiable king's fool should not be put higher. I would like to close this short homily by glancing at certain of the motives.

The vanity of most intellectuals manifests itself in a pursuit of power, which they commonly prefer to disguise in the finery of ideals, ideals of scientific progress, social reform, infallible therapy, blinding wisdom, and so on. The engineer seeks the power of the back-room, inventing world-revolutionizing technology or process, or as a diplomat moving the world-players, perhaps becoming one himself. The chiliast designs the systems of our future, redefines our past, and exhorts us to follow him, the omniscient one, out of our degrading present. The shaman seeks power over the underworld of the individual soul; he has the unique power to exorcize the demons that cause mental or physical disturbance; as the Prince of Light his politics focus on redeeming the chaos of individual life.

Engineer, chiliast, shaman are all Napoleons at heart. So is the king's fool, the trickiest of the power-seekers. For one reason or another he has withdrawn from the squabble for tangible power – likely he does not have a stomach for it. He seeks power of a higher order, influence over the power-holders, the kings. His power is that of a peculiarly pungent type of understanding, and it is recognized by the king himself. The fool is the only one that a king will tolerate as an equal, or even a superior. Because the fool sees all he is above all. He himself has the conceit to imagine that he has already occupied all the weighty offices of the world and subsequently retired, to escape from the petty routines and disgusting conflicts of real politics into a privacy in which he can amuse himself by observing the all too predictable antics of those more innocent than himself. The one person with any significant power in Sophocles' *Oedipus* is the old fool, Teiresias.

The mandarin is more elusive. He takes us to the border of a different although allied territory, inhabited by those preoccupied by the obsession to control their immediate environment and thus overcome their constant fear that they personally will disintegrate. It could be argued that these people who are threatened by loss of control seek 'power' over themselves and their own incipient aimlessness, but this would be to employ the concept in an eccentric manner. It is not power over others that they are interested in: they are too self-absorbed, too ungregarious. The chess player is the outstanding intellectual representative in the land of the control obsessives. His single goal is order, command over his own chaotic impulses; he dreams of the intoxicating harmony of the perfectly executed strategy. The mandarin is another obsessive, a fetishist for ritualized order, but he remains worldly enough to project his obsessiveness on to the pursuit of influence, power over the institutions of learning and the cultural heritage of the society. In the Chinese case he sought even wider powers, an example that our modern Western bureaucrats show all too many signs of following.

The chess player is one type of intellectual whose vanity is not that of power. The Galahad is the other. His heart is pure, and he does not even suffer from the chess player's primitive longing for control. Whether any flesh and blood man has even been purely of the Galahad essence is another matter.

The Galahad's heart might be pure, but we should not bow our heads too low, for his saintliness makes him the least resistant of the whole intellectual species to the most common of its pathologies. That is the pathology of detachment, of losing contact with every-day reality, with the down-to-earth joys and woes, conflicts and comforts, achievements and degradations of the human condition. Other intellectuals lose themselves in their lust for power, or fame, or become the well-drilled instruments of their obsessions. The Galahad's detachment, because it is inspired, is all the more dangerous: gazing at the past or into the beyond for a glimpse of the Truth can become totally entrancing. There is retribution in store for all intellectuals, but especially for the Galahads. As the ancient Greeks put it, by arming their Goddess of wisdom, Athena, with a Gorgon-head, he who dedicates himself to intellect should not become too hypnotized by his vanities lest he finds himself turned to stone.

Appendix: three case studies

This is all very well, these stories of great adventurers, conjurers, charlatans. We have indulged our fantasies long enough; any shirker can daydream of a grain of sand as more than a grain of sand, even a universe. It is now time to come down to earth, take a look at our contemporary reality, and find out what sort of rope these many wonderfully coloured threads have entwined together.

The first case is an odd fellow, representative of the fortunate fact that life is sometimes, especially perhaps amongst intellectuals, richer, more exotic, than it appears on the ordered surface – usually, of course, it is even more limp and dreary than its outward appearance. The case is not obviously typical of our times, and might have been met in more or less any period during the last two hundred years. If our lives were in better shape we might well feel pity for him.

My second specimen is all too familiar, all too contemporary, all too symptomatic of the future, and he goes to prove that if you try to ignore the cliché, for its banality, that cliché is all the less likely to ignore you. About this case, the facts say more than enough.

The third case is a lady. Whether her sex has actually added colour to the traditionally male fief of intellectualdom, or simply contributed to its emasculation, should be left for the reader to answer.

Case 1

The case of Max, who could be seen on occasion strolling along King's Parade in Cambridge, smoking small cigars held with a Bourbon ostentation in his long, pale fingers. The slight tightness with which the elbows were tucked into the sides, the slightly too ironical twist to the mouth, above all the blush that would break out whenever he collided in public with the slightly unexpected, and light up a galaxy of pimples through the light powder on his cheeks, hinted to the curious passer-by that he was not made for this world. He spent his twenties wandering, studying philosophy, lost in the gargantuan abstractions of his hero, Hegel. Hegel stood for Max as the figure of God stands for a devout Christian; by means merely of his abstract presence, his divine prescience, the self-acclaimed world-philosopher endowed a threateningly random world with meaning. A world in which Hegel had lived and worked made sense, and permitted Max a context, in which this giant of his dreams watched over him, urged him on through his doubts to begin his own great synthesis, promising to accept it as a gift, value it, and through it give, at last, recognition to the long-orphaned son. Max, what can one say – yet another mouse, with visions of a Shakespearean homecoming; and he never came within sniffing distance of a girl until he was thirty.

Having taken a lecturing position in Durham, he found lodging in a squalid boarding house. The landlady naturally had a daughter, the unlovely Agnes, a blotchy-skinned dumpy creature whom the gods had totally overlooked on the day of creation, but who had enough animal cunning to sense that with poor pallid Max, unversed in the ways of the world, and in particular of the flesh, but whom nevertheless she looked upon as a Greek god cast magically in her midst, she had a chance. Suddenly Max found that he was not alone, not unrecognized; and in the warm glow of admiration that now

surrounded him he started to feel abdominal twitches he had never
felt before. The intimacy was clumsy, fumbling, but for all that the
more intense. Our Max became so absorbed by his Juliet, and by his
redirected fancies (now seeing himself as a cinema Casanova, an
intellectual Clark Gable), that his luminous blue flower was
pregnant before he even suspected that mostly flesh is merely flesh.
So, married at thirty-one to a virtually illiterate proletarian, and still
beaming with gratitude for what his Agnes had done for him, still
faithful to the tradition of the one true love, he turned in the dank
Durham winter to his masterpiece.

It took him two years, this work that would bring him a brief
notoriety on publication, and then decades after his death establish
itself as a minor philosophical classic. Its theme was the superhuman
potential of the lonely individual; it filed away one by one at the steel
threads that society spins to tie him down. Among the countless
Romantic exiles who have littered the presses of Europe for the last
two hundred years with their frantic compensations for what they
were not, Max was one of the few who rose above the cliché. Neither
his situation nor his character differed from the lowest common
denominator. But he was the one who was graced by that inexorable
appendage, talent.

And he knew it. He was a dedicated teacher. His vanity was of
the variety that required that each lecture he gave be a brilliant
performance. He could bear flaws in other areas of his public life
with slightly less shame. He seemed to need constant reassurance,
from an always changing gallery, of his virtuosity. As a result he was
an excellent lecturer, and even, in smaller groups, a good teacher. But
those who were close, his mother and his Agnes, were treated coolly
and carelessly, that is once first passion had died; they were no longer
included in the charmed circle of his omnivorous narcissism (not that
anyone would ever hold their place for long), and they inevitably
became a burden to him, intruding upon his fantasies, and thereby
upon his work. Crisis was delayed until he finished his manuscript.
While the two forks, as it were, of his spirit had been fully employed,
in his devotional book and his teaching, the rest of his life could be
accommodated as an incidental distraction. But, once his spirit
became half unemployed, it seeped vagrantly into areas in which it
no longer belonged. It forced him to take a look at his wife. At first he
was puzzled, at the sight of this utter stranger, to whom he vaguely
recalled having once felt very close; bewilderment soon turned into

disgust. Concurrently his teaching seemed to be losing its appeal. Now he would spend his mornings at the university, return home for lunch, then, overcome by a stifling tiredness, retire to bed. A late afternoon walk, an early dinner, and he was again exhausted, and had to retire. But after a month or two of mounting melancholia he was re-awakened by a letter from the publisher, accepting his manuscript. Asking himself what a man of talent, soon to be famous, and rich, was doing wasting his gifts on the semi-literate rabble off-spring of this god-forsaken northern town, Max resigned his job, told his sobbing Agnes that he had had enough, packed his books and papers, and headed off for the London train.

There are many to witness that he lived for a year on his royalties in London, trying to insinuate himself among the literati. He had expected to be lionized; but, perhaps due to his urgency, or his gaucheness in society, perhaps simply because fate is cruelly fickle, he was barely recognized. His royalties soon became a trickle, and the few who bumped into him in later years tend to agree that he lived on the dole, a broken man. There is even a rumour that ten years or so after his arrival in London he contracted some exotic disease from an insect bite, and died.

Case 2

He became famous almost overnight in all the progressive sociology departments of the Western world for his theory of the 'undifferentiated nexus', a tool by means of which he managed to lay bare hitherto undreamt of facets of family life, of impotency among the upwardly mobile in rural Ohio – a brilliant paper in which he introduces the complementary concept of 'estranged intercourse' – and finally the tool by means of which in 1963 he provided us with definitive hypotheses on deviancy drawn from his situationist study of affluent blue-collar shift-workers at their morning tea-break in a tractor assembly plant. This man seems to have caught the contemporary sociological imagination, embodied those diverse talents that make a master in our discipline today: he passed through the sociological midst, a Napoleon astride the horse of our time and its leading human science. Some sociologists have pondered on the roots of this success, and the consensus seems to be that this intellect, really no more than a peer, achieved that rare combination of versatility with a sophisticated scientific method (nobody can match his speed at regression), and at the same time he was able to tie the multiple strands of his interests together with a simple yet novel theory, that of the 'undifferentiated nexus'. This theory bears some attention, not simply because by now thousands of doctorates, from the University of Botswana to Massachusetts Institute of Technology, are being researched on the nexus, applying it to every known type of social situation. No, the nexus, like the 'role', the 'free-floating intellectual', and the 'generalized other', is here to stay. The crux of the theory, as much as I understand it, seems to be that, in spite of the growing differentiation of institutions, jobs, roles, perceptions, individuals that has marked the rise of capitalism, at the core of each social entity there endures a special something that defies dichotomization. It is this something that makes us human. Thus, for instance, in the tractor assembly plant, workers suffer from chronic ongoing alienation; but, during the morning tea-break, a spirit can be observed that has not been contaminated by the degrading work experience. Those, however, whose own individual nexus does not slot into the collective nexus in a mutually legitimating and synthesizing relationship are forced into deviancy, the crucial leisure situation reinforcing rather than relaxing their estrangement. And so on, through the tractor plant and beyond, from one entity to the next, along the myriad tentacles of society's vast network, the dialectic of nexi works out its logic.

Heavily bearded, a ruddy complexion, stockily built and usually dressed in a check sports-jacket, one size too large, an open-necked lumberjack shirt, and green corduroy trousers, our subject's fancied image of himself was ruggedly Lawrentian. The fact was, however, that the spirit of Dionysus never ran less in a man's veins. His large reserves of energy were fed almost exclusively into his work, to which he strapped himself at dawn every day, very much as an ox to a plough, and then proceeded methodically to trudge up one furrow and down the next, until dusk. Out of his harness he was a restless, moody man, unable to sit with his family for longer than the main meal. He would spend his evenings in his study catching up on periodicals, at socialist meetings, or on a rare occasion out with some of his academic or political colleagues, drinking himself resolutely into a lighter mood, when his greatest pleasure was to sing vulgar shanties. His character's sheer lack of complexity was enabling; he was untroubled by those melancholy doubts, that botched crisscrossing web of half-hearted passions that have traditionally marked the temper of the intellectual. His life exhibited one theme, in terms of which his every movement could be understood: he had no ambition, no goal, no strong desire, other than to climb. He had left his rude petty-bourgeois parents far behind in Cleveland, Ohio, and compensated for the ruthless single-mindedness of his rise, the insensitivity to all those close to him, with his socialism. The eddies of guilt that turned in the wake of the giant wave of his career could not stay his momentum, as he shielded his eyes from them with impassioned cries for universal equality. He used the ideology, additionally, to lever himself through difficult points in his career, successfully budging those in his way; he used it again later when he had become a man of moment to camouflage his own authoritarian political tactics. He was the hero of a time addicted to democratic rhetoric, a time that would lightly give away almost any liberty in the name of equality, a time that sensed in this individual's manner an exemplar of its own contradictions, its naivety and its ruthlessness, its idealism and its insensitivity, its sentimentality and its philistinism – ultimately it approved of the resolution that was his work.

His work was his own umbilical cord. He had no other ties; he recognized no traditions, of life or mind; indeed he shuddered to know of any past that had worth, for that might incriminate him, not merely bringing back what his life sought to deny – his origins – but, far worse, implying that there was virtue there in Cleveland, and he a bastard prodigal just ran and ran. The future was his only belief. One of his quirks is of some interest in this regard. He would take a rather hysterical delight in demeaning revelations about those in authority, the more smutty and sensationalist the exposure the better. It was as if those who remained above him, whom by definition he respected, and who trod with some pleasure and dignity other foyers than that of the parvenu, were a singular threat. Their authority had to be discredited if his future were to be gilt-edged.

He seemed to find a substitute for the intimacy of which he was not capable, for the restless rootless nervousness of his life, in his sociology, in poring over the disappointed ambitions and daily miseries of groups of people like himself who had been ripped away from traditional moorings by the workings of industrial civilization, but who, unlike himself, had failed, as he saw it, to adapt. He controlled their lives with his theories, setting himself up as the divine arbiter on the day of judgment, assessing the quality of their nexi, the quantity of their estrangements. And the power gave him a sense that he himself was firmly placed, for how else could he judge.

So this sociological luminary doggedly drew his plough towards his chosen future, through the chosen clay of equals who had failed to be equal.

Case 3

A slender body, classically structured face, and long auburn hair provided the lineaments for a striking appearance. But something failed. It was not the sallow tinge in her complexion, nor the raw pig-flesh eyelids, the slight stoop, nor even her discordant, jerking gait. These blemishes withdrew behind an energy of spirit, an alert eye, and a kind of physical warmth that she carried. Her enigma was a reminder that physical features never stand for themselves, a nose is never just a nose; they are as lifeless as Pygmalion's statue until we populate them with that crowd of fantasies that improvises as our view of the person. And slaves of our unconscious that we are, an unconscious far wiser in its judgments than all our higher faculties, so wise that like Teiresias it usually forces our hand into banishing it; such slaves we are that we select one feature, or movement, and spotlight it as the essence of our impression. So we unwittingly, despotically caricature all those whom we know. In the case of our intellectual it was her mouth that was called upon to stand as sovereign symbol. The mouth was not sensual, and yet lacked firmness. The bottom lip skewed slightly to the right, and when she was nervous, in blurting something out, would sag and become very moist.

She taught English literature, and her guilt was of the variety that demanded she devote herculean patience and attention to those on the margin of her care, in particular her students, persons who were not of importance in her life. She would spend hours of rapt devotion with her waifs, and out of them create a magic circle in which literature took on the numinous quality of holy books containing the deepest secrets of life. Certainly her readings were transparently autobiographical, and her judgments erratic, but this mattered little compared to her strength – that she handed on the flame, and her students read furiously and would, each week, bring their new flaring passions to share with the brotherhood. They could never complain, as many do, that university literary studies reduces inspired classics to dusty fossils.

But some days there was a slightly musty tang to her. Every now and again it was there, a hint in the air, of some stagnancy of spirit, some as yet small corner of the character that was not stirred by her powerful passions, a scent of the old maid wafting through the fragrance of young and vitally independent womanhood. There was a Victorian strain to her personality, a George Eliot emanation.

Her students cushioned her against her punitive disposition and its deepest wish, which came in the form of a recurring yearning for a benevolent father who would appear and take her curled up in his arms, making the world secure. With him there would be neither judging scrutiny nor sexual demands: only tenderness. The image of submission to kindly authority dominated her life. It found illustration in her fear of intimacy with equals, indeed a timidity before peers in general. A demoralizing ambivalence was at work: she was not yet so musty that she did not harken to the call of serene evenings in a lover's arms, and occasionally would yield to the impulse of romance, although less and less. But each time a threshold was reached at which she panicked, as if the lover had attained a point with his last step towards her at which he was close enough to peer over the rim of her soul, and look inside. The thought terrified her, and she would flee, battered, disoriented, and try to piece herself together again with students, or women friends (although the same law prohibiting closeness applied to them), or with men of a completely different disposition, who were neither interested in, nor capable of recognizing the deeper strata of her nature. She fitted, it must be said, into that large category of people who, underneath the preening, do not like themselves. She feared that down in the depths of character there was some dark stain (on bad days she was obsessive about physical cleanliness), some terrible canker (periodically she developed an obsessive fear of disease, especially cancer, secretly eating her away); or she feared that some ghastly crime marked her past and slung a shadow forward across her entire life, a crime for which she must eternally do penance, for example in devotion to her students. Intimacy's curse was that the more receptive her ear became to its whisper the closer she was brought to herself. Intimacy cut through the inner dyke, freeing long-stemmed passions which flowed out and bathed the lover in their intensity; but once the out-pouring flood began to ebb, the breach left in the dyke appeared, and cold, murky tides began to surge around menacingly outside the unguarded entrance.

She did not write much herself. What she did write was very close to her, produced at great cost, days of obsessions, prevarications, clutching at distractions until she was tightened to such a pitch that another turn and she would snap. Then it would start to come. But the actual writing was only the first torture. She projected the fears she held about herself on to her work, and thus would face her peers when giving a seminar paper with a paralysing timidity, imagining only disaster, that the rotten heart of her creation would end up lying naked on the table under a spotlight. Afterwards, her relief was that of a mother finding her only child returned from the dead, as she withdrew into the cosy circle of her own students. Understandably she wrote less and less, she appeared before her peers less and less, and she poured the more energy into her classes. Fate treated her badly, for if there had been a senior man of stature in her department, a professor who could have filled the role of father, encouraged her, known when to take her hand, when to let it go, she might have overcome her disability. And a gain in confidence in her work might have served as the thin end of the wedge into prying the clam of her guilt a little more open.

Just as in the lives of many, most unions appear in retrospect to have been ephemeral, even trivial. There were only two men whom she had known who had left a mark on her imagination, whose memory endured and influenced her present; in both cases their importance derived from their benign and distant paternal flair. With her students she managed to recreate the enabling cocoon of authority, by reversing roles: she played the nurturing mother, on whose fortified estate the foundlings flourished. Although their only desire was to please her, it was not altogether a delusion that this was freedom, and they were discovering themselves.

Lecturing did not suit her. When alone in front of a lectern, her students now at a distance, it was as if some witch cast a spell over her, freezing her warmth towards literature; she became a strident moralist. Now when she talked about 'intelligence' or the 'felt response' it was like the screech of chalk. She suddenly embodied the split of mind and body, such a sensitive issue amongst literary intellectuals, and would even, in true bluestocking manner, take to lecturing with Lawrentian fervour on civilization's last hope being the emergence of the unashamedly sensual woman, whose erotic sources combined the intuitive depths of the dark rock-pool with the musk, oriental mystery of the Venetian courtesan. Actually, in her case, work and sexuality were strictly separated. The tender emotions with which she bound her seminars made her, for the duration of the teaching term, abhor the anarchic violence of fornication; the tension of lecturing confirmed her celibacy. Consequently, a promiscuous vacation did not help to resolve the fissure of mind and body; indeed it was only in the arms of the surrogate father that there was peaceful respite.

4 A modern marriage

He has not lived up to her ideal. He did not prove assertive at key moments in his career; talents that she once saw as potentially rich did not develop. His failure to move calmly and commandingly in his public world has carried over into an indecisiveness and detachment among their friends and even within the humble circle of their family. She did not become motherly enough in their relationship to keep respect for him, although the loss did not happen in any dramatic way — it crept upon her through the years, a bit like the slow deterioration of sight. She has not been unaware of a trough of indifference in her feeling for him deepening as she withdrew her earlier enthusiasms, and like a peeved god shifting his patronage she turned some of her hopes to shine on her children, kept a few for herself, to brighten the gloom and lost the rest in a strain of weariness, of resigned melancholia, that has started its relentless dimming work on her spirit.

But she has not given up. She worries about the loose flesh that has developed around her abdomen since her two childbirths, and the pockmarks that have started to disfigure her thighs. Each morning in the shower she examines these signs of spreading decay with a fearful fascination. There is a queer passion to the ritual, a perverse sensuality, as she draws her fingers rhythmically back and forward almost caressing the regions of her physical flaw. In fact she remains pretty, and with careful preparation and confidence could walk into any crowded room and cause a stir. But the confidence is no longer there; she cannot sustain enough pleasure in herself to make the effort to face the world at her best. That best is no longer she, if ever, once upon a time, it had been.

A part of her longs to try again, to seek adventure. It would boldly walk out the front door of her domesticated family routines for

good, and have her fling herself into the arms of a wild young
cavalier. She could have at least accommodated, if not satisfied, her
rebellious stirrings with affairs, as many of her married counterparts
had done. But she has a certain Puritan disgust for half-heartedness,
for compromise excitements, and she imagined the wife-swapping
parties that some of her friends described to her as sordid and
prosaic, so limited in their choice, so literal in their sexual aim, as
merely to replace one routine by another, and pretend this is living
out their high-school dreams.

However, Puritan single-mindedness is not the only restraint
upon her fancy. During her last year at school she had once passed an
old woman sitting hunched in a gutter, wrapped in a filthy tattered
overcoat, toothless, and muttering to herself. Passers-by quickened
their pace and avoided noticing. She is pursued by this image, nagged
by the fear that if she were to break the security of her marriage – and
after all her husband is devoted – she too would end up in that gutter.
In the slow stroking of her marked thighs is the intimation of what
ties her, the personal loathing cultivated by ten years of battling with
the realities that were unleashed on her once she was freed from the
protection of her childhood home.

In more bitter moments among women friends she joked that she
had a husband, but needed a man. It was true. She had been let down
more profoundly than by his public failure. In the beginning he had
invited her to a ball. She had gone, full of trepidation, about him,
about the importance of the occasion, and about whether she would
be equal to it all. Once through the door, however, she was ushered
into a sumptuously decorated hall whose magnificence echoed with
the excitement of moving clusters of elegant people, and she found
herself drawn out of her bashfulness. She was thrilled by a sight
and a mood such as she had never imagined. Her wonder was transformed by stages into a more mellow enchantment as she became
accustomed to a splendour that seemed to have been provided just
for her. It slowly dawned on her that she was the guest of honour. As
they sipped champagne, she and her escort, and strolled among the
beautiful women and handsome men, and as they danced so lightly
through the open arches, his hand gently guiding her motion, she
released herself to the moment and to him. Thus it was that she lost
her girlhood bearings, and went with him, aware through a glowing
haze of the outlines of what in reality was happening to her, yet
powerless to use that awareness to check her desire.

Entering the ballroom had meant that at last she had been intro-duced to depths in herself that made the finery of the occasion, the elegance and the manners, seem nothing more than tinsel, although charming and memorable tinsel. The occasion had in one sense duped her, he had duped her, by leading her in a direction that she had not anticipated and for which she felt herself ill-prepared. It had introduced her to forces in herself that at first frightened her by the vehemence with which they asserted their presence. But these were the passing fears, and the exhilaration that followed soon drowned them out.

Her feelings were not focused exclusively on him; she also felt herself united with her own female species, in an unbroken re-generative chain moving down from primordial time. She had been welcomed into a tribe much larger than the circle of her friends, her city, or her epoch. It was an awesome expansion as resources of feeling that she had never experienced opened their gates, and she knew that she was now alert and generous enough to encompass anything. They would breakfast at leisure in her warm kitchen; she would bake; she would sew. They had discovered a cosy completion, bound by her new-found womanhood. She conceived. But even-tually some adamic restlessness entered their private nest, and the ballgowns, the dinner-suits, and the music started to fade.

She braced herself. Whatever supportive maternal warmth she could still find in herself she devoted to her children. It was a second-best, and satisfied but one part of her. Her yearning for lost passion began to transmute itself into a more abstract longing, one she vaguely remembered having felt as a girl, a longing for recognition. She had been touched by perfection once: a warm wind had blown through her window carrying exotic perfumes, caught her up, draped her in silk, intoxicated her with wonderful inti-mations as it carried her along. Now she knew the starkness of its absence, the bleak patience with which one had to gird oneself in its wake. Whoever it is who determines the course of an individual's life, his disposition, whom he meets and in what circumstances, had forsaken her; whether it was fate or fortune or the gods, they were no longer drawn by her charms; and was their neglect not perdition? In her misery she searched for some reason, why she had been rejected, some explanation. If she understood, then there might be some way out. As her joy had been sensual, seated in her body, so she sought in the same regions the stain of evil that must have blighted her. She scrutinized her flesh like a detective scouring a neighbourhood for a murderer. She became self-conscious about her movements, her walk, her gestures; they began to feel awkward. That she had been renounced unstopped her guilt. Her guilt made her ugly; it marked her thighs. She liked these emblems, these marks: she was drawn to her guilt, to caress it, as if to nourish it, as if it were her most intimate possession, her richest resource. And it was. Her guilt was the most clever and perverse of all the humours that coursed through her veins. In its many disguises it was capable of playing any role with consummate mastery and deception. And it was real, more real than the perfume and the polite chatter. It was not ephemeral, like an embrace. It was her constant companion, giving a powerful connecting theme to her otherwise seemingly haphazard life. Its resistance set the struggles through which she had achieved the finer moments that she had known, the memorable ones – thus it also constituted the thread that linked and animated her cherished recollections, that kept her in contact with her past. What is more, by taking a physical form, this guilt allowed her to experience in a concrete and immediate sense the demon of worthlessness that had cast her down, that had made her ashamed, and ensured that her fate would not be easily borne. In being able to plunge her hand into her wound, and feel its contours, she remained in ghastly touch with the drama that keeps death at bay: her sensuality stayed alive, sustaining her, saving her withdrawing from her present misery, giving her the chance to be ready and able if the wind changed. The one hopeful sign in her life was this masochistic sensuality; without it she would have been vacant, the winds of time and possibility blowing through her unresisted, unutilized.

All, however, was not for the best. These marks, she sensed, would not be caressed away. They were there for life. The mute irreversibility of fate, whenever she paused to consider it, terrified her. In her terror she craved the more for recognition, that the gods would see her once again, take her up in their arms, and approve. Who would the gods send as emissary? In her case it had to be some worthy man. She would give up everything for him, everything if the one she endowed with virtue might welcome her. He had to be an equal; he had to be able to stand alone. He had to recognize her calmly, astutely, with warmth, and not from below, cowering and clutching. She had had enough of mothering, of bearing the full brunt of necessity. She had had enough of being the sole point of equilibrium, of sanity. She had always been the responsible one, the one who understood, the one who restrained herself, the one who sacrificed herself. And for what? It had turned out to be a hollow heroism, producing either indifference or sourness in her husband. But she was trapped, in that her terror was that the new man, the saviour, would walk straight past. Even if he stopped to talk, he would be sure to move on again soon: what did she have to appeal to him? She dared not risk that. Were she again to enter the gates of love with full seriousness, to stake all on the plea, am I worthy to be loved, were she in other words again to bare herself to the judgment of the gods, she would fail, she would be rejected, so she is now convinced. She has become an onlooker at the dance of life, standing effacingly at the back as the couples whirl past.

There was some feeling for her husband. She after all was hardly a more appealing sight: her morale was little less frazzled than his after ten years together. And he did touch a maternal nerve, moving her to protect this pathetic child who had somehow landed on her door-step. The guilt she would feel if she abandoned him would be acute. And it was no illusion that he would be far worse off without her. She had enough guilt to accommodate as it was, without adding another layer. Moreover, she might, in pushing him out into the hostile world to fend for himself, gain nothing for herself but an intensified feeling of guilt.

She had reached a turning point. She was thirty. Certain patterns had emerged and begun to look set in her life – her husband was not one of them. She feared that a nagging element of dissatisfaction had entered her veins and would not be flushed out. On the other hand her motherhood was an enduring consolation. Linked to her dis-satisfaction with another characteristic that she was coming to regard as part of her: her moods would often switch quite erratically from an extreme of confidence into an acutely self-effacing shyness. In certain situations, above all with her husband or her closer women friends, she was assertive, quick to express her assessment of people and their actions, severe in her judgments. Her conversation was becoming more spiked with bitchiness: she would sustain a petulant monologue through the pauses in the general banter of her friends, continuing on and off for half-an-hour running through the inadequacies and failures of those whom she knew, and of the state of the world. In other situations, however, especially out in public, she would fret, speak only with great timidity, and generally try to make herself as invisible as possible. She tried to avoid occasions such as formal dinner parties where there might be unfamiliar people.

While certain elements in her character seemed to consolidate themselves, there did remain openings. She had been looking around for a couple of years for some occupation to engage her during the day. She had gone as far as to spend six months in part-time university studies. Some of the subjects had interested her and she had liked the challenge of working at a discipline with given rules, and having to produce work of her own for assessment. Nevertheless she found the academic world too abstract; she was not so taken by ideas in themselves; ideally she sought something more vocational, more practical. She had also dabbled in pottery, but given it up, finding that it was no more than a hobby, and she wanted something more serious. She made inquiries about other options, such as social work and occupational therapy, but in both cases was reluctant to throw herself into the lengthy training that they required. In part her doubts about herself made her cautious about testing herself in too many alien fields, in case she were found wanting. On the other hand her hesitations were justified: she was past the age for heedlessly flinging herself into the training for a career without a careful examination of whether that career would in fact suit her – she just could not be sure.

Her own discontentment made her sympathetic to many feminist ideas in vogue at the time. Like a lot of educated women she was torn between family and career, and had not been able to find a workable accommodation. More importantly, although she herself would not have admitted it, she shared with many feminists the frustration of not having a man that she respected. But she knew herself and her situation too well, and was too honest with herself, to be keen on blaming outside forces. She knew that her social world was free enough to allow her to become what she wanted, if only she could find out what that was, and had the courage of her convictions. If she were to find out, and were not able to live up to her recognition, then on her best days she would admit that it was she who was to blame.

His brows are now permanently knitted, deep vertical furrows branded between them, a grim modern mark of Cain. But what was his crime? Ten years of constant petty worry have tautened his face: a net of fine lines stretch across it pinning the skin down in a fixed expression of troubled earnestness, troubled resignation. It is a heavy visage, making him look much older than his age; yet it is also a brittle visage, deterring anyone from approaching too close in case the surface might fracture, and one might be forced to witness the raw pulp of blood and tissue held together by its vulnerable form. Then again there are moments when it is the face of a stunned child that stares out through the branches of a fate that has proved so hostile. What have the gods been avenging in his seemingly so harmless case?

In the beginning together they had talked, of how their lives so far had merely been a preparation for this event, their meeting. They had talked about their friends, their parents, spinning out of their happiness a myth, that they had been favoured above others. He talked of his ambitions, of the path of his career, of his experience in general, and encouraged by the devotion of the listener he began to take a pride in sounding and feeling worldly wise.

Somehow they had not been able to sustain their companionship. In the first years of their marriage the challenges of setting themselves up in their social world, of finding a house, and settling into it, above all of their children, had swept them along. And one thing that he had retained was an interest in his children: indeed his one pleasure when he got home in the evening from work was to find out from them at the dinner table what had happened to them that day. He would often reflect later, when he had sunk into his armchair in front of the television set, how marvellously curious his children were, how much excitement they found in their days, and how free they were from the burdens that weighed down the two adults, his wife and himself, who had produced them.

As for his wife and himself, a stifling chill had set in, and it hardly ever lifted. Sometimes when he was alone with her he felt as if he had been injected with a drug that rendered him limp and lethargic, without any vitality, only wishing to drag himself off somewhere by himself. It was at times a nightmare, his inability to take a step towards her, to relax himself into some gesture of kindness. Although there was some respect on some occasions, it seemed that he could not like her. An intense hatred had built up within him, choking him: he dared not show any emotion in case it was a flood of aggression that streamed out. The concealed dislike and his own frigidity made him acutely guilty: he ought to love his wife, he ought to feel friendly feelings. The chilled emotional paralysis intensified the guilt, which in turn reinforced the distance. So he withdrew. So he closed off all means of appeasing his guilt, leaving it to sit back on its haunches and gnaw away.

He had no idea where the hatred came from. It had sneaked upon him and clasped him to it when he had been absorbed by other things. It happened with the receding of the founding flush of passion. The reaction in which chemical agents from both sides are attracted, mix, and ferment, that ultimately imponderable reaction that determines all in human intimacy, had stopped. He felt himself trapped in a stagnant emotional solution. He blamed her; he hated her. In his more honest moments, however, he did wonder what had really happened. Was it that he did not in fact like the person whom he had at the outset so overvalued. Or was it a more general disappointment, that the carefree life of adventure was over and obligations had arrived. Everything was now so predictable; she was so predictable. He was bored. He had expected to be continually surprised and excited by the woman he married; and he had fallen for the clichéd delusion of eternal intimacy. The small things of daily living together had turned out not to interest him. He was extreme: once the passion failed then everything failed, everything became humdrum. He wished that she had kept some of the aura of sanctity, of a remote yet sympathetic understanding, of womanly depth, that had so taken his imagination at first. Maybe a woman needed to be for him like the Romantic archetype of a mist-shrouded mountain that he was driven to keep climbing, ever onwards, rounding new outcrops, rising over new ridges, always new vistas unfolding and with them new unknowns. If he were ever to reach the top he would be lost, for that great truth he sought would turn into one specific outlook, breathtaking for a moment, and then ever after prosaic. Something of such an ascent had occurred, and he could no longer look up to his wife.

Although the whole business wearied him too much to care what had in fact caused it, boredom was not his only affliction. He also knew terror. At times it felt as if he had been abandoned in a small field high on another mountainside, and had no idea of how to descend, of where the path might lie, if it existed, of whether he could negotiate the descent even if there were a path, and even of whether he wanted to get down to the valley he saw in a distant bluish-grey haze – it looked so unreal below, a collage of farm-houses and fields. It was cold on the mountainside and he felt sick with giddiness. Some moments he was caught by the beauty of the alpine flowers, and localized; his attention would jump to the hues and shapes of trees swaying in the distance, and the fading sun would warm him. It was a Van Gogh landscape, brilliantly clashing, fervid with wild harmonies, on the edge of splintering into madness. The giddiness increased; so did the quiet gnawing panic; he felt weak at the knees; he turned, walked a few paces, hesitated, turned, and walked back. Night was coming on. His nightmare had found him, trapped him in this mountain field. He needed his wife to warm him, to earth him, to hold his shivering hand. A woman, a mother, a wife, the particular person did not really matter. Thus he was not tempted at root to break his marriage; it was the woman essence that he needed. And anything would be better than being stranded alone on this mountain.

The terror indicated that it was not just that he was poorly equipped for everyday reality, and bored by its routines. There was a more insidious canker at work on his soul. A deeper and more inscrutable vein of guilt darkened his spirit. But it was that formative guilt whose sources are so close to preconditioning our existence that we cannot gain enough distance to understand them. What he could see, and what was clear to those who knew him, was that he suffered from some form of depression, the symptoms of which were all too clearly marked.

A general moroseness clouded his presence. He could not be entertained readily, nor distracted from his meditations. The normal forms of human relief, such as social chit-chat or pottering around the home, did not engage his interest. But there were certain great purposes the thought of which could animate him. What did absorb him was his driving belief that he might atone, he might rise above his burdensome heritage. It was less a belief, for it was not conscious, than a kind of instinct, an instinct on which all his hope and vitality was dependent. There were two courses that promised him total remission and therefore happiness. The first involved a woman. But it seemed not one single woman, or at least not for life. He could not sustain enough interest in the same woman to keep the guilt at bay. It was as if a moment would inevitably arrive when the cord of passion that tied him to her became too weak to hold against the heavy seas surging beneath the normalcy of his surfacing moorings, and he would find himself drifting off into remote waters by himself, lulled into a sombre dream by the turbulent roll and pitch of his movement, again lost to his guilt.

His guilt funded an essential insecurity, one that forced him to seek again and again recognition and acceptance by *Woman*. The archetypal female figure could take the form of many particular women, as long as they fitted within the contours sketched by his fancy. What he fancied above all was the situation in which a woman who caught his attention remained remote and aloof, cool towards him, absorbed by her own life and people whom he did not know. He was moved to win her attention and gain her intimate recognition. However, once he had her attention and separated her from her independent life, and once her ways had become familiar to him, he lost interest – as much we may deduce from his marriage. The single interruption to this pattern occurred when the favoured woman turned against him; his anxiety at the threat of rejection and abandonment would rekindle his interest, and move him to restore the intimacy.

His need to find a woman to accept him, and his fear of separation, were overpowering. Without the benign gaze of a woman watching over him, interested in what he did, approving of it, he could not live: he was cast back into his nightmare on the mountainside. In short he doubted his own worthiness; he feared that he was without value, and required virtually continuous reassurance to the contrary. The umbilical cord had never really been severed, at least not by him. Such an insecurity at the core of his being indicated severe guilt, a black veil hanging over his inner being. The guilt was so severe that he was not free to do anything with relish apart from seeking atonement. Now, after ten years of marriage, the process of atonement had broken down; his wife no longer caught his fancy, and so the main lifeline holding his head above the sea of his guilt was in shreds.

The second course that promised relief was work. To his own mind he had done fairly well at his job. He had been advanced in his office, although not as far as a couple of his contemporaries. What he supposed that his superiors had been impressed by was simply his intelligence; he was gifted in the speed and clarity with which he assessed problems. He suspected also, however, that financially buoyant times had helped him: profits had been easy to make and the firm could afford to be generous to its employees. He knew that he had not been promoted for his zeal. His work hardly ever challenged him; it was rarely that his intelligence was stretched, that he had to exert himself. Consequently he had never been able to devote himself fully to his work; it had become something of a routine, something from which he felt the better parts of himself were detached. At best it gave a structure to his life, determining his hours for most of five days a week. He did not have any close friends in his office, but his relations with his colleagues were cordial – occasionally he would lunch with them or have a drink after work. However, the comfort of his job rituals did not serve to mitigate the tragedy, that he was a man who could have devoted himself to work, and found in it, if it had challenged and absorbed him, a means for proving to himself that he could do something well. Doing something well was the second path he might have followed to the recognition that he was worthy.

Where he did find relief from the disappointment of work and the failure of marriage was at his golf club. He would spend most of Saturday and sometimes Sunday afternoon at the club. The course was an oasis to him, separated from the rest of his life and its various pressures: there he was his own master. Moreover, at golf he was tested, and in serious competition with other men. Success depended on skill and tenacity, especially when things had been going badly for a few holes. There was no pleasure equal to the sequence of meditating on a long iron shot from a difficult lie in the rough, selecting the right club, angling himself into position for the shot, then keeping his head down, swinging back slowly and striking through the ball with perfect timing, his wrists firm, standing back to watch the ball speed in a long arc across the valley, over the bunker, to pitch on the green and run up close to the hole. Here was perfection, and he had only himself and his technique to blame for failure. At golf failure hurt him in a healthy way, nor forcing him to withdraw in a depressive self-pitying mood, but rather making him writhe, and talk out his frustration with his friends in the bar after the game. Failure made him the more eager to return to the course and avenge his humiliation; it revitalized the challenge.

At golf it was him against nature, in the form of the course and its hazards, the weather and the seasons; against man, in the form of his opponents; and against himself, in the form of his own limitations of skill and concentration. He shared the challenge with his fellow players who were bent on their own parallel endeavours. It created a solidarity between them in spite of the fact that ostensibly they were in competition. He enjoyed the rituals that followed the game: first the hot shower which eased the slight ache in his muscles, and reminded him how pleasant it was to feel the weariness that follows

physical exertion. Then he would spend an hour or so in the bar
drinking with his competitors, chatting with other golfers going past,
relishing the atmosphere peculiar to a gathering of males who are
relaxing after having undergone some tough endeavour together. At
the golf club he was a different man. He was outward-going, urbane,
at times witty; and he was generally well-liked for all that, and
regarded as an amiable man, a reliable citizen.

But golf was not enough to sustain him. Its role was more to
provide a day of respite from the brooding tones of his week.
Moreover, things seemed to be getting worse as time passed. It was as
if there were a price in accumulating guilt that he had to pay for the
years he had spent hanging on to a relationship and an occupation
that had lost their founding principles, that at best occasionally
provided a bedroom-slipper cosiness. It looked as though he had
been held responsible for the continuous procession of minor
decisions, never faced, never recognized as important, taken tacitly
as if they were not decisions, but rather mere acceptances of the
normal course. It looked as though he had been held responsible, and
now suffered from the guilt, of an entire ten years of ambling along,
happening from one moment into the next because to do anything
else did not cross his mind. Comfort turned out to be all that he
had been left to pursue. But he did not particularly want to be
comfortable. Comfort did not ease his frustration; it had no steel
edge, it brought no impassioned will to strengthen his sinews. It left
him defenceless against hardship. And in the end he was not
comforted, and started to resent things.

He became more irritable, more remote, less able to take pleasure
in his family. He lost hope that he would rise again under the
mysterious burden that had descended upon him. When he arrived
home the atmosphere became tense. He grumbled, he moped. He
would finally settle into his armchair with the evening newspaper,
and the rest of the family relaxed a little, and on good days returned
to what they had been doing. But they could not entirely escape the
presence of this dark figure, central to their lives, slumped at the
heart of their home, his bitterness overspilling the high-walled cup
and lightly tainting each room with its odour.

He was on the verge of giving up, retreating into himself, which
was retreating nowhere, for that self was mutilated by the very
events that made him need it, as a last refuge. It too failed him,
unconsolidated as it was, rather like a long track meandering across

an infinitely extending flat-ploughed field, a track which months of drizzling rain had turned to mud, which now offered little foothold, and as his panic increased his tread became less able to resist the temptation to slide out from under him. So his retreat into himself left him stepping gingerly along a track that was losing its definition, merging with the field, his breath drawn, expecting any moment to lose his balance, no longer caring where he went as long as he stayed on his feet.

The husband of this story was not alone in succumbing to guilt. He was assisted by his wife, who out of her own resentment, compounded by his, suffering from his, reacting to it in kind, joined the plot. They were their own victims, as were their children, the seeds of the fall thus being watered in young innocent hearts. It was a mutual crime. And as in the case of many group crimes the guilt generated served to bind the felons together. There was a new ground for intimacy, not an intimacy that was easy to enjoy, nor indeed even to recognize. But intimacy it was. It provided them with a mutual past far less ephemeral than one illuminated by happy memories. And although they were not good at sharing their suffering, and although on the surface there was little to be witnessed other than a dour prickly hostility, a bond had slowly formed, forged by mutual guilt. They were judged together. A shadow had fallen across them that singled them out, isolated them, made them look fearfully around as with one pair of eyes. Moreover, while there was on the one side of the scales so much hostility, so much blaming of the other for their common circumstance, this was balanced by a certain attraction that their dismal condition with its fraught and lonely distances held for both of them. One of the manifestations of their guilt was the feeling that they did not deserve better, that what they experienced together was their appropriate lot, and they should make the best of it (they did not, however, show much inclination to put this ideal into practice). On bad days one of them might even consider that he or she had been lucky, that things could have been much worse. A part of each of them was drawn to their misery, embracing it as an achievement in realizing, in bringing to fruition, their destiny. If they had been allowed entry into a serene and joyful garden each of them would have soon been inwardly driven to start trampling the flowers, for neither could have lived up to the expectations of such an environment, neither felt good enough for such grace, neither would stand the shame of having their despoiled beings shown up by the contrast with perfection. Indeed, their own real-life story was of a fall from paradise, and the strange bond that now held them together was very much strengthened by the sense that this story touched a deep chord in both of them. There was something decisively appropriate about their experience together, as if they had fulfilled the profoundest ambition lodged in their dispositions. The story carried for them the resonance of ultimate truth. So it was that they became a couple. And unless one of them were to catch an optimistic virus from their housing culture, and forget their disposition, a couple they would certainly remain.

In a way they depended upon one another. Companions in guilt, each needed the other to share the burden, to witness its cost in nervous strain, and above all to provide a definite area of reality in which to articulate that guilt. Their relationship gave them an arena in which to try out their ambitions, their responsibilities, their beliefs, and, in the form of a countermanding principle, their guilt, this guilt that both fed off and reinforced the failure of their purposes. It was far better to go through perdition as a couple than alone. Recognition of such a reality meant that the relationship kept a certain dynamism: the moment one of them became too distracted, too detached, the other would start to fret, and work for a reconciliation.

As a couple there were moments when the black brooding skies cleared and the heavy surging, grey-green seas stilled, and they rode smoothly through their daily business. But in general their intimacy was sombre, leaving them blank, with their most promising resources unexploited, their lives disquietingly untested.

None of this was recognized. As products of their time they were chosen to deny the reality of their misery in public, and between themselves, by proclaiming that they were comfortable, that they had their family, their steady income, and their friends. Their children do moderately well at school; he does not do badly in his job; she is respected among the women she knows. There do not seem to be any hitches; most people appear worse off to them. Around them they see cautionary tales of what happens if you jump out of the moving carriage – and after all the horses have not really bolted. He has his golf club and his newspapers. She has the children, the house to maintain, and her friends. It is all very normal. They are well-off.

5 Shopping World: the palace of modern consumption

They come for their groceries, for their socks, for their sherry, for their cassette tapes and their dry cleaning. They also come quaking for excitement. It is a large unremarkable building about the height of St Paul's Cathedral in London, and covering twice the ground-space. It is set in the middle of a plateau of asphalt covered with rows of parked cars, the whole strangely out of the scale with the miles of sedate suburbs in which it is set. The sun shines, there is a slight breeze, one can see the low mountains in the distance, and the mood is of a quiet carefree tranquillity, with people here and there going about their afternoon business, in no great hurry, paying no great attention to anything beyond the path in front of them. A large neon sign over the entrance we approach reads, 'SHOPPING WORLD'.

Pushing open the door, crossing the threshold, we falter in astonishment at the exotic new world that confronts us. We have entered a long hall, skirted by an upper balcony, connected by staircases and spiral walks, the entire space as far as the eye can see draped with fairy lights, neon signs, and richly coloured hangings, interspersed with fountains, split-levels, kiosks, merry-go-rounds. The soothing, gently exciting throb of contemporary pop music fills the air, picking up the warm ochre tones that back the kaleidoscope of bright lights and determine the visual texture of the surfaces. Then there are the people crowding, milling, walking, loitering, some hanging over the balustrades, watching, daydreaming or whatever, altogether forming another dimension of shapes, movements and colours.

Shops flank the hall and the balconies. They open directly on to the central space without doors or windows, forming a line of elaborately decorated alcoves, each with its specialized textures of posters, signs, hangings, and goods. People seem to wander in and out of them as a diversion from the central parade, as one catches their fancy or they feel like a monentary withdrawal.

The clues to the essential truth about a society whose individuals devote a major part of their energies to fulfilling the goal of consumption must lie within the walls of the institutions that service that goal. Shopping World has become the leading representative of such institutions. Each week 400,000 people pass through one of the larger Shopping Worlds in Melbourne. Moreover, each new Shopping World that is built is bigger, grander, and more extravagant in the distractions that it provides. Shopping Worlds are now planned with twenty-year build-ups to full capacity in mind. They are the shopping venues of the present and the future, and almost inevitably their existence leads to the running down of the shopping streets and even the single supermarkets doing business in their surrounding suburbs.

Most of the reasons for the success of Shopping World are straightforward. Compared to the local shopping street a greater variety of shops is provided; there is plentiful car parking space, which is safe and of easy access; the whole centre is enclosed and kept at a constant temperature, thus providing insulation from climatic variation and protection from the nuisance and danger of car traffic. Compared to city shopping it has the advantage of being situated relatively close to the homes of those who use it. In short, Shopping World is convenient. However, there is one major reason for its success that has nothing to do with convenience. I wish to suggest in this essay that Shopping World provides us with a clue as to the deep motive behind consumption, and indeed indicates that a new direction has been taken in the evolution of Western consumption. I shall not be at all concerned with Shopping World's convenience.

Let us return to where we had left off, having just entered Shopping World. There is suddenly a general movement of people towards the centre of the hall where there appears to be a raised platform with rows of seats surrounding it on three sides. It is three o'clock in the afternoon and here at the core of sedate suburban life the spot-lights go on and a *Vogue* magazine stereotype of forty walks across the stage to a waiting microphone and announces her privilege, in a voice whose tones are like the facets of a severely-cut ostentatiously large semi-precious stone. Her privilege is to be here and introducing the latest fashions in wool. More lights come on accompanied by pulsing rock music, a makeshift curtain opens and a model prances forward on to the stage, her long slim legs sending her skirt out in swirls of pleated colour. A hush of surprise murmurs through the audience, partly seated, partly stopped in their passing-by, partly hanging over the balustrade of the upper level which encircles the central stage in the form of a gallery. The impression is strong, set in the midst of such everyday ordinariness, the music, the fashion lights, the nakedness of this single young woman dancing alone so close that it is possible to see the veins on her wrist, the slightly clenched hands working to the beat, the forced smile beneath the heavy make-up.

After half-an-hour the parade is over. The lights go off, the curtain is removed, the crowd disperses, and the carpeted stage is left bare waiting for its next event, which might be a quiz, a boys' choir, or a cosmetic demonstration. With the heart of Shopping World now stilled we wander off further along the main hall. The leading sensation suddenly becomes olfactory. The smell of warm bread, and then of freshly-ground coffee draws the mind away from clothes and svelte girls. A car is on display, repeating its demand for attention with a sign advertising that it is the first prize in a lottery. On again, past a news-stand, stopping in front of a furniture shop inviting the passer-by into any of its simulated living rooms, one of which is guaranteed to suit 'Your' individual taste. Chairs and couches matched to coffee tables, wallpaper and hanging lights to vases and standing lights, ashtrays to reprinted paintings, a world in suspended animation waiting to have life breathed into it by a family walking into its space, occupying it and making of its designed harmonies something more personal.

A small crowd is gathered around a stall across the way. The strains of rumba music drift through them, with what sounds like a harpsichord backing, interrupted now by the rhythms of a dixieland band starting up from the near front of the hidden shop. Pushing through the cluster of spectators we see at the centre of attention a woman seated at a piano-size instrument with two rows of keyboards above which rows of brightly coloured plastic buttons and levers in red, yellow, powder blue, leaf green, grey, white and numerous other colours, with writing on them, some in, some out, some up, and some down, this complex of controls which seem to operate both the music and another row, this time of flashing button lights. The woman appears to toy with half-a-dozen keys and miraculously the entire sound of a jazz band results. The audience is entranced.

A little speculation, confirmed by one of the salesgirls, tells that these, the most popular of contemporary technology's domestic novelties, are 'electronic organs'. They are wonders of simulation. with rotating speakers their only moving part — rotating we are informed in order to produce the echo effect, 'the full quality of concert hall sound'. At the flick of a lever one has drums or violins, trumpets or piano, banjo or xylophone. This remarkable computer, if that is what it is, makes it possible to create 253 million tone combinations. The brochure boasts that one simply chooses the rhythm that one wants: 'then play a chord, corresponding pedal and hold. And the organ takes over ∴. . the chord and pedals automatically follow the rhythm pattern selected.' There are sixteen rhythm patterns from classical and polka to rock and afro.

The second miracle offered by this instrument is that skill is redundant. Gone are those long hours everyday of practice in order to gain moderate command of one instrument. Now hardly any practice and one has sixteen types of orchestra at one's finger-tips. As the brochure proudly asserts: 'a Sweeping Commitment to Today'. The salesgirl, after having spent a half-hour with us explaining with great animation the advantages and disadvantages of different organs, confides that she herself came from the country to the city four years ago and immediately fell in love with electronic organs. She has worked selling them ever since, and has slowly graduated, both in skill and in what she could afford, from one of the simplest to one of the most expensive. She adds shyly that she spends much of her time at home playing, and smiles at the poster above which commands 'Bring Romance back into the Home'.

What then is Shopping World? What is really going on here? In this, the modern market-place, the ratio in size and importance between the public space and that occupied by stalls or shops has been inverted. The central hall is the enthralling area; it is the focus of activity and attention. The shops are subsidiary, rather like the side-chapels in a gothic cathedral. The change in the use of space indicates a change in the priorities of the shoppers. Shopping has become of secondary importance. Shoppers are drawn by and large to Shopping World by the promise of a consumption more meta-physical, more quixotic, than the purchase of soap and socks. Indeed it is as if in those moments they actually spend in the side-booths filling their shopping bags they are purchasing their entrance tickets.

To what world offering what metaphysical allures have they bought tickets? Shopping World is first a fairground, with the intimacy of a cabaret. As at a fairground the visitor strolls around, alternating at will, or on whim, between being spectator and performer. He is always a part of the performance, but sometimes he merges with the crowd, or disappears through a tent door to watch the bearded lady. At other times he becomes a more prominent part of the play, throwing balls at coconuts or driving a dodgem-car. Then it is the performance that matters. It counts for little whether he carries off a coconut or has lapped the other dodgems: what is important to him is that for a moment he has been at the centre of the action, utterly absorbed in handling the challenges of his act. As he steps out of the car and returns to being a spectator he can relax a little, daydream about his time at the wheel, walk on watching others, seeking new absorptions, daydreaming further. Shopping World is much the same. The performances might seem less explicitly defined, but in fact there are merry-go-rounds, there are electronic organs to play and furniture displays to occupy, and there are market surveyors who interview and wine salesmen who tempt. Shopping World provides a range of events, from the grand and glamorous to the local and incidental; it invites each shopper to participate as she will.

On the other hand the boisterous, gypsy elements of the fairground under the night sky are not here. Shopping World is enclosed, and its lights, music, and orchestrated happenings, its more precisely lit and defined roles, make it more reminiscent of the modern cabaret. The one who goes to the cabaret becomes a part of the glamour. The event is unique, not recorded on disc, film or video; the singer is singing to him personally; the lights include him. Here he is invited into the foyer of the house of celebrity, almost famous himself. The modern media emphasize that it is the show that is important: at Shopping World everyone is in a small way on show.

The fairground-cabaret is popular not merely because it provides entertainment. It provides much more. Indeed I wish to suggest that it is within its walls that we may witness some of the lineaments of contemporary hope. Here some of the gropings of wishes unfulfilled within the frame of the monotonous stability and incipient aimlessness of suburban life leave traces as to their ultimate purposes.

That hope and those wishes are not directed towards consumption, or at least not the consumption of material goods. Buying is something to do on the way, a nervous mannerism at a moment of hesitancy, like scratching one's nose. It is the way that is important to the shopper, and for us to concentrate on the shopping-bag would be to take the person merely at face value. Maybe there was a brief period in the history of capitalism that was more obsessional, when the sociologist had reason to identify commodity fetishism as a central passion, and to see self-esteem linked directly to social status which in turn gained its most secure demonstration from the ownership and conspicuous consumption of material goods. Presumably material possessions have always been and will continue to be taken in part as emblems of power and prestige. And in a few cases, for instance of deprivation in early childhood or of living through economic depression, they may satisfy a deep need. But in general they do not answer any essential wish, they do not water the roots of well-being. This is clear today at Shopping World.

At best material consumption offers a substitute satisfaction, a palliative to the wish to possess a thing of ultimate importance. The redeeming possession that is the true object of consumer desire may take the form of a beautiful moment, a taste in the mouth that awakens all the senses, a feeling of self-containment, of increasing pleasure in the person's self, of regained vitality and purpose, or finally at the end of the aisle the possession of love. Such a possession is rare, especially given that its binding threads are spiritual, and that it must unite heavenly aspiration with earthly activity. Gratified desire, the goal of so much of human endeavour, is tantalizingly elusive: our richest image of it comes from the mood in which fairy-tales end. However, there are moments in which every individual achieves that treasured state, and those moments cast the lines of hope that govern life through the long in-betweens, and pattern the way he will at once compromise his deepest desires and console himself for the discontent that the compromises cause him. Consumption has taken over from religion as the main source of compromise and consolation.

There may be moments when a new pair of shoes or a standing lamp so catch the purchaser's fancy that she does feel that the gods have blessed her with one of their finest gifts. But she has deluded herself. Genuine gifts carry the receiver into new areas of experience; they challenge her current assumptions about herself;

they announce new possibilities, as the angel Gabriel, portrayed by fifteenth-century Florentine painters, announced to the Virgin Mary the miracle that would change her destiny; above all they are memorable. Consumption does not have any of these qualities. The most it can satisfy is a satellite wish that moves in the reflected light of its sun.

There is nothing new about the quest for palliatives. Freud saw the whole of culture as a substitute gratification, a sublimation of frustrated desire. What is changing is the nature of the palliatives themselves. Shopping World represents a significant change in the history of consumption in our culture: its design recognizes and exploits the wide gap that usually exists between the wish and the commodity. It fills that gap with activity that is more conducive than basic shopping to arouse the wish, to clothe it in a whole range of exotic guises, and to carry it into the realm of possibility. Shopping World tries to play the role of the eternal seducer, arousing extravagant expectations, and then keeping just enough interest and just enough distance not to break the spell; it offers neither total consummation nor total rejection. Although its own sole motive is to increase sales, the hall of consumption supplies many activities to keep its captive's wish alive. Buying is merely one of those activities, and consequently the shopper does not expect too much from it; as a result she is less likely to be disappointed. The history of consumption has now advanced to the point at which the commodity's main function is to serve as a background ritual, and a rationalization.

Buying's function at Shopping World is to provide a context for exciting experience, in fact for experience that is quite the opposite to the useful, dutiful collecting of provisions. If we choose to retain the term 'consumption' then we have to disregard completely the Marxist emphasis on commodities. In a sense what the shopper wants, as Max Stirner would have put it, is to consume herself; she wants to be eaten up, absorbed by a larger universe than that of her lonely self; she wants to be consumed by a captivating moment, a moment that resonates past fantasies and may imply a future quite different from the mundane present. What she seeks to purchase is experience, a release from what she knows into something larger and richer. And she is now too mature to be duped into believing that commodities alone can help her very much.

This is where the electronic organ has special appeal. She wants her ideal commodity to be suggestive, suggestive enough for her to believe in the fantasy that it supports. She does not want a compromise, although that is in fact what she gets, with the consolation that she has been entertained. She does not gain a momentous, a memorable experience, but she has at least been taken out of herself for a while. So her culture remains materialist only in the sense that material consumption contributes the form of many of its rituals; the form of the ritual should not be confused with what it enables. Even on Christmas Eve, when the pressure to buy is at its strongest, the ambience of the great modern market-place slows the dense crowds of shoppers down to a stroll. The shoppers are calmed within its spaces. Their eagerness is not for purchase.

Emile Zola has provided us with a yardstick for measuring the degree to which the nature of consumption has changed. In his richly sociological novel *Au Bonheur des Dames*, written in 1882, he described the advent of the great department store. The new emporiums were eclipsing all the small traditional shops in their neighbourhoods. Zola attributed their success to two factors. First they exploited the 'bargain', seducing women into buying things they did not need by making them seem so cheap that the customer imagined every time she bought that she was bringing off a brilliant economic coup. The stores created a frenzy of buying. Second, because of their size they could offer an unprecedented range of merchandise. However, the important thing for our deliberations here is that the commodity itself remained the focus of attention in the department store. Although the director of Zola's store knew that his success depended on him capturing the imagination of the bourgeois ladies of Paris, playing with their fantasies and drawing them in at just the right moment, he did so purely through his goods. The shopper's mind was concentrated on the article of consumption; it had not yet started to stray into more abstract fields.

People do, of course, buy at Shopping World. Moreover, not all their shopping takes the form of an incidental dropping into an alcove as a relief from the central parade. There is some serious shopping, carried out with matter-of-fact efficiency. It seems common, for example, to proceed on arrival to the supermarket section and speedily purchase the week's groceries. The full bags are then deposited, to be collected later when the shopper finally leaves. Her duty done she can throw herself with a good conscience into the pure pleasure of Shopping World. Indeed it is essential to the success of Shopping World that it cater to the guilt of a utilitarian culture. Ladies can pretend to themselves that their motive for coming here is to do something useful, even necessary – an obligation that in reality they choose to get out of the way first. Once they have done their serious shopping and thereby absolved their utilitarian guilt they can relax, having successfully rationalized an hour or two at leisure in the fair. Moreover, there are no clocks here to remind them of duties that await elsewhere.

If Shopping World is first a fairground, with the intimacy of a cabaret, it is second a meeting-place. Occasionally the shoppers do meet friends; then they stop to gossip, or stand together and wistfully gaze around them. However, such meetings are not sought, and the shopper is likely to get impatient fairly quickly with such collisions with familiarity. If it were familiarity that she sought she would stick to her local butcher, who knows her personally and likes to chat. She comes here to escape her private suburban circle of known objects, reliable people, and predictable situations. If it is a meeting that she seeks it is one of those surprise intersections of fate whose possibility the image of the fairground or the cabaret conjures up. If the shopper were able to confess, and clarify those vague metaphysical longings that have driven her here, then the shadow of some stranger might be made out beckoning to her. She is protected enough at Shopping World by the deliberateness of the space, the anonymity of the people, and the concreteness of her own motive for being here, to dare the unfamiliar, to loosen slightly the halter on her most deeply unconscious intention. Is she not in fact flirting with the fancy of a mysterious and enthralling encounter, the passage to an alternative life? Is there not a wayward impulse in her that she is indulging this afternoon? Were some real opportunity to confront her (which is unlikely because most of the people here are other suburban wives) she would probably flee in agitation. But living out a fantasy is not everything; the experience she is in search of is a feat of the imagination, and if she can live through it during an hour at Shopping World then she will return home satisfied. Shopping World provides her with the props that allow her to stage herself in this play of her imagination, an experience that releases her, if only temporarily, from the carefully defined finite surfaces of her life.

Maybe it is even more ethereal, the wish that Shopping World alerts. Maybe it signals to a long-subdued childhood or adolescent image of adult omnipotence, of having the power to attract at the right moment in the right place the people and the circumstances that would make of her life something royally glamorous, that would draw her into a mystery of exquisite splendour and significance. Where better than here, where there is the atmosphere, the crowds of strangers, and dancing models who stimulate dreams of stardom, of elegance and influence?

So she wanders around, gazing through a veil of reverie at the particular goings-on. She can lose herself on occasion, in the fashion parade, or hidden in the crowd around the electronic organs. Being in the mood for a cabaret, the music helps her to imagine that she is there. The organs can so seduce her with their echoing beat that she envisages her own home transformed, the excitement of the night-club superimposed on its securities. The Promotions Manager of one of the Shopping World chains in Australia has speculated that these centres may replace Valium.

After an hour or so she starts to feel pains in her legs, the large space and the crowd begin to look alien, and she recalls that chores await her at home. Soon it will be time for her to start preparing the evening meal. With the aura of Shopping World fading fast she heads off to collect her groceries.

Well over 80 per cent of the people buying at Shopping World are suburban wives, thus the justification for having followed one of them around. However, there are other people whom we could have observed. There are the young married couples, sometimes with an infant or a small child, who can most typically be seen in one of the simulated living rooms in the furniture shop. They are lightly intoxicated by the vision of their own living room furnished like this down to the minutest detail, down to the style of the modern baroque mirror. Then in the late afternoon or evening there are the groups of teenage boys lounging around. Shopping World is their street-corner meeting-place. Finally one further qualification needs to be made to our having concentrated on the suburban wife in our attempt to discover the peculiarly contemporary nature of Shopping World. In earlier times the more affluent suburban wives would have satisfied similar needs by travelling to the city centre and spending a few hours wandering along streets and arcades, in and out of shops and cafés.

We should not leave Shopping World without questioning our initial assumption, that here we are in the modern agora. The agora of the classical Greek city was similar, in being the market-place and yet serving as much more, indeed as the most important public space. When a citizen left the privacy of his home, wishing to engage in public life, most likely he went to the agora. Shopping World at its most general is a public space. It answers to one of the most basic of human needs, that for society in the sense of a defined space among people in which to see and be seen, in which to move and to meet, to linger and to evade, a space at the same time in which to conduct some of life's important business – in this case shopping.

The Greek agora, however, was different in one crucial respect, a difference that highlights a momentous development in modern life. It was surrounded by civic buildings and temples; it served as the daily centre not only of commerce, but also of religious, political, judicial, and indeed general social life. To be in public in ancient Athens meant to be a citizen, and likely enough to be engaged in civic duties. In modern life, by contrast, the areas of political action have become so remote that to be in public for a person has lost all connotation of being a responsible citizen with duties to his community. Being in public has become completely abstracted from having power over the commanding political, legal, and economic institutions of the society; it has been focused back on private life. Shopping World is designed to encourage narcissistic fantasies about the future of the least political of all interests, those of intimate personal life.

6 The soap fetish

WE VACUUM your skin to beauty with an ingenious machine designed in Europe for our skin spa treatments. It's positively uncanny what it sneaks out of your skin. Vacuuming is just the first of 6 unique stages in our hygiene skin renewal clinic. We also oxygenate and polish your skin to shining. . . .
Advertisement, Herald, Melbourne, 18 July 1978

OMOmatic contains ingredients to remove dirt from clothes (anionic and nonionic surfactants); soften water and disperse soils (sodium polyphosphate); break up fatty soil (sodium silicate); remove bleachable stains (stabilized sodium perborate); modify foam (long chain soaps); provide a special brightening effect on cotton (triazolyl stilbene fluorescer) and improve product processing (sodium sulphate); also small quantities of normal fabric brightener, soil suspending agent, colour and perfume.
Statement on a soap packet

You're very particular about the outside. Choose Harpic for the inside.
Harpic Powder toilet cleaner: *It power cleans, kills germs and freshens above the waterline, and through the S-bend where ordinary scourers and brushes can't reach.*
Harpic Thick Liquid toilet cleaner: *Squirt it on under that hard-to-get-at rim. Thick liquid clings to the bowl, cleaning continuously and killing dangerous germs without the need for hard scrubbing.*
Advertisement, Australian Family Circle, 30 June 1978

To know a society means above all to know its irrationality. Sociologists might do well to take as their exemplar the haughty Madame in Louis Malle's brothel, in his film *Murmur of the Heart,* who claimed that she could tell a man's perversion at a thirty-second glance. Presumably she would have read in these men's so-called normal daily gestures clues to their deepest wishes. And it is true that there are few of even the most humdrum everyday activities in the life of a society that are not deeply veined by the irrational. However, in this particular essay I am not choosing an ordinary gesture as the starting point for the enquiry. In a more cowardly style I shall go in search of a fully-fledged dodo specimen, something so perverse that it defies all reasonable attempts to give it a purpose or a function.

In the quest for his dodo specimen the sociologist in the latter half of the twentieth century cannot do much better than watch television. If there is a leading clue to be found to collective out-landishness in a consumer society then it may well lie in the more extravagant fantasies that advertising agencies can stimulate in their audiences, indicators of the degree to which the average housewife – the target for at least eight advertisements in ten – can be coaxed beyond the perimeters of reasonable need. Moreover, as Vance Packard taught us in 1957, in *The Hidden Persuaders*, modern advertising agents have developed an acute talent for getting at the unconscious wishes of the potential consumer – the student of the irrational can learn much by simply paying attention to the images they employ. Now if the industrious sociologist were to follow this advice I am sure he would end up at the spot I have reached, admittedly by another path (for who arrives rationally at the scene of their enquiry): that is at the soap fetish. My subject, more specifically, is the Western middle-class housewife and her pathological levels of anxiety over cleanliness.

On Australian television during July and August 1978 roughly one advertisement in four during the afternoon, and one in six during the evening, dealt with cleanliness.[1] Yet the average family spends around one per cent of its disposable income on cleansing agents.[2] Thus the intensity of advertising is completely out of proportion to the percentage of their budget that people spend on soap. This is not because of a peculiarly high degree of competition among the manufacturers. On the contrary, the market is almost entirely controlled by the two multi-national corporations, Unilever and Colgate-Palmolive.

That extraordinary sums are spent by the soap industry on advertising is confirmed from the other end. The Chairman of

Unilever in 1958 in a speech headed 'Advertising' announced that his company spent £83 million on advertising in 1957, an amount almost equal to the trading profit for the same period. I have been informed by Unilever that the situation is not significantly different twenty years later.[3] The same speech argued that a product that is not advertised will lose sales.[4]

The Trade Practices Commission in Australia investigated the soap industry in 1975–6. One of the Commission's more interesting findings was that many of Colgate and Unilever's products are virtually identical, containing additives in such miniscule amounts that their widely promoted uniqueness is almost negligible. Unilever admitted during discussions that their products, Omo, Rinso, and Surf, had a substantially similar ability to clean. The Commission concluded that the manufacturers had been able to boost the over-all demand for soap by creating 'artificial product differentiation by misleading advertising'. They had been able to convince housewives that they needed two or three finely differentiated detergents where they had previously used one.[5] The advertisement for two types of toilet cleaner quoted above might well fall into this category.

For our purposes here we can draw two conclusions. First it is necessary to advertise in order to sell. Second, it is possible in the case of soap to inflate demand by marketing a range of products that in essence are virtually the same, but whose image varies enough from item to item for them not to be regarded as substitutes for each other.

We are then faced with the question of why soap manufacturers can manipulate demand in this fashion when manufacturers of other goods cannot (cosmetics is one exception, but then, as will become apparent in the following discussion, cosmetics are closely related to soap). There seems to be a peculiarly high level of consumer gullibility here. This is where the soap fetish enters. The manufacturers are able to address a thick strain of irrationality in modern western societies. They have cleverly exploited a growing obsession with cleanliness. As the saying goes, where there is smoke there is fire.

The exaggerated sway that soap holds over the consumer imagination is manifest in the range of available products. The contemporary supermarket, selling food and household goods (excluding clothing, appliances and hardware), will have five rows in twenty-five devoted to cleansers of one type or another. Laundry detergents, to take one category, have proliferated to the point that 105 different brands and packages may be found in a large American supermarket.

Of course the accusation of being 'unclean' is age-old. Concern with purity and contamination is universal to all men, although beliefs and customs vary widely from culture to culture. Mary Douglas has effectively knocked on the head the view held by some anthropologists that the concern with purity in primitive societies is rooted in medical knowledge. She demonstrates the general social function of discriminating over cleanliness, that of maintaining order.[6] I am concerned only with modern Western societies in this essay, but while accepting the universality of a preoccupation with the metaphors of dirt and cleanliness, wish to argue for a peculiar level of irrationality in our own concern with purification. Which is not to suggest that other societies have not gone to absurd lengths to sweep their stables.

There are certain examples of a contemporary concern for cleanliness that I shall not consider. It has been standard among the Italian, Greek or Turkish peasants who have migrated to Australia since 1945, as soon as they finally own a house of their own, to put linoleum on all the floors, to laminate all the working surfaces, to protect the furniture with plastic covers, to concrete the garden, and then to keep everything immaculately clean and shining. This is not irrational behaviour. They have come from areas where the local poverty and the nature of the housing made it difficult to keep dirt – perhaps disease – at bay. They see themselves as having risen out of squalor, and like to celebrate that rise by creating the most tangible of all gleaming symbols. What they have done is rational in terms of hygiene, and understandable from the standpoint of theories of upward social mobility.

Medicine has made the links between dirt and disease obvious to Westerners for over a century now. We have learnt that our own preservation depends in part on a clean environment. However, we have gone far beyond what reason could recommend. Once we had sewers and health inspectors the battle against disease-carrying dirt was largely won. Today a doctor receives something like one patient in ten who is genuinely in need of medical attention This is by and large another story, but it does indicate the degree to which the West has overstepped the mark of a rational concern for health. It is the overstepping that I am interested in here, in the related field of cleanliness.

I am not concerned in this essay with people who keep reasonably clean. There is one other species of motive in relation to dirt that I shall likewise pass by. In the nineteenth and early twentieth century there was, behind the pride members of the middle class took in their order, neatness and cleanliness, a distinction they were drawing between themselves and the grimy, sweaty and vulgar working class. They were asserting a hierarchy of privilege, illustrating to others and confirming in their own minds their superior status. This is not to say that hysterical elements did not abound in their attitudes to dirt.

Finally, I shall discount the cases of the males of the species who demonstrate an excessive interest in the smutty and the tainted, the innocent and the pure. Certainly there remain cases like Jonathan Swift, for whom excrement figured large in his imagination,[7] or John Ruskin, who was rendered impotent in his marriage with disgust at the first sight of female pubic hair.[8] But they are not common, and they are psychologically quite independent from the soap fetish as I shall outline it. What may be significant is that a male concern with purity in woman will reinforce the woman's own concern with the state of her body and soul. It is likely, however, that such a concern has lessened in the last hundred years.

(a) Water

To soap requires water. Water is one of the four primal elements, with fire, air and earth, and abounds with symbolic resonances. Water is the purifier, enabling baptism or the washing away of sins. In special circumstances it becomes 'holy water', when touched by the divine presence; or it may be the 'water of life' or the source of the 'fountain of youth', in either case promising to wash away the degradations of ageing. The ancient Greeks identified one of their rivers, Lethe, with oblivion or forgetfulness. Water is also of course a preserver of life, the slaker of thirst.

I wish to focus here on one only of water's images, that of its power to soothe. Inundation provides an archetypal pleasure, contrasting with the equally deep fear of submersion and drowning. A person suspended in water, swimming or bathing, finds himself in harmony with the element that contains him – it moves with him, in immediate perfectly malleable response, supporting and caressing. He does not clash with water: the boundaries of his body, and by extension his self, which are normally carefully guarded against possible threats of physical or psychological collision, are less necessary. In water he can fuse with a wider universe, releasing himself from the defences he must keep up at other times. The security he feels in water draws on another source: plunging into water has a symbolic identity with plunging into the unconscious. Just as it is dreams that relax him at night, when he lets himself go in sleep into the hands of his unconscious fantasy life, so during the day bathing in deeper and less trammelled mental life eases the pressures of conscious living. Being in water is one of the best ways of inducing the state of relaxation in which daydreams can flow at will. Being in water carries an additional symbolic connection, with the womb: it is suggestive of a return to the first and probably the most momentous of all experiences of security.

The pleasure of water is further related to the harmony achieved through sexual release, a sense of loss of self and free-floating fusion with a larger world. Moreover, the feeling of water washing off the body is deeply sensual – soothing, caressing, making sleek as it flows, laps and splashes. We have John Masefield's image of the stately Spanish galleon 'Dipping through the tropics by the palm-green shores'.

I have opened my interpretation of the soap fetish with water because it acts as a complementary factor. Water brings its own pleasure quite independent from a desire for cleanliness. The pull of this pleasure may well reinforce the drive for purification, a fact that many soap advertisements exploit to their advantage. However, there are deeper links between a delight in water and the wish to be pure, and not simply the fact that it seems universal among men to identify water in part with purification. The soothing power of water, as I have already outlined it, appeals to a need for security; a similar need lies beneath much of the obsession for cleanliness, as I shall argue in the following sections.

There are many contemporary examples of the pleasure of water as a soothing element being integrated with the wish to be clean. The shower has virtually replaced the bath in Western societies as the major means for washing the body. The shower is soothing and cleansing, with gushing warm water streaming across the body which is being soaped sleek and clean. Many advertisements extend this image to shampooing, showing a turbulence of perfumed foam in hair, with the associated sensual image of the result, the silky sheen of freshly-shampooed long hair wafting in a light breeze. But the shower is less soothing, and more cleansing, at least in its symbolism, than the bath. If we can imagine the soothing and the cleansing as overlapping areas then there has been a shift towards the right-hand side of the picture.

The fusion of the two pleasures is illustrated in washing machine advertisements, especially for machines with a glass porthole in the front. The image of dirty clothes tumbling around in hot water and suds, and finally emerging clean, dry and warm has an almost magical potency. To wear clothes that have been so generously purified is to gain for oneself some of the virtue and the pleasure of the process that so redeemed them.

Similar things may be said about the washing of crockery, tiles, oily hands, windows and motor cars. My sole aim in this first section has been to note, before turning to the cleanliness wish itself, that the use of water in various methods of purification carries its own pleasure.

(b) Inner barrenness

> The very strong need which women feel to have a beautiful body and a lovely home and for beauty in general is based on their desire to possess a beautiful interior to their body in which 'good' and lovely objects and innocuous excrements are lodged.
>
> Melanie Klein

Melanie Klein argues in the eleventh chapter of her major work, *The Psycho-Analysis of Children* (1923; third edition 1949), that a woman's deepest fear, paralleling the male fear of castration, is of her inside being robbed and destroyed. This fear originates in the young girl feeling guilt over her own sadistic fantasies of attacking her mother and destroying her inside. She fears retaliation. Her hostility to her mother is often expressed through excremental imagery, of poisoning with urine or faeces. In turn she fears that she might have been despoiled by having had 'bad' objects put inside her. According to Klein girls feel an intense need for children, a need greater than any other desire, in order to overcome their anxiety by proving that they can produce 'good' children, that they have not been contaminated inside. In adult life for the woman to have an abnormal or sickly child is likely to confirm her worst fears. A bad child is likened to a poisonous excrement.

The woman's anxiety that she may be innerly barren is intimately tied to a fear that her inside is dirty, polluted or ruined. She readily projects this fear on to her immediate external environment, especially on to her own body and her home and family. She fights her anxiety by trying to ensure that that environment is clean, hoping that if the outside that she is responsible for is pure then so will be her inside. A fresh complexion, a beautiful body, clean and healthy children, and a lovely home stand as symbols for the necessity of the truth that she must be pure herself.

Projections of the anxiety about inner barrenness come in many forms. The need for a beautiful body carries with it the more specific desire to wash and make-up first thing in the morning in order to gain greater confidence to face the world. Phobic fears of mice and spiders are by and large the preserve of women. These creatures are seen as dirty and disease-carrying, and what is more having the ability to crawl up inside. After a house has been burgled it is the wife who has more than the rational concerns about what has been taken: she frequently suffers from shock that her private space has been violated, intruded upon by an unwelcome stranger.

Another projection is to be found in the stereotype of the 'old maid'. The peculiar stigma attached to being a spinster is of being wrinkled, scrawny and dried up, a sterile husk that has above all lost its nourishment. A spinster is without children. In contrast to the earth mother she is nervous, dithering and brittle. Thus the most pejorative image of womanhood is one that stresses inner barrenness. The stereotype has a more sinister representation in the fairytale image of the wicked witch. And Hansel and Gretel's witch entices the good children with the succouring offer of gingerbread in order to cage them and eventually force them into a womb, her oven, that will destroy them.

The argument draws further support from the common strategy of women under stress: to restore their self-esteem by trying to increase the narcissistic pleasure they gain from their own body and its image. They take especial pains in making-up, have their hair coiffured, or buy a new dress; at the extreme they want, in spite of the mixed metaphor, to play the peacock. Men under strain seek to improve their morale by countering their own leading anxiety, that of castration. They attempt to assert their potency, by taking their car out for a fast drive, or by arguing aggressively with friends, involving themselves with a fierce determination to win in competitive sports, or by going out to seduce a woman. It is often assumed that a woman's desire to be more beautiful is primarily a desire to be more sexually alluring. This is partly a self-congratulatory male prejudice. I would argue that a second, but not altogether independent, wish is more important, the wish to be elegant, spruce, graceful and blooming with youthful gaiety. Vance Packard recounts the results of a study carried out by an agency marketing lingerie: a woman first of all wants to be able to look approvingly at herself. Second, she wants the approval of other women. The approval of men comes a poor third.[9] These conclusions are confirmed by those who work in *haute couture*: in public it is by and large the scrutiny of other women that counts. Quentin Crisp claims that in fact the great female stars of film were objects that women identified with rather than men were attracted to.[10]

We can conclude so far that a narcissism spread across the whole body is vital to a woman's sense of well-being. She wants to enjoy her own image in the mirror; she wants the begrudging admiration of that highly critical group, other women. This narcissistic emphasis is directly related to the anxiety over inner barrenness. Melanie Klein notes that a girl cannot test her inside in the way a boy can feel his penis. A boy can master his anxiety in part by phallic attacks on the outside world. The girl's situation is more difficult, tending to foster in her both an introspectiveness (and a more intuitive mental style) and the generalization of her need to feel good inside to her whole body.[11] She defends herself against the anxiety accordingly.

The most pervasive projection of the anxiety about inner barrenness comes in the form of the soap fetish. Cleanliness compulsions are typically female. Sexual fetishism seems to be the preserve of males,[12] as do many other forms of extreme behaviour – for instance it has usually been men whose fanaticism has driven them to lead religious or political movements, or alternatively to reach the frontiers of scientific research. It may indeed be that the one female fetish is that of soap. The somewhat old-fashioned neurosis of feeling compelled to scrub the kitchen table every hour was a female preserve. So was the obsession with dirt in the house, leading for instance to the insistence of anyone changing shoes every time they moved from one room to another. It was Macbeth's lady who under the strain of their mutual guilt started frantically washing her hands as she descended into madness.

One type of soap fetishist is the woman who is driven to shower three times a day to wash off the chaos of her life — best symbolized by the inside of her handbag, which is a clutter of broken pencils, leaking biros, open cosmetic tubes, stained lipsticks, torn and grubby crumpled notes with telephone numbers scrawled on them, obsolete keys, money caked in various congealed residues, handkerchieves, tattered notebooks, a brush tangled with hair, two marbles, a make-up compact, a wallet and a purse. In the hot shower she finds a moment of release from her inability to make any headway in gaining some harmony in her life. It is not just that her cares are washed away; there is a moment when the inside of her treasure trove is sleek and clean, soft and welcomingly sensual. She endeavours to sustain the moment by putting on scrupulously clean clothes and taking great pains with her make-up.

Another inflexion that the anxiety over barrenness gives to the fetish is the concern that soaps be soft and gentle. It is not only dish-washing detergents that promise not to wrinkle the hands. A range of cleansers emphasize that they are mild on the skin, and will leave the hands tender. One dandruff treatment claims special ingredients that 'help your hair from being damaged or dried out'. Many cosmetics promise to oil or cream the skin into a pristine velvet condition. There is a great concern above all through these advertisements not to damage the skin. The fear of pollution that lurks here is that the skin will become stained, hard, dried-out and old, thus losing those properties that are identified with generativity. The peach must not wither.[13]

The washing-machine is a womb symbol. The mother controls it. Dirty objects are squeezed inside which later, as if by magic, come out clean and warm — and after a further period in an ancillary cavern, dry. In the window model the mother can watch this extension of herself working to prove how well she cares for her family. The washing-machine contributes to the range of securing images: producing good babies, transforming dirty products into clean ones, and literally keeping her family looking, feeling and being good.

Another domestic symbol for the inside is the toilet, and in a moderately masochistic mind it may even carry womb associations. The third advertisement quoted as an introduction to this essay takes as its headline: 'You're very particular about the outside. Choose

Harpic for the inside.' The advertised powder is professed to clean 'where ordinary scourers and brushes can't reach'. The cleanser gets at regions that cannot be seen, and more, regions that are inaccessible to normal techniques. The advertisement implies that there are heavily polluting dirts in these remote and forgotten regions that it is essential to remove. These dirts are so powerful that only scourers and brushes can move them. If the image of the scourer sounds too harsh to associate with such a tender region as the womb I would remind the reader of the first advertisement quoted as an introduction to this essay, which suggests that the delicate feminine face needs vacuuming and polishing if it is to regain its spring bloom.

The vacuuming advertisement highlights another irrationality connected with the fetish. Cosmetic ideology, concerned with preserving and rejuvenating the face, plays upon extreme fears of the spetic juices that may course beneath the surface, of the poisons that inhabit the air, of the desiccating power of the sun and of 'the thousand natural shocks that flesh is heir to'. It is not enough to caress with oils and cremes. It is necessary to vacuum and polish, to remove the old scum and scrofula, a sadistic process that presumably leads to additional pampering processes to soothe the rasped face. Moreover, freshness's image is as important as its reality: so cosmetics are applied in the morning to serve for the day, but they in turn require a shelf of cleansers, moisturizers, powders, additional cremes and oils for the evening. That it takes a thief to catch a thief in the case of a woman's face is illustrated by the alternative to vacuuming and polishing, the mud-pack.

An allied irrationality driven by anxieties over inner barrenness is hypochondria, the prevalent fear of inner contamination in the form of disease. Hypochondria may precipitate frequent visits to doctors for inspections or the keeping of a vast range of pills and medicaments in the bathroom to ward off the threatening pollution. Alternatively hypochondria has increasingly erupted as a passion for special vitamins to counter impurities in ordinary food, and a preference for whatever is labelled 'pure' or 'natural'.

We are now confronted by the specific sociological question of why the soap fetish has gained a peculiar intensity in contemporary Western societies. What is it in the development of advanced industrial societies that has served to aggravate the universal female anxiety about inner barrenness? How is it that the anxiety has developed to pathological proportions? The way into answering these questions lies in the recognition that the woman's most effective defence against the barrenness anxiety is to procreate and nurture, and thus to be proved fecund and generative.

The industrial revolution and its various economic consequences – above all the division of labour and tasks, increasing specialization, and the growth of the vast modern metropolis – has meant that many of the nurturing and tending activities that most women would have had in pre-capitalist societies have been removed. Women have seen their generative opportunities radically reduced. The family itself has got smaller: she gives birth to fewer children. Because of crêches, kindergartens and schools the mother sees less of the children she has. When a child becomes physically or psychologically ill she has become more dependent on the advice of specialists in caring for it. Her greater distance from her children is due not just to their going to school; she is more and more likely to take an independent job herself. No more does she have food-producing animals to tend; nor does she grow vegetables. Moreover the hens and carrots that she buys come already plucked, gutted, chopped, cleaned and sometimes even cooked. Machines mean that she has less and less physical contact with food, with preparing it, cooking it or disposing of what is left over. She does less sewing: she buys clothes that are already made and tends, when they wear, to throw them away rather than mend them. Cleaning itself has become less and less a sensual, physical act for her: she no longer scrubs or even sweeps, and if she polishes she uses modern agents that do not require great exertion. She cleans in isolation, rather than gathering with other women at the communal well.

The wide range of tasks that confirmed a woman in her generative role has been decimated. Her anxiety is left at a loose end. Her guilt is augmented by the absence of signs that her fears are groundless; at the same time it is detached from traditional methods for sublimating it – above all working hard at domestic tasks. She has less to do, maybe two hours per day of real tasks. That her guilt derives from anxiety about inner barrenness means that it will surface in a related neighbourhood. It surfaces above all in an obsessive concern that she, her children and her home be clean, that they show no external signs of impurity. This concern is manifest for example in the irrationality of her being driven, the less her hands get dirty in the modern kitchen, to concern herself the more with further techniques for preventing the invasion of muck.

We have reached the masochistic element in the fetish. The woman becomes so clean that she is sterilized. The obsessive drive to purify her home is associated with a nervousness that disturbs her capacity to be the nurturing mother and wife. The obsession reinforces itself, making it more difficult for her to be the person that she above all wants to be.

Ambivalence veins the cleanliness obsession. Cleansers must be harsh on the dishes yet gentle on the hands – an absurd contradiction. The wish to be clean, when highly charged, militates in its practice against generativity. In fact the biology of copulation and procreation makes them most unclean in the range of fluids and smells that they produce. Thus we have, in addition to considering the fetish in itself, to take account of its acutely masochistic nature: in practice it may inhibit the cure for the very disease that has infected it.

In contemporary Western societies women could counter their anxiety about inner barrenness more rationally: they could have more children, they could grow their own vegetables and keep their own hens, they could sew in the evenings, they could reject many domestic appliances, and of course some do. But the majority seem to be moving in the opposite direction, one that will inevitably aggravate the anxiety. To understand why they act in ways that seem directly against their own interest would take us into the most difficult of all psychological questions, that of masochism. This is not the place for such a discussion.[14] Let me merely note that masochism may be witnessed in many other corners of our social life, for example in the cases of individuals choosing tasks at which they are certain to fail or be hurt, or choosing again and again the same type of punitive relationship that seems to bring them only misery. We know that animal species when they are put under enough environmental strain stop reproducing. The human capacity for selecting self-destructive courses of action is much more generalized.

An associated expression of masochism in women is the eating compulsion. The anxiety about inner barrenness can carry with it a feeling of emptiness, and the drive to take in narcissistic supplies to soothe the anxiety. The compulsive eater is symbolically filling herself with milk, penis or child, the 'good' objects that she fears she has lost. But in over-eating she makes herself fat, disgusting and dirty. Discussion of this masochistic theme, however, belongs, more properly to the next section, on sexual repression.

(c) Sexual repression

The cleanliness obsession at times reveals a quite different motive, that of purging dirty wishes. Men are as much driven by this motive as women. I shall consider now the nature of the case when those forbidden wishes are sexual, and leave to the next section examination of the case when they are aggressive.

When a person is tempted to do something that would make him ashamed, that would contravene one of his most deeply held moral beliefs, the repression of the wish may lead to reaction-formation, to the wish surfacing in the guise of an opposite, passion for purity. In different historical periods prohibited sexual impulses have appeared in reaction in the form of pledges to chastity, of fasting, of self-flagellation, or, more recently, of strictly held beliefs in the necessity of confining copulation within the bounds of marriage and moderation.

Throughout these different reactions the themes of purity and cleanliness have been marked. Constraints on sexual urges have commonly been accompanied by moralistic hostility towards others who fail to conform to the same code, branding them as depraved, filthy and so on. Moralizing about the squalidness of others employs another psychological mechanism, that of projection. One of the vivid examples of the tension caused by repressing sexual wishes being relieved through projection is that of a common type of racism. The Nazi stereotype of the Jew, as represented for example in the magazine *Der Sturmer*, was of a short, dark, hairy creature who came out at night, who lived in slummy conditions and smelt evil, who was promiscuous and sought above all to seduce and defile pure Aryan girls. Hitler referred to Jews as an 'emasculating germ' and a 'dirtying contamination'. Racist Germans projected on to Jews their own dirty wishes and assumed that by eliminating the Jew they would rid themselves of those passions within themselves whose stirrings disgusted them. To purge their own repressed wishes was the leading motive that lay behind the slogan 'racial purity' and the drive to clean up the polluting minority. Similar associations may be traced in much white American hostility to negroes, the black man being feared as a sensual, uncontrolled seducer of good white wives and daughters.

With the progressive relaxation of restraints upon human sexuality through the twentieth century it has become more difficult to moralize about the erotic depravity of others. There is much less social support for the ascetic line; if anything restraint has itself come to be seen as contaminating. Thus one of the avenues for gaining relief from the tension set up by repressed sexual wishes has been largely closed off. Traffic on the main alternative avenue, that of the cleanliness obsession, must inevitably increase.

It is a widely held belief that the holding of more tolerant attitudes to sexual practice indicates that levels of sexual repression must have gone down: there are fewer erotic impulses that shame, and when they do shame they do so less acutely. However, ideology is quite a different thing from practice. A culture that proclaims itself as permissive may well continue to behave in a guilt-ridden manner. And indeed in the contemporary West the absence of a climate of relaxed carefree sensuality and the predominance of the depressed mood within intimate relations are strong indications that sexuality remains deeply infused with guilt. It may well, nevertheless, be the case that there is somewhat less of a bad conscience surrounding sexual experience than a century ago, and to the degree that this is true the influence of the factor of sexual repression on the soap fetish has lessened. As a result I take the theme of sexual repression as a minor one in my analysis, minor that is in comparison to the theme of inner barrenness.

There remain other things to be noted about sexual repression in relation to the soap fetish. The need to restrain sexual urges is in part bound up with the universal human conflict between on the one hand the primitive, natural, animal, spontaneous, unbridled, Romantic and Dionysian and on the other the civilized, artificial, cultivated, controlled, classical and Apollonian. Both sides of the conflict have many symbolic extensions. Psychoanalysis discovered an identity between ugliness and sexual excitation:[15] a woman's feeling of being dirty and unattractive was at times stimulated by sexual urges. Furthermore there is a symbolic equation of odour with escaping sexual longings. Thus the fear of ugliness or smelling bad may clothe a more basic fear of exhibitionism. A person with such a fear is indicating an unconscious striving to show her sexual excitement, but is afraid of being rejected or punished as a result.[16] The translation of troublesome sexual wishes into anxieties about uncleanliness will very likely increase the need for soap and various purification rituals.[17] The more acute the sense of bad desires the harsher the cleansing agent – thus sexual repression may well strengthen the masochistic element in the obsession.

One of the more extreme consequences in women of the blocking off of threatening sexual urges is frigidity (analogous to impotence in men). Frigidity indicates that the woman has become estranged from her own body. The fear of being soiled by her own deepest impulses may again surface in reaction-formation, in an obsessive wish for cleanliness, and indeed there is a popular wisdom that links hysteria, frigidity and compulsive cleaning. When Hamlet discovers that Ophelia is as fickle as his mother in the allegiances of her heart he berates her dishonesty. He equates purity with frigidity in his curse on her if she is to marry: 'be thou as chaste as ice, as pure as snow, thou shalt not escape calumny. Get thee to a nunnery, go; farewell.' The frigidity-purity-dirty-promiscuity linkage is asserted in the ambivalent image of the 'nunnery' – in Elizabethan English slang for a brothel.

(d) Guilt: where work was, let there be soap

Behold, I was shapen in wickedness, and in sin hath my mother
    conceived me.
But lo, thou requirest truth in the inward parts: and shalt make me
    to understand wisdom secretly.
Thou shalt purge me with hyssop, and I shall be clean: thou shalt
    wash me, and I shall be whiter than snow.

Psalm 51:3

Christianity has not differed from other religions in identifying the sinful with the unclean.[18] When a man falls from grace he sinks into the mire, he becomes marked like Cain, with the stain of sin upon him. He must somehow purify himself. Within Catholicism those who are closest to the divine lead chaste lives; the highest ideal of womanhood is the Virgin Mother whose virtue is spotless. Protestantism went a long way towards secularizing the imagery of dirt. It was one of John Wesley's sermons that introduced the famous Victorian maxim that 'cleanliness is next to godliness'. After the Evangelical and Puritan revivals the Victorians began their moralizings about 'filthy minds' and started the practice of washing children's mouths out with soap and water after they had spoken tainted words. In 1866 John Morley described Swinburne's imagination as putrescent, his *Poems and Ballads* as worse, in their sensuality, than vile and filthy prints.[19] In a more sentimental vein Tennyson had his Sir Galahad proclaim:

My strength is as the stength of ten
Because my heart is pure.

The leitmotif of the *Idylls of the King* is that civilization declines from loss of purity, in the Arthurian case primarily as a result of Guinevere's adultery. The knightly vow has it: 'To lead sweet lives in purest chastity'.

Christianity has deeply embedded in the Western psyche its own equations of sin and guilt with pollution. Moreover the further secularization that has reduced the Christian religion itself to cultural marginality has done nothing to uproot the metaphors of despoliation that it bequeathed. We may no longer think or speak in terms of 'sin', but we still feel guilt, and sometimes even recognize the fact, although we usually prefer to call it 'anxiety', 'restlessness' or 'depression'. In spite of remissive ideology the sexual remains coated in taboo, a quagmire of threatening degradations. The erotically inflected adjectives 'obscene', 'loose', 'rough', 'sluttish', 'bitchy' and 'depraved' are still applied in tones of high moral disgust. People are still accused of having 'dirty minds'.

Guilt in the main (some psychoanalysts claim wholly) derives from anxiety about expressing hostile impulses. An aggressive wish that is restrained by conscience in turning inwards will cause guilt. Now it is not only the case in the modern West that pollution imagery has kept its force in the field of sexuality. In the more general moral arena, one above all in which aggression has to be combatted, there remain countless associations of wickedness with having a stained character. We still talk of 'foul deeds', of virtuous men having 'got their hands dirty' in the pursuit of their goals, of 'blotted copybooks', of 'slimy behaviour', of 'tarnished reputations', of a 'lousy thing to do', of a 'grubby affair'; we refer to someone being a 'swine', a 'rat', a 'worm', a 'dirty animal', a 'rotten egg', a 'filthy wretch'. We 'smear' someone's name, or 'throw dirt' at them: their name becomes mud; we are 'mud-slingers' or 'muck-rakers'. If someone is innocent before the law, slang refers to him as 'clean'; 'keep it clean' instructs someone at sport to obey the rules – again transgression is dirty. The police 'clean up' the remainder of a criminal gang; when a criminal confesses he 'comes clean', or 'makes a clean breast of it'.

Having established that sin and guilt continue to carry with them the imagery of pollution, I can move on to the second part of my argument. I want now to suggest that guilt is not on the retreat in our civilization and, moreover, that as many of its traditional outlets have been closed off one of the remaining ones, the cleanliness obsession, has been forced to carry a heavier load.

Freud named guilt as the central question about civilization. In his work there is the speculation, taken up later by Theodor Reik,[20] that levels of guilt in a society increase in proportion to the advance of civilization. Increasing levels of differentiation and complexity in work, institutions, values and individual sensibilities indicate gains in man's ability to control, through sublimation, his primitive instincts. They indicate at the same time higher levels of self-restraint, a more diverse and intense conscience, greater difficulties in finding straightforward methods of expressing passion – in short, more inner tension and more guilt. Freud talked of 'civilized nervousness'. The guilt question is far too large to go into here. I would simply note that some of the main symptoms of guilt – tension, anxiety, restlessness and depression – are showing no signs of easing in our civilization. The carefree, easy-going and flamboyant manner of the guiltless does not immediately hit the eye in our cafés or along our pavements. And it may well be that in spite of remissive rhetoric levels of guilt continue to increase.

Let us accept the more moderate speculation, that guilt is not on the wane. A person burdened with guilt is in need above all of two things. He needs an explanation of why he feels bad, and some means for sublimating his guilt. With the decline of Christianity the West has lost the traditional cultural forms that explained to men why they felt anxious, and what they ought to do to atone for their sins, and thereby get relief from their troubled consciences. The new secular culture that has subsequently arisen has been notably weak in its interpretations of guilt.

On the second front, that of finding some activity through which to sublimate feelings of guilt, there is a parallel problem. The decline of the work ethic has meant that the main Western technique for releasing guilt, for finding some means for acting it out, has lost much of its moral backing. Although this loss may have been most serious for men, it has also affected women. Their domestic activity, before the latter half of the twentieth century, was rationalized as contributing to a diligent and virtuous family life. The low status of housework today is in part a consequence of the failing belief in work for its own sake – work now has to be 'creative' to be valuable.

The two main defences against guilt — understanding it and being able to transform it into work – have been severely impaired. As a result other, and more self-destructive, defences have had to carry an extra burden. A leading candidate for this role in the case of women has been the soap fetish.

Given this general cultural background the reasons for the rise of the soap fetish are not hard to find. We have the equation of sin with dirt. Unexplained guilt is experienced as a sense of feeling ill-at-ease, discontented, or nervous – more specifically, inadequate, insecure, doubting of one's purposes, low in morale, as if having committed some serious crime and being in danger of being caught (Kafka was the great psychologist of such guilt-feelings). The lurking sense of unworthiness, of having done something terribly wrong, of having sinned, carries with it the drive to atone, and the imagery of purification.

Guilt, as one of the propellers of the soap fetish, does not confine its thrust to the desire to wash dirty hands or erase the blots from the copybook. It also drives through the more generalized need for order. Mary Douglas takes as the leading theme of her anthropological study, *Purity and Danger*, that impurity is 'matter out of place'. She argues that dirt and pollution are perceived in areas in which social control either is breaking down or is disturbingly imprecise. She links together dirt, obscenity and lawlessness, all of which generate moral sanctions to which men on the margins of society are vulnerable. In short, a disquiet about order will very likely turn into some form of drive for purification.

Guilt causes in the individual a state of psychological disruption that readily feeds the worry that things are out of order, rotten, falling apart. The restlessness that results carries with it a need to restore order, or in Hamlet's words 'to set it right'. One example of this relevant here is the woman who keeps an impeccably neat kitchen and bathroom, who is nervous to leave the dinner table as soon as the coffee is served in order to wash the dishes and return them to their proper place, and who fusses around as soon as the guests have left, and sometimes before, straightening chairs and fluffing cushions. She cannot relax until it is as if nothing has happened during the evening. She feels an acute disgust whenever she sees other women with chipped nail-polish, laddered stockings or even slightly soiled clothes. Her guilt is so severe that she fears that were she to disturb order even in one of the smallest and most remote corners of the universe she would be tampering with the grand design of a very harsh, persecuting God, and would be direly punished. She feels an overpowering timidity before the order of things. Her fear that she might put matter out of place translates directly into an obsession about cleanliness, including a hatred for others more casual about their habits.

I want to turn finally in this section to look at some further examples of the fetish, behind which the grim visage of guilt can be made out. In the modern home the sight of immaculately white sheets drying on the line, or of the white glazed or enamel surfaces of refrigerators, washing-machines, toilets and basins, tiles and baths, all gleaming with a spotless radiance, such a sight is the flag of innocence. Is there not encouragement in the very term 'stainless steel'?

One sophisticated variant of the fetish is the passion for airing – to air rooms, to air laundry, to air oneself. Another variant is the passion for wrapping and packing. In an extreme case dust is kept at bay in the living room by covering unused furniture in plastic; clothes too may be put away carefully wrapped in plastic bags.

The fetish has extended beyond the front door of the family home. Our modern ideal of beauty is a soaped one. The international beauty contests emphasize a surface polish achieved through carefully prescribing physical measurements and proportions, styles of make-up and hair. Irregularities of feature are absolutely prohibited, and accordingly 'character' is down-played. The ideal was so successfully maintained that to look at photographs over a twenty-year period is to find it impossible to distinguish one Miss World from any other. The image of clean beauty, with the purity of an asexual synthetic substance, mass-produced in a hermetically sealed environment, was disseminated downwards to air-hostesses, receptionists and shop assistants. Those pastel-tinted and sculptedly bovine dolls of the 1960s, the Playboy Bunnies also projected the image of innocent and passive nudity, as unsensual as Manet's *Olympia*.

But *Playboy* was ostensibly an erotic magazine. While this is true, the *Playboy* ideal of female beauty was dictated more by fear of women than a desire for licence. If sexual repression is to be detected here it is as a derivative of guilt. The ideal was of the admiring, submissive, pliable, intellectual inferior woman, part mother, part companionable mistress. She was never to be demanding, sexually or otherwise; she was to be there when desired. Her image is indicative of a male fantasy that belies a fear of being engulfed, dominated, castrated by women. The single heterosexual situation that attracts this male without cross-currents of fear or guilt is that of masculine power over a 'bunny' type. Marilyn Monroe had earlier exploited that same fantasy.

This example reminds us not to neglect the male influence over a culture's ideal of female beauty. In this case guilt weighing on the male loins indirectly adds strength to the clean beauty image: a part of the male fear is of the uncontrolled, over-sexed, over-emotional, devouring woman. As we have already noted a passion for cleanliness and order is often employed as a restraint on raw instinct.

A British equivalent to *Playboy* was David Hamilton's photographs of adolescent girls posed affectionately together. The girls were clean, when naked showing no bodily hair, their mood tender and gentle, utterly without desire. They were photographed in misty, leafy bowers as pre-pubescent innocents: one can imagine a light and pure fragrance. Again the image indicates the fantasy of men in flight from the mature woman. The girls would have suited John Ruskin.

The clean-cut look has also entered the domain of popular music. A successful group of the 1970s, Abba, coming from one of the heartlands of the cleanliness obsession, Sweden, projected themselves as four innocents, untainted by the moral laxity and rebelliousness of many of their contemporaries. They were sterilized against either knowledge or sin. They appeared on 'Keep Australia Clean' posters. Moreover, their music sounded as if it had been washed, triple-rinsed and spin-dried.

There have been some rebellions against soaped stars. The 'natural look' in feminine charm has made various assaults on the citadel, but without great success: for one, the advertisements have not changed in essence. However, in the domain of popular music the attempt to put matter out of place was highly successful. The Beatles, Rolling Stones, Bob Dylan and a horde of imitators capitalized on a youthful revulsion at the cleanliness of their parents to make of soap something evil, symptomatic of an obsessive, over-regulated, conformist society. Here was the fetish used against itself.

I take my final example, to close some sort of circle, from television. Between the soap advertisements there have been many dramatizations of the past. It is significant to note that in the 1970s when there was a strong emphasis on the documentary and on 'realism' these programmes were careful not to show the real dirt, disease and squalor of the medieval peasantry or even the eighteenth-century aristocracy. What was portrayed was modern standards of cleanliness and comfort neatly dressed in the garments of the past, themselves laundered. The 1977 American series on the Jewish experience of Nazism, *Holocaust*, while pretending not to gild any lilies was most unrealistic in its reconstruction of the Warsaw ghetto. What was cleaned up for the modern audience was not only the physical conditions and the overcrowding; the series also avoided showing the internal bickering, the selfishness, the resentments within the ghetto provoked by putting a confined and crowded group of people under great physical and mental strain. The desire not to know about the possibility of aggression between members of a community under duress reflects an anxiety about the individual's capacity to control his own violence. This anxiety becomes particularly acute when it is the family, or its symbolic extension the community, that is involved. The guilts developed in childhood associated with the attempt to restrain hostile wishes return with a vengeance. *Holocaust* scoured away any contamination which might have issued from this the most basic of all guilt-feelings. As a complementary purification it showed the physical conditions as equivalently clean.

I have attributed the soap fetish to two major motivational factors: the anxiety in women over inner barrenness and a generalized guilt in modern civilization whose major traditional outlets have been closed off. These two factors reinforce each other. Guilt contributes to paralysing a rational counter to the anxiety and increases the nervous intensity of the obsession; obsessive cleanliness in failing to reduce the barrenness anxiety adds guilt. The fetish draws additional strength from the universal pleasure of water, and from another fairly universal source of pollution imagery, that of sexual repression.

My argument has been that a universal female anxiety about inner barrenness has become severely aggravated in the advanced industrial societies with increasing levels of civilization. History was the catalyst acting on elements that have always been present. The significance of the cultural factor may be illustrated by contrasting peasant women in the countries round the Mediterranean, who pay attention to their appearance only during the years in which they seek a husband. Once married they let themselves go, growing fat, dressing in drab clothes, showing indifference to gaps in their teeth. Soap is another pathology that they do not share with northern middle-class, ancestorially Protestant housewives.

Mary Douglas's interpretation of impurity as 'matter out of place' applies with only partial success to the modern soap fetish. This is because the links here between psychological process in the individual and the cleaning rites themselves are much closer and more important than in her examples from primitive societies. Ironically, if my argument is correct, the modern woman is closer to nature in what drives her need to clean than her primitive counterpart who comes from an incomparably less differentiated society.

I should like to close with a note on national characteristics. It seems unanimous amongst tourists that Switzerland heads the ladder of nations most diligent in their pursuit of cleanliness. And there is surely no earthly peer for the country that has machines specially designed to clean road signs, that has restaurants with their own forms, headed 'Toilet Control', that are signed every two hours by waiters attesting that the toilets remain clean, and that has public swimming pools that do not need chlorine. On Swiss evening television, viewed for one week in February 1979, one advertisement in three concerned cleanliness. The other finalists in the soap competition would be Holland, the Scandinavian countries, with West Germany and the United States just scraping in. Protestantism does seem to be a common theme, reinforcing the guilt hypothesis. The German sense for order is a northern, Prussian derivative. Belgium must have been contaminated by a French, or perhaps to go further back, a Spanish Catholic, carelessness about dirt. Indeed the French must be given the wooden spoon among the nations of the civilized world: there is no finer symbol of their lack of concern about muck than the toilet *à la Turque*. The French might well reply that none of the clean nations is known for its great sense of humour.

Postscript

Before any reader gets over-excited about this essay displaying a mean bias against the gentler sex let me admit both that many Western men are vividly compulsive about cleanliness and that in some other cultures obsessions over dirt seem more the preserve of men. However, our story here has been complicated enough without qualifying or complementing it further. The case of middle-class Western men is a story all of its own, better left for another time, a story that would, I suspect, concentrate on obsessions about order, and find that cleanliness was merely one sub-species of the need to put matter in the right place!

7 Automobile culture and citizenship

The question when is a citizen most irresponsible would today commonly elicit the reply: when he is driving his car dangerously, drunk on the roads. Moreover, those times when the modern citizen acts as a criminal and is apprehended and charged as such, relate almost exclusively to motoring, above all to the offences of speeding and illegal parking.

That motor cars pollute the air, fill cities with noise, carve up suburbs with highways, create in the factories that produce them the most inhumane work conditions experienced in modern society,[1] and that they maim and kill a significant proportion of those who use them – all this is accepted and well documented. It is also a commonplace that a majority of owners project on to their machines their unfulfilled ambitions of power, adventure, mobility, even of sexual release; some take out their frustrations on the road. A wide range of literature, for instance John Keats's *The Insolent Chariots* (1958), attests to the corruptions of the automobile culture. Less well recognized is a quite different development: that the main opportunity for a person to demonstrate that he is a mature citizen has become the driving of his motor car. I wish to focus in this essay on the curious fact that the automobile has become indispensable to the modern individual's sense of well-being as a responsible adult member of his society.

When he buys a car a person gains a range of powers. He has gained mobility: he can travel farther, faster, by his own route, and when he chooses. He has gained access to remote landscapes, to golf clubs, and to the houses of all his acquaintances who live within a couple of hundred miles. He has also gained access, in the quite distinct moral sphere, to the major social arena in which he will be tested against the laws of his society and the judgment of his fellow citizens. He gains by this last boon the inestimable power of feeling confirmed as a competent, participating member of his society.

What is involved here is an elementary sociological case of norms being reinforced, and the individual thereby coming to feel more at home in his world, less restless, less aimless, more attached to the spaces and habits that surround him. The modern citizen is never less self-conscious in his obedience, never less hesitant in his responses, than when faced by a red traffic-light. Automatically he stops. The same holds for much of the traffic code. Driving becomes a ritualized sequence of responses to an almost entirely predictable sequence of events, governed by a set of laws and conventions that are so well internalized by the driver that they are 'second-nature'. Out in public, driving, the modern citizen is unwittingly soothing all those latent fears that he is alone, disconnected from other men, other groups, even from his own purposes. He has introduced himself into a central social ritual, as surely and with as much faith as his ancestors stood humbly in their churches singing hymns. He has relaxed in the sea of social life, and now alternately swims and drifts with the ebb and flow of its currents, no longer fighting against it, no longer in fear of sinking, or having to flee to the beach. He is in harmony with his social environment, co-operating, understanding intuitively the movement of things, moving with them, part of that movement, recognized and respected as such.

Driving allows the modern citizen to act in public, and is cathartic. It is cathartic first of all because it is action: it is movement, its routine motor-activity of working pedals and steering is relaxing, it requires concentration, and it draws the driver out of introspection and indecision. Certainly if he drives well he will daydream at the wheel, and rely on his trained reflexes; but light daydreaming is quite different from nervous introspection – on the road it gains the rhythmical quality of reverie. Driving, the world is ordered. Decisions are made according to specific rules and reasonably exact predictions. There is an informal science to driving, a science that includes knowledge of the car's performance: how quickly it can stop, how well it corners, its power for overtaking. The driver has to gauge the different factors influencing the situation he is in. Driving is not the passive ritual of the church service. It is a ritual that at the same time requires active responsibility. Responsibility too is cathartic. Driving is an experience of risk, of the testing of competence: to be proved competent is satisfying. The more competent, the more relaxed, and the more the ritualistic element in the experience dominates. The competence of the driver is something like the courage of the soldier, in that most of the time it lies dormant, as routine processes are followed; then it is needed, at an instant's notice, and it is decisive. In driving, responsibility depends on competence: and it is the duty of he who lacks the ability or the temperament for this civic ritual to renounce the wheel.

With the village green asphalted, with shopping centres of Colosseum size and anonymity, with politics conducted at a great distance and by inscrutable giant bureaucracies, and with privacies guarded by the family home, the main experience that people have today of being out in 'public', in the great classical sense of the term, is driving on the roads. One of the indices of the 'public' realm is being vulnerable to the inconsiderateness of others, and being free to sanction that inconsiderateness; it requires a consensus over right behaviour. On the roads one is in public in this sense all the time; each driver has a horn with which to moralize to others about their misdeeds. In the event of an accident the interdictions are more concrete. In short, the responsibility exercised every day at all times on the road is real, a far more tangible and established part of everyday life than the responsibility for choosing political representatives.

Motoring brings modern man into a unique proximity to his law, and thereby places him squarely in public. This being in public means that there is a time when his liberty may threaten that of others, a time when the mutually accepted constraints are close to being broached. At this moment his society as a collectivity is alive for him: there is a real tension between himself and the legal code. The fact that fellow drivers will in their own ways assert that code if he infringes it further illustrates the vitality of the collectivity in this sphere of its life. It is not merely the large bureaucracies of state that serve as the watchdogs of motoring conduct.

There are many sources of tension between one motoring citizen and another and they often involve the wider moral universe. Some are accused of being too irresponsible to be allowed on the road. The charge is in effect that they should not be accorded the status or the full rights of the mature citizen. Families usually find it difficult to suggest to aged kin that they ought for the safety of all to retire from driving: this would be tantamount to depriving them of their citizenship. That citizenship is involved here is confirmed by the fact that, at the other threshold of maturity, modern male youth attaches far more importance to reaching driver's licence age than becoming old enough to vote. Moreover, it is commonly more dangerous to criticize a man's ability as a driver than to express doubts about any other of his capacities or achievements, except perhaps his sexual prowess.

With the growing importance of the practice of driving to the moral experience of community it is inevitable that the car itself should have come to stand as an emblem of citizenship. It plays something of the role that property played in times when its possession was a prerequisite for political rights, and more generally for virtue. In this connection it is not irrelevant that the car itself is a significant item of property. In the West, however, the period of the car's novelty has long past. It is the few devotees these days who lavish accessories on their prize chariot, or who devote their Sunday mornings religiously to cleaning and polishing their brightly painted pride. The car today is more like a house that has been in the family for a few generations: it is taken for granted, but nevertheless remains fundamental to that family's sense of time and place, of order in its deepest ramifications.

The automobile as taken-for-granted does not imply that it has lost its place at the hub of the consumer society. The car industry is certainly in decline, and in some ways as seriously as the Lancashire textile industry in the 1890s.[2] However, we are even less likely to give up our cars than our ancestors gave up wearing cotton. The current troubles of the automobile industry are less to do with consumer rejection than with the market being saturated, with competition from Japanese manufacturers, and with certain technological problems within the industry. That the automobile has undergone a certain demotion in the palace of consumption is nevertheless indicated by the car industry having lost its glamour, first to plastics, then more recently to electronics, and by the fact that consumers are more likely today to spend their marginal dollar on air travel or dining out. The motor car's image as the emblem of consumerism is somewhat tarnished; but I want to suggest that it remains an emblem, and has gained new colour from the fact that it has come to satisfy genuine human needs.

The car is still today, apart from the house, the largest item of expenditure for most families. It is needed first of all because it provides mobility in the consumer society, a society that has as a part of its essence that very mobility (there are the rare exceptions of environments less dependent on the motor car, for instance the central areas of old cities like London, Paris and Vienna). This need is in turn amplified. Most consumer items are for the house, for the passive enjoyment of privacy from society at large. The car fulfils a similar and yet different function, extending the virtues of the home out into public. It offers comfort and isolation from others, compared above all with public transport; and yet, at the same time, it carries these domestic values out into the bustle of the public world, into situations that can be far more discomfiting than tram travel. As work is losing its value as an expression of human endeavour, and as the true public realm, that of politics, has become the preserve of very few, consumption has become more the means through which fantasies are stimulated, wishes induced, and achievements realized. The car is crucial to the versatility of consumption: it keeps modern man engaged in his profane lifestyle of repeatedly finding new clothes in which to dress the same wishes. It does this above all by taking consumption beyond a purely soulless hedonism into the realm of morals, thereby giving it a dignity and attaching it to a deeper, more troubling and absorbing level of the human condition. As a passive consumer, whether buying cashew nuts in the supermarket or lying in bed watching football on colour television, the modern individual is granted no more responsibility than a child; his freedom is restricted to asking for more, or for this rather than that. As the possessor and driver of a motor car, by contrast, he finds himself treated as a responsible adult.

There is a further dimension of a truly liberal society that is preserved on the road. Drivers form a community of equals. They have equal rights and they are equal before the law as practised. Individual responsibility is not token. This may be important psychologically as well as morally. The driver may experience the most significant other parts of his life, whether in his office or among his family, as a subordinate or a superordinate. The road then provides the balance of a longed for power and responsibility, or a salutary constraint. Here too it serves as an important practical model for a liberal society.

A first consequence of the car having become a certificate of citizenship is that those who do not drive condemn themselves to social marginality, a pariah experience of modern life. They distance themselves thereby one significant pace from the social world in which they live, and on which they are dependent for work, for regular supplies of food, clothing and shelter, and for culture in its widest sense. Already in the 1920s Robert and Helen Lynd, in their classic study *Middletown*, reported that the average American was asserting that he would go without food rather than give up his car.

We have now stumbled upon the heaviest obstacle in the way of convincing more people to use public transport. To choose to travel by bus, train, or tram, except in extraordinary circumstances, is to accept one further encroachment of the State into the realm of individual freedom: it is to give up one more sphere of independence from the suffocating maternal authority of central government bureaucracy. The decline of individual authority, and responsibility, whether of father, teacher, or civic leader, and the complementary increased authority of institutions, particularly large corporations and governments, has been accompanied by the social and psychological importance gained by consumption. Automobile consumption is one of the last bulwarks against the total passivity that threatens to follow these developments. In the case of public transport, one of the signs of the presence of the maternal State, caring for its child dependants, is the safety of that transport. Private transport has always been dangerous, the horse, or the horse and carriage, as much as the automobile. Ironically, it may be a mistake of the advocates of public transport to stress safety. To take a risk requires a kind of individual choice, and in a world increasingly devoted to comfort it may be necessary to keep alive the choice to be reckless, to retain the motor car not only as a vehicle for exercising personal responsibility, but also as one for experiencing adventure.

Offering a type of adventure, the motor car is violent. It has come to supply the main outlet for many people for the expression of their aggression, for the displacement of their frustrations and resentments. Here is another reason why personal responsibility is so important on the road. The driver must control his own hostile, anti-social impulses if he is to retain acceptability amongst the motoring citizenry. Innocent people are at his mercy.

The violence of the motor car, unlike that of the saddled horse, is not restricted to he who travels by it. Another dimension of the moral significance of the automobile in modern life is this violence. Whatever images may recur in the nightmares of modern man his real contact with objects and situations powerful enough to maim him will almost entirely involve motor cars. He may turn pale when his Jumbo jet takes off, or swim with trepidation because of the thought of sharks; but if he dies violently it will almost certainly be in a motor car. If he sees mangled bodies in the flesh it will be near car wreckage strewn across a highway. Moreover, if he is tortured by loud noises or dense fumes they will surely emanate from motor vehicles. As a consequence, the important moral discussion of how, and in which situations, the law and its agents ought to protect citizens against violence shows signs of coming to centre in the near future on automobile traffic and its movement.

In the proliferation and deepening impact of the roles of the automobile lie the roots of the feeling of despair and depression that frequently follows damage to it. It has been said that a dent to the car is like a bruise to the body of the owner, the identification of man and machine being so close in this case. The explanation does not go far enough. The dint is usually far more painful in its psychological consequences than a minor assault on the flesh. Moreover, it is hard to accept as fully adequate the rational explanation that the owner becomes overwhelmed by imagining the trouble that a minor accident will cause him, in contacting insurance, arranging repairs, losing the use of his car for a couple of days, and so on. I am familiar with a number of cases in which the inconvenience has been minimal, and the psychological shock bewilderingly severe.

The car-as-an-extension-of-man theory works at one level. The driver imagines that he is insulated from the potential violence that surrounds him; his car shields him; this shielding is one of the factors contributing to the relaxation he experiences at the wheel, in his air-conditioned cabin, listening to cassetted music. A sudden blow from the side is utterly unexpected, like a sharp knock in the middle of the back when walking along the pavement. His peace of mind is shattered. His personal space has been violated.

But the shock is not simply that of one individual intruding upon another. It carries with it a battery of moral charges, an arsenal that the automobile has accumulated with its growing social importance. A dent to the car breaks the reverie of driving; suddenly the driver is really in public, and something has gone wrong. In fact a crime has been committed, and he has to leave his car where it is, awkwardly placed in the middle of the road, blocking traffic; he has to get out of his car to face the other driver. He sees himself becoming the centre of a public event, surrounded by spectators, and the growing number of irate drivers who are being held up, some of them eager to intrude their judgments of the accident. He has to think quickly. Was he in the wrong, wholly or partly; what should his approach be; doesn't he need witnesses; should they call the police; he had better first examine the damage; now he is going to be late. The anxiety over lateness cloaks the real source of unrest, that his so comfortable, so smoothly running ritual has been destroyed. It is like waking from a deep and very peaceful sleep to face an interrogation, instantly in need of all his wits. Moreover, this public event is highly un-predictable: will the other driver be aggressive, is he drunk, will he have insurance? Someone has been irresponsible; maybe they were both partly to blame. All drivers are at times lazy, careless, off their guard; now he has been selected as the one to suffer, the one to be punished. To possess a motor car means inevitably to become a criminal at one moment or another in a driving career. The worries pile one on top of the other, in the instants as he collects himself to get out of his car, to step out into the public spotlight that is turned on a crime that so many passers-by identify with, for they themselves would many times but for the grace of God have been in a similar predicament. (As a corollary to the linking of violence with automobiles, it may be that the crowds that form around an accident are the modern equivalent to the masses that used to be drawn to watch public executions.)

For some a dent in the precious body is enough punishment for a lapse on the road: the perfect surface has been flawed, thus atoning for the black streak across the driver's virtue. These are the happy ones, those sane enough to recognize their own mistake, or bad luck, that a price has to be paid, but a price that, like the dent, is easily repaired and once repaired may be forgotten. For others, however, punishment comes in a severe and inscrutable form, as intensified guilt, guilt flowing from the suspicion that there was a moment in which the driver's self-control weakened and violence resulted. The guilt commands that there must be much more self-control in the future, or some catastrophe will result; it attacks the person's sense of their own competence, of their worthiness to pretend to be a mature citizen; it makes them more hesitant, more indecisive, less controlled on the roads; and it induces a slough of depression. This is especially the case when the criminal is a woman, more likely to feel her citizenship as a precarious status, and to doubt her driving competence. For the guilt-ridden there remains the physical reminder: every time they pass the dent they are confronted with the stark emblem of their inadequacy, their failed control.

The moral centrality of the car, its potential violence, and the responsibility or irresponsibility with which it is handled, are themes which converge in the question of automobile suicide. Some doctors in Houston, Texas, conducted 'psychological autopsies' on people killed in crashes, and concluded that one in seven road deaths should properly be called suicide. This would mean that one-quarter of American suicides are carried out on the roads. Without taking the figures themselves too seriously there is little reason to doubt the broad conclusion that they lead to. Indeed it would be surprising if many of those drawn towards self-destruction, the ultimate violence, did not find themselves tempted by the sphere of modern life in which the ordinary citizen has power, instant power. This is taking to a parodic extreme the boast of Harley Earl, General Motors' first stylist: 'you can design a car so that every time you get in it, it's a relief.' Suicidal depression can be transformed into an act of bravado. In a carefree, careless spasm of masochism he who has lost the will to live can hurtle himself along a highway testing how much fate is on his side, whether or not it is intended that he survive. With respect to his own life such an act may be a worthy and even responsible way of assessing the quality of existence, of whether he is to continue – for we are all ultimately in the hands of the gods, it is they alone who determine the major turns of destiny, so why not this one. His high-speed spin may on the other hand be merely reckless foolishness in a moment of impassioned despair.

The act from every point of view other than that of the driver is intolerably irresponsible. How many innocent victims were trapped by all those automobile suicides? As we noted at the outset, there is hardly anyone more deserving of the condemnation of modern society than the reckless driver. Caring little for himself he is careless towards others. His action contravenes the first axiom of liberalism. The law should treat him harshly (in most Western societies it does quite the opposite, proving very lenient). However, the very fact that the reckless driver is allowed the means to be so effectively irresponsible is one of Western society's great remaining freedoms. If he were restricted to trains, or some futuristic compromise such as an electronically controlled bubble car, there would be one less sphere of social life in which he found himself thrust together with his fellow citizens in situations in which his own authority counted for something. For individual liberty to be a reality there must exist situations in which that liberty is in peril and even destroyed by free individuals, acting independently of large organizations.

The reader who finds the linking of automobile culture and liberty far-fetched might argue that there are motor cars in the Soviet Union, where their existence does not appear to have had any moderating influence on the State's tyranny. It is too early to tell: cars are still rare, too much a novelty, too little an integrated part of the average citizen's life to have unfurled their true colours. It remains to be seen whether the freedom of movement, physical and moral, that car ownership brings will feed a growing sense of political suppression. A Russian who visited my university in Melbourne photographed the car parks with great enthusiasm; she was not really interested in anything else. Certainly she was motivated to a large degree by an unashamedly blunt materialism, jealous of the West's superiority in this sphere of consumer durables, imagining how nice it would be if she and all her friends could have their own cars. But there is a chance that there was something more to her yearning for ready access to the motor car.

I have sought in this essay to establish that we have come to belong to an automobile culture in a more profound sense than we commonly recognize. I have left aside many aspects of automobile culture, not being concerned with such phenomena as the focus on car sales as the leading indicator of a nation's economic vitality, as the car salesman being the businessman that Westerners most distrust, as the role the car came to play in adolescent courting. I have also avoided certain areas closer to my own theme, for instance the possibility that the automobile has contributed to the uniformity, rootlessness and anonymity of modern life. (This particular possibility is offset by the contribution the car has made to family life, confirming the nuclear family as the fundamental social unit in modern society.)

My concern has been exclusively with the moral consequences of the motor car. That concern finds Marshall McLuhan's prediction that the wheel is obsolete in the electronic age peculiarly ominous. McLuhan has also prophesied that the individual will be obsolete in the electronic age. But if he is wrong about the individual he will also prove wrong about the wheel. For the car has become to the modern consumer perhaps the most vital effective element in his struggle to keep his liberty intact.

8 The tourist

Faust has become a tourist. That eternal striving that drove westerners through their industrial revolution and hurled them on forward into a dizzy rate of social change has finally, late in the twentieth century, come to focus much of its energy on the search for the sight of some physical landmark that might put this madman at his ease. At his best today he roves the globe after that experience or revelation that eludes him at home, and whose absence makes of his domesticity a restless misery.

The ultimate offerings of the consumer society to its satiated credit-card holders are dining out and travelling. The further capitalization of these two industries in the last quarter of the century is as inevitable as such things can be. Tourism, the big brother of the two, is a peculiar achievement in offering the excitement of the exotic unknown in a form that carries with it the very securities whose tedium it is intended to relieve. It has brought to the many an experience that they imagined to be the privilege of the few. Moreover, it has done this with extraordinary success by stimulating a range of glamorous fantasies in the mind of the modern citizen. Let us look first at the dream and then enquire into the reality.

I shall not be interested in this investigation in holiday-makers, those taking their annual vacation and who by and large seek relaxation. It is that side of tourism that offers the journey of a lifetime, and that has nothing to do with relaxation as a goal, with which I am concerned.

The dream

The tourist is first of all an *adventurer*. The dream is of the pioneer, the explorer, the great voyager or the conquering emperor. He leaves the security of home far behind and sets out beyond the perimeters of the known world for fame, fortune and excitement. He wants to take on the minotaur, scale the Matterhorn, discover a lost Amazonian tribe or sample the delights of a Thai brothel. His heroes are Marco Polo, Napoleon, Dr Livingstone, Ernest Hemingway.

The tourist is, second, a *lord*. As soon as he leaves home he becomes a man of distinction. He stays in first-class hotels; he uses taxis; he employs porters, guides and interpreters. In short he is served: his every whim may be instantly satisfied by a grateful and deferential servant. His pleasure is the goal of all those around him. He has the authority and power of the medieval lord.

The identification with the upper class carries over into the glamorous image of travel. The 'jet set' move at will from one international playground to another. The wealthy cruise the Mediterranean in their luxury yachts. The tourist takes a step into this world. On the terrace of the Oriental Hotel in Bangkok he can sip cocktails and gaze across the river just as Joseph Conrad, Somerset Maugham and Noël Coward would have done from exactly the same spot.

The tourist may be, third, an *aesthete*, travelling in search of the beautiful, and of knowledge about the finest of human or natural creations. Through knowledge of other cultures and other epochs he gains a sense of the richness of human achievement and the range of human refinement. For the tourist in this role cities are museums in which he seeks enlightenment and inspiration. He seeks cultivation. He may seek to become a connoisseur in some special field. He does become cosmopolitan.

The tourist may be, fourth, a *Fletcher Christian*. He may mutiny against the manifold constraints of civilization and its cool climates. He may seek to escape the cold and at the same time go in search of a grander vision, that of the tropical paradise. He imagines himself in Tahiti or Barbados sun-tanned, lazing on golden beaches under palm trees, gazing out across azure lagoons, with sultry, dark, sensual women strolling past.

The tourist may finally be lonely and in search of company. He travels in order to meet fellow tourists, to become part of a group, or in the hope of romance. Many advertisements stress that the restraints on amatory possibility that he experiences at home are suddenly cast off once he goes on tour.

The reality

Travelling is a great art. Many people travel to escape from a difficult period in their life or to patch up a cracking relationship – nothing could be less wise. Travelling brings with it an inordinate level of strain. Day after day has to be filled from scratch with different activities, testing both concentration and interest, never mind the feet. A tourist without an organized tour is confronted by a constant sequence of petty worries: where shall we stay tomorrow, where shall we have lunch, do we have enough money, how do I ask for antacid tablets, where is that museum, is it worth the effort, if we are exhausted this afternoon what shall we do, and so on. The strain of touring often dims the eyes, meaning that the tourist loses his main resource, the desire to see new things and experience strange situations. An Austrian psychotherapist has even discovered that the tensions of holidaying readily precipitate psychotic breakdown. [1]

Whatever their fantasies, not many could take adventure as the Victorian explorer knew it. This is no reason to be snobbish: one man's routine is another man's adventure. However, what is less relative is that the modern tourist adventurer suffers from a lot of common nervousness. He is constantly threatened by the unexpected. It is not simply knowledge of other cultures that he lacks: in a more general sense he has no traditions, no skills, in short no culture to prepare him for new places, new languages, new customs. It is therefore little wonder that he becomes so attached to his castle and demands that it not vary too much from Manila to Salzburg – he is able to master the workings of the international hotel, and asks that beyond the uniformity each one should incorporate just a little local colour, to protect the illusion that he is in exotic parts.

The tour is the greatest of modern saving lies. The dream promises action, excitement and revelation. There is no *action*. Tourism in its purest modern form, that of the package tour, has been fitted neatly into the model of consumption. The itinerary is planned down to the last detail: the consumer should ideally just sit back and enjoy it, leaving all the worrying to the agent. The battery of books, guides, brochures and magazine articles become an elaborate extension of the instruction manual for the latest domestic appliance. The consumption model, with its excision of action, is most obvious in the sphere of service. The tourist may be attended like a lord, but he has none of the power and responsibility that went with the manorial privileges. In effect it is the guide who orders him around, leads him by the hand, advises him what to see and where to eat. If London catches his fancy and he would like to stay longer, or he is bored by Munich and would like to cut short his visit, it is very unlikely that he will have the power to act accordingly. In fact he is not likely to rebel against the planned itinerary, preferring to sit back and tick places off as they pass, and not bothering to reflect on what *he* would do if he had the choice. Daniel Boorstin, in his fine chapter, 'The Lost Art of Travel', demonstrates the historical development in which the traveller turned into the tourist.[2] He illustrates the old world of the traveller, a man who worked at something, for whom things were not easy, and who acted. The tourist by contrast is a pleasure-seeker, used to a world of packaged commodities, one of which he has almost become himself.

That the tourist is the product of a society that has made consumption sacred is borne out in other ways. One aspect of the lord fantasy is that the tourist wants to spend extravagantly, royally – use up all of his budget. One of his leading interests is in shops, bargains and trophies. At another level one of his favourite topics of conversation, and of anecdote when he is back home, is the relative price of things – how cheap pineapples were in Bali. Like any person he carries his interests with him, as essential a part of his luggage as his underwear.

There is *excitement* but it is the excitement of anxious expectation. Taking the prototype for postponed gratification, that of romantic love, it is as if the tourist went through all the strain of building up courage to meet and to invite to find that the event had fallen through, and he gained none of the joy of consummation. It is very unlikely that any of his extravagant touring fantasies can be satisfied, given the way he travels. So he gets the nervous tension, and with it some excitation, of flirting with the unknown, but he misses the balancing gratification. The excitement he gets will make him nervous rather than sustain him.

The essence of the tourist adventure is exhibited in the contours of the excitements that it provides. And these contours are best inferred from the stories that are told and re-told with animation to relatives, friends and colleagues at home. It is virtually never what has been seen that is recounted with enthusiasm. When the sites are described it is in the form of ritualized clichés: the Eiffel Tower really is a wonder – we went up it, and you get such a nice view. It is rather the personal moments of the tour, moments of near-crisis, that in retrospect were exciting: when one of the suitcases failed to arrive off the luggage chute at Frankfurt Airport. Touring has itself been turned into a routine, restricting adventure to those moments when the routine breaks down. But again what sort of excitement is this? The tourist might as well be confined to a repeating sequence of jumbo jet flights, international airport interludes, air-conditioned taxi rides and International Hilton stops. For what he remembers, and therefore for what in fact he sees, there is no point in stepping outside this carefully controlled and secured touring capsule. Moreover, the fact that so much fuss can be made about a minor inconvenience suggests the level of free-floating anxiety besetting the tourist, which finds outlet only here, ridiculously exaggerating the event.

Because touring is consumption there can be no *revelation*, only repletion. Tourism is the largest and richest cake at the end of the meal of modern life. Virtually all consumers want to taste this cake, but it gives indigestion to many of those who do actually indulge. The media give a strong boost to the assembly of influences that build the tour up as a grand event. Thus the consumer gets talked into trying it; and he cannot think of anything better to save up for. But those who enjoy events have to happen upon them spontaneously, or be comfortably seated – above all they have to understand and like what is happening. The tour is typically like that allied activity, the highly publicized visiting art exhibition. When a large exhibition of obscure Chinese pots of archaeological rather than aesthetic value came to Melbourne, a fanfare of publicity led hundreds of thousands to queue for hours and then file past at an enforced pace in a bewildered throng. There was neither enlightenment nor pleasure in this staged cultural event. Moreover, those few who were actually interested in the pots were crowded out.

The saving lie of tourism is often in danger of straining credibility to breaking-point. Above all the hapless tourist has to cope with the shock of what the tour is in reality, how far from its publicized ideal. The tension between dream and reality builds up a crisis of legitimacy. But a range of defences is provided, the most important of which is the camera. The photograph is an aid to authenticity. He really was there: see him photographed next to the *Mona Lisa*. It really was grand: see these famous places, so widely written and spoken about, do they not look exciting here in his colour slides. A bit of their magnificence brushes off onto him; their consequence extends a hand to he who has witnessed it, he who has now walked amongst the great. The colour slide, especially when shown to friends two months later, blown up on his living room wall, makes it seem real. Those moments in his heart of hearts when he was tired and aggravated, wondering what the fuss surrounding these lumps of stone was all about, are now forgotten.

Clicking the camera also gives the tourist something to do. It is a duty that gives greater definition to his role and makes him less at sea than he would be otherwise. Moreover, this duty takes his mind off whether or not he is inspired, or even interested; he can at least enjoy the action of getting it on film, even when he has no idea of what the 'it' is, whether he likes it, what he is doing spending a fortune getting to see it, or indeed what possible relevance it has to his life. When in doubt, which he is most of the time, he can fall back on the role of tourist, and he is provided with the props, the costume and the make-up for this role – he also has a reliable prompt constantly in the wings. The guide himself prefers it that the tourist sticks to his role: he is easier to organize. When things are running smoothly the tourist does not have to worry about whether he is living up to his own expectations on tour. His task is to recognize the famous sites, with cues from the brochures and the guide if necessary, and then photograph them. The job done he can move on to the next, or retire for a well-earned dinner and rest.

There are complementary aids to authenticity. The string of postcards launched at those back home serve a number of purposes. They confirm the umbilical cord, the ties to a familiar place where he can relax and know what is happening, where things are not alien and forbidding, where he belongs and shall return. They affirm the importance of where he is, and what he is doing and seeing; here is not one suburb amongst thousands but a great and unique cultural site. They confirm that Rome *is* Rome and exciting, that he is here and here is Rome, that he is enjoying Rome and the trip is marvellous. One of the advantages of the postcard is that there is so little writing space that he can lie with a good conscience.

Finally the postcard, like the slides two months later, like the unique presents bought near the pyramids, and indeed like the entire tour, is an act of aggression against those at home, designed to stimulate their envy. After all it was jealousy of others who had already gone, stimulated by their stories and the glamorous advertisements that had sent him in the first place. He can at least have the pleasure of revenge through encouraging the illusion, and stimulating in the next generation of potential tour consumers the same urges as had driven him. Moreover, there is probably some universal fantasy in that part of the parable of the prodigal son that has the one who goes out and travels, whose travels are by and large a misery, returning home to be welcomed by the father as the favoured son. Then there is the son who dutifully stayed at home and his envy. The modern western tourist carries this Romantic theme of recognition on return from great and difficult adventures with him, and may well suffer deeply when on return there is no father to welcome him – at least there are plenty of brothers to envy him.

Insecurity serves to further reinforce the need to keep up appearances. The tourist's first worry when it dawns on him that he is not enjoying himself as much as he had hoped is directed against himself: what am *I* doing wrong? His deepest fear is that he is bungling it, he is failing to live up to the role. His worries about legitimacy increase. One defence is to convince those back home that it is working marvellously. In fact the number of postcards he sends may be taken as an indicator of his level of insecurity. If those at home believe in him and his tour then he can have a little more confidence himself. On the other hand, his worries may readily be turned against the tourist agency: the tourist, because of his insecurity about his role, fears that he is not really being treated like a lord, that the service should be better, that maybe this is not really a first-class hotel, and he is being duped.

Indeed much of the paraphernalia of tourism is designed to help the tourist to keep up appearances. There are the stickers for the back window of the car to indicate which towns have been visited. There are detailed maps across which the person with Magellan or Cook fantasies can mark out his route in coloured ink. There are the hotel matchboxes and sundry other knick-knacks that vary from place to place, the contemporary replacements for the tusks and tiger-skins displayed by the big-game hunters. The tourist is primarily keeping up his own morale, and true to modern life this means keeping up the image of his tour. If he returns home deflated then the gossip will start and he will be tarred by his tour's failure. One piece of West German research indicates that nearly 90 per cent of holiday-makers claim to be satisfied with their travelling experience. This statistic indicates nothing directly about the tourist's reality; it is a statement about the need to live up to the dream.

It is significant to note what is photographed. The hotel is itself sometimes the main focus of camera activity. The lord of the manor fantasy is here at work: this splendid building is where I stayed. Some tourists have been known to treasure on film the bedroom in which they slept for one night. Is a comparison being made with the ordinary bedroom back at home? Or is not a telling confession being made, that the hotel bedroom was the part of the tour that was most enjoyed, a refuge in which the weary couple could retreat into privacy, relax a little because they were no longer on show – the bedroom serving as the private dressing-room where they could step out of their role and regain a semblance of their ordinary selves? Moreover there was some novelty in this hotel bedroom, in its luxury, in the services that were provided, allowing them to indulge in the lord fantasy and yet at the same time take it easy.

Having said that the typical tourist does not get much pleasure from his tour, it must be added that the tour may nevertheless have been important for him. For him it was an adventure and he was treated like a lord – to the degree of enjoying criticizing the hotel service in Florence. The most significant factor is the unknown. The things he saw and the way he saw them are far from unknown: in fact he went where he did because it was so well known. He travelled in a secure manner. He was never in the slightest danger. He knew exactly where he would be at noon tomorrow or noon in seven days' time. Nevertheless it was all unknown to him. In his own modest way he was daring the uncharted. Even if his favourite topics of conversation when he returns are the six-hour delay at Athens airport or the stifling heat on the bus from Avignon to Paris in which one woman broke down in hysterics, or the price of whisky in Madrid, he did leave the routines of his normal life behind, he did go on a journey, and he did subject himself to acute nervous strain on a number of occasions. He did take some initiative to go on this tour; there was a type of action involved in taking the decision. Above all he went in hope: he entered that very human cycle of taking on something different in great eagerness, of experiencing it and finding that in many ways it proved to be a trial rather than a joy, and finally of a returning home tired and wanting only to relax and recoup his strength. This is the prodigal son again. Moreover, as a footnote, it is quite a feat of the imagination to see in the plasticated comfort of the mass-produced modern hotel bedroom the sepulchral splendour of the medieval chamber.

Dean MacCannell has argued that 'touristic consciousness is motivated by its desire for authentic experiences.'[3] It is getting at how the natives really live that is of first importance for the tourist. I doubt this. Certainly there is a corner of the tourist mind that searches out the real thing, and does not want to be faced by substitutes. However, the desire for the authentic is subordinate to the deeper tourist goals, of adventure and so on. Moreover, although MacCannell is right to suggest that what tourists usually get is staged authenticity, it may well be that they get what they want. They do not want things too authentic. To take an extreme example, how many Anglo-Saxon tourists in France have any desire to eat frogs' legs or snake? Or again, it is obvious to American tourists in a New Orleans restaurant that the waiter is a fellow American faking a French accent and French gestures in accordance with the stereotype familiar to them from television comedians. They like the familiarity. They prefer the fake to the real French waiter they might encounter if they strayed off the tourist track in Paris, a waiter whose alien customs and expectations would only make them nervous. As a final example, the very American bar in the Vienna Hilton is partly decorated in Jugendstil to suggest the city of Klimt. The hotel provides a known environment with a hint of the exotic. Tourists accept far too high and obvious a degree of stagedness for their true desire to be for unadulterated authenticity. There may be those occasional aesthetes hot in pursuit of the natives, but my suspicion is that even in most of their cases they prefer the natives tidied up a little, and visited with prior instruction of what to see and what to avoid, of how to proceed in such a dangerously unfamiliar environment.

The ultimate truth is that the modern tourist remains a Faust. When he travels he cannot linger; he has to keep pushing on. Some tours visit five European countries and ten cities in two weeks. Nothing really moves this man; nothing so arrests his attention that he wants to stop and spend a few hours in its presence, meditating, losing himself in its beauty, releasing himself to the rhythms of its symmetries. There are no moments of joy, no moments of humility. He is not carried away, out of himself; on the contrary, when he is touched it is by anxiety at the mechanics of the tour, and his sense of himself as a vulnerable isolated organism becomes the more acute.

Moreover, he has become a mundane Faust, able to recount at home only the most everyday type of interruptions to his comfort, interruptions well understood because of their mundanity. The traveller belonged to the age of conversation; he was a story-teller.

The tourist has lost all resemblance to his noble ancestor, the religious pilgrim. Compare the Western tourist, staggering up the long dragon staircase to the Buddhist temple of Doy Sutep near Chaing Mai, with the devout Thai making a pilgrimage to this very important religious site. The Westerner knows it is a temple and has been told that he ought not to miss it while he is in Chaing Mai. He climbs the hill, takes off his shoes, enters the temple, speeds around photographing the gold Buddhas, takes a quick look at the view, then descends and returns to his hotel. The Thais are highly self-possessed and do not seem to mind the intrusion of these busy Westerners. They come piously to this temple. They offer prayers, burn candles and stick gold foil on to some part of one of the icons. A priest says a prayer for them. The visit to Doy Sutep is of especial significance in their lives. They too presumably have their worries once they are away from home – are their fields being properly tended in their absence, have they brought all their medicaments with them, is their son keeping up his religious duties, and so on. But they are in contact with greater than human forces at Doy Sutep and are humbled by the experience. The temple is also alive with historical importance. In marked contrast to the western tourist the Thais find a confirmation of their deepest beliefs and moral supports, and they gain some sense of tranquillity. Their example should re-awaken in the minds of us Westerners that question that so troubled the founding fathers of modern sociology, where will it end, this terrible gnawing restlessness that is our civilization?

9 On homecoming, or man's tyranny over space

Arrogant we humans are, so lacking in self-restraint, that we can't leave it at inflicting our inner lives on others, we also have to muffle and smother trees, birds, and valleys with our private obsessions. Physical domination of nature is not enough for us; we refuse to recognize anything that we haven't already given a human shape. Thus a mountain is never simply a mountain, a house never a house. The Greeks called this narcissistic possessiveness *hubris*; Freud included it under *neurosis*. Others, like Byron, have praised it as the core of our humanity, our unity with nature, our godlike imagination: 'Are not the mountains, waves, and skies a part of me and of my soul, as I of them?'

This essay concentrates on one of the ways in which men exploit the spaces in which they live – their need to project their unconscious wishes for a home, for homecomings and goings, on to their environment. There is psychological centrality to the home fantasy, something formative and inescapable about the movements it induces, the spaces it defines, and the valencies it attributes. Moreover, its consequences provide a beautiful illustration of man's incapacity to view spaces, objects, landscapes, cities for what they are, in their uncomplicated objective thereness. Man's tyranny over his environment is not restricted to economic exploitation. But much that we regard as human, and approve of, has as one of its sources this discrepancy between the sense impressions that stimulate a person's retina and what he thinks he actually sees.

When are we at home, and what does it mean? Rilke wrote that one's home (*Heimat*) changes. Toledo today, Paris tomorrow, most men live abroad, in an alien place (*die Fremde*), and the homes are empty. Home thus for Rilke means 'spiritual home', a place where the rhythms of one's being are for the moment in harmony with the environment, where one belongs. Should we then be so general as to equate home with a context for well-being? What can be said, at the outset, of a general nature in relation to well-being, is that a man is blessed who in his life manages to find and inhabit most of the home spaces to which his disposition makes him susceptible. This is one of my theses.

In a sense this essay belongs to the newly emerging discipline of 'environmental psychology', whose range of interest, and current level of achievement, is well summarized by W.H. Ittelson, *et al.*, in their *An Introduction to Environmental Psychology* (1974). Environmental psychology is still in its early days, and that is one factor making it adventurous and challenging. However, past trends in other branches in the social sciences suggest that almost inevitably it will take the plunge into hard-core science, as its leading aspiration, and in applying the screws of rigour end up losing the juice.

The essay is divided into three sections. The first discusses homes that take the form of sublime spaces, arguing that the experience of such spaces, heightened and inspired as it is, lives off the yearning for home, a space in which one belongs. The second section focuses on the alternative, quite different experience of home, that of familiar space. As much as humans need the excitement of the sublime they need to be able to relax in familiar surroundings. The third section looks at the dynamic process of homecoming, the journeying itself and what it might mean, how readily it turns into a tormented experience, especially when men lose contact with either of the fundamental types of home.

1 Home as sublime space

Caspar David Friedrich's painting *The Cross and the Cathedral in the Mountains* (*c.*1811) provides a readily accessible example of how we personalize space. Space here takes the form of a mountain landscape shadowed by a cathedral, which substitutes for the mountain peaks.

The foreground is an arrangement of rocks, grass, and dead branches sloping down on both sides to a mountain pool. The composition is wild, without straight lines, or planes, apart from the surface of the pool. The background is dominated by the cathedral, defining the central axis of the painting, its focal thrust up the same vertical line that passes through the centre of the pool. Fir trees stand as sentinels, reinforcing the cathedral's image of powerful height. A third space within the painting mediates foreground and background, while remaining independent; that is a crucifixion.

The mood of the painting could easily be sinister, its cathedral overbearing, its nature wasted, its Christ a symbol of human impotence, its brown tones coldly foreboding. But this is not the case; it rather impresses a mood of serene melancholy upon its viewer, some strange harmony, as if potentially devastating forces have been tamed, and come into balance. The key to this compelling equilibrium lies in the symbolic content of the painting's elements and the manner in which they complement each other.

The foreground is disordered, wild, and yet not unsettling in the way that chaotic things are. The pool gives it a still point, that orders the forces around it, making them its garments, outlining its form, that of rankly unformed, deeply sensual nature. The foreground is utterly female, to the literal extreme of taking the shape of a woman's genitalia. It is internally balanced by having the wild undisciplined energy of its surface elements, its craggy rocks, its jutting branches tied to the inscrutable stillness of the deep pool. The two archetypes of sensual womanhood, the wild-cat and the earth-mother (itself the complement, in another direction, of the virgin mother), are united. Thus the foreground taken by itself has its own harmony, its own level of integration.

The background is assertively male, to the literal extreme of the phallic cathedral, unlike any real gothic cathedral, whose towers were usually left truncated. Its force draws to a minor degree on its representation of soaring human endeavour, the striving for the infinite. But it stands more as a guardian of the foreground than as some Faustian spirit reaching out of the painting. Its presence is above all that of authority, the ambience of the father. The authority is benign, its vast and solid immovability set back to convey that its power is latent, ready if needed to protect and defend; what it provides is security. There is nothing in this presence of the authoritarian; it does not tower threateningly over the foreground, and the crucifixion. Indeed it rather contributes a strength to the Christ, by its vertical backing. By contrast to the foreground it is pure artifact, the geometrical precision of its vertical lines vigorously man-made. But rather than being heavy it is finely worked, especially in the spires, suggesting a refinement and elegance which softens

what otherwise would be a somewhat forbiddingly massive masculinity. (The attraction of ruined cathedrals or churches is that the
decay takes an edge off the formidable patriarchal force of the
building, making it more friendly.[1])

Friedrich has here created the perfect resolution of what Freud
established as the crucial childhood ambivalence, the ambivalence
that in its many shadings governs all adult relationships. What is
resolved is the conflict between the two wishes, or needs, that in their
different ways hold men, and thereby their societies, together; these
wishes float the fantasies that make men, at the psychological level,
need each other. On one side is the authority wish, the longing that
all men have to submit themselves to the benign and inviolable
authority that they ideally experienced in infancy within the family
circle. The longing is for the emotion of tenderness, which is only free
to flow in its purest form within the security of this relationship,
unthreatened by possessive or competitive forces from within or
without. It is this type of authority that the cathedral in the painting
embodies, implicit, unassertive in the light mist, the sun just behind
its topmost spires, a quietly inviolable form; and it subdues the
viewer into a mood of tender well-being.

On the other side of the ambivalence is the erotic wish, carrying
with it the desire to compete and to possess, to rebel rather than
submit, to assert rather than consent. Its emotional pull is not
towards tenderness, but towards the more direct, impulsive release
of sexuality, of wild, uncontained sensual abandon. The erotic wish
carries with it a desire for independence, for equality, for the end of
authority. In the painting the rebellious element is reduced, neutralized by the pool, and its secure, deeply founded sensuality, and by the
fact that the image of authority is benign, itself contained and with
no sign of intrusion into the foreground.

The centre of the painting holds the most fragile of human
representations, Christ on the cross, suspended precariously, as it
were, between the forces of authority and eros. The fine human
qualities, of a sensitive, knowing assurance, of compassion, humility, and of reason, that Christ embodies, are, like the ego in Freud's
schema, easily crushed by either of the two great primary forces.
Equally, it is only when authority and eros are in equilibrium that the
values of the Christ may emerge; they need a relatively untroubled
sea. The fact that it is the crucifixion, rather than other gospel
scenes, adds the element of man released from guilt; the uniqueness

of Christ's death, as indicated by the assertion 'he died to save us all', is that, unlike the death of any other intimate, or maybe anyone, we are not culpable. Even if we have wished his death, we are forgiven the inevitable guilt that follows its realization. Now the situation of death without guilt may occur in reality only when the primal forces are in harmony, when aggressions against authority, or flight from the erotic, are stilled. Finally, the complete harmony of authority and eros is attained only in death, the ultimate peace; the melancholy mood of the painting derives from its last determination, that its stillness is the stillness of death, and thus it plays upon the Romantic 'half in love with easeful death'.

But the tones of death in the painting are not restricted to the Christ figure. There is a remoteness about the authority; the sun carries little warmth; the father's benevolence is not of an effusive, emotionally generous type. Equally problematic is the cathedral's lack of any driving muscular strength; its masculinity is somewhat pallid, enfeebled. Moreover, the sensuality of the foreground is tempered by the deadness of the branches, and a certain frigidity in the shape and texture of the rocks; the femininity is not of an opulent or nubile variety. Thus Friedrich counters his own resolution of the two primal forces by abstracting them from any direct emotional strength or warmth; he makes their balance precarious, and ensures that the mood of melancholy serenity remains aware of its proximity to a petrifying death.

Interpretations of the psychological meaning of this Friedrich painting vary. Some individuals respond to the darker undertones, and see the cathedral as forebodingly dominant, or alternatively coldly impotent; some see the foreground as fetid, rank, frigid with decay. These opposite responses serve to confirm the psychological weight of the painting's elements, and the degree to which personal projections bias perception. Friedrich has facilitated this variety of response by severely qualifying the polar elements in the painting, thus imposing his own ambivalences, and making plausible projections of either longing for or hostility to authority, of either attraction to or fear of female sexuality.

The painting personalizes a landscape; it also goes some way towards creating a home. The longing for authority is a longing for the protective circle of the early family, at home. As much as the painting appeals to this longing, and induces a mood of well-being, it does so by putting the viewer at home in its spaces, protected by the benign paternal form of the cathedral. The viewer belongs. This belonging is qualified by other elements and tones in the composition, by Friedrich's ambivalence; but then real, as opposed to ideal, homes usually arouse ambivalent feelings. Let us turn now to a less ambiguous image of a cathedral, and use it to enquire more thoroughly into how the pursuit of sublime space constitutes a homecoming.

On entering Amiens Cathedral, one is seized by a rush of light down a thousand slender vertical planes, as if a thousand giant and transparent crystals were suspended there and light played a Bach fugue on their faces, drawing one inevitably up, past the piers, through the triforium, up continually, along the shafts of the clerestory, until just short of where parallel lines meet at infinity they sweep across forming the vault, as if a light veil of stone had been draped at this high point to shield the eyes of humble man from looking directly into the face of the divinity. This veil halts our ambition just short of the unlimited, and holds us, now stunned, self-conscious, as we become aware of the stone, that here it is not heavy and implacable, but light, with the delicate lines of an angel's flight, and yet firm, solid, nothing would move it. The experience changes into a quieter more contemplative mood, as the light grey hues of this heaven-bound colossus assert their still eternity; time and movement are suspended here, as in a deep cavern we are separated from land and sky, from history, and only the timeless echoes, the spiritual. The temple is austere, bathed in cool grey light; walking along its aisles, between giant piers, out into the nave, along to the transept, nothing distracts from the sculptural lines of the stone. There is an archetype of spatial perfection that has been created here in what Panofsky referred to as the inordinately slender nave of Amiens. Breathless, from within the spell of the sacred, for to breathe is too human, and in God's presence one is drawn a little out of one's disposition.

But there is something acquired about a taste for Amiens. Spengler contrasted the Gothic cathedral with the dark cavernous womb of the Magian mosque, and the noontide Euclidean elegance and finitude of the classical temple; he saw it as the leading visual metaphor for the Faustian spirit that has driven Western man for the last millennium. What a culture does with its spaces is one of the keys to its nature. Amiens is an exemplary representation of the restless, powerful, striving for the infinite, the nature-defying confidence that has funded European progress. But it may nevertheless be the case that Amiens is strong enough to be universal at the broadest level, to be able to touch all men, through the various filters of their cultural backgrounds.[2]

(The taste for Amiens reached a peak among the Victorians. Ruskin wrote a book, *The Bible of Amiens*, in which he concurred with M. Viollet-le-Duc's judgment of the cathedral as the Parthenon of Gothic architecture. Proust translated Ruskin's work with great enthusiasm into French. Then Walter Pater wrote of 'the greatest and purest of Gothic churches' in his essay, 'Notre-Dame d'Amiens'.[3])

What more is this cathedral to us than an impressive stone edifice? Why are we compelled? Is it only at the general level, of Faustian striving, of the phallic triumph of creative man over passive nature, that the symbol of Amiens works? Or do we have more specific associations? It is both: the general itself contains the lineaments of many particulars, the cultural archetype can be traced like a symphony theme in each element of the culture. For example, Amiens enthralls by its representation of Western man's ideal human relationship: awesomely uplifting as one tentatively steps over the threshold of a new space, and the imagination is captivated by new dimensions, of scope, of height, where in the flush of the moment anything seems possible, a space that is at the same time containing, defined, giving a specificity to what hitherto were rather formless, chaotically vaulting dreams. Here stone is transformed into flight, flesh into sensual rapture. Amiens reawakens a fantasy, gives it new weight, elaborating its form, so that henceforth whenever that same fantasy is touched it will arrive with a stronger charisma, its face showing the added depth of the moment inside the Gothic cathedral.[4]

On our ransacking of our external world for our psychological convenience, Freud says the following:

> The contrast between what is subjective and what is objective does not exist from the first. It only arises from the faculty which thought possesses for reviving a thing that has once been perceived, by reproducing it as an image, without its being necessary for the external object still to be present. Thus the first and immediate aim of the process of testing reality is not to discover an object in real perception corresponding to what is

imagined, but to *re-discover* such an object, to convince oneself that it is still there. (*Negation*, 1925)

Amiens provides a new and vivid form for the image or fantasy that derives from early experience of key objects (mothers, cribs, prams). If we were without that early experience, if it had been different, then Amiens would not exist; we would detour in annoyance this absurd pile of stone blocking our way.

In Amiens Cathedral one may feel at home. One belongs, if only briefly; one does not wish to be elsewhere; that agitated restlessness that gnaws one often into moving on is stilled. What does it mean this *home*?

It is something to do with the space being personal, an extension of oneself, with which one is immediately on terms of intimate rapport. And it is a larger, grander self. We are taken beyond the narrow confines of our own everyday egos, and connected with a wider universe. The sensation of transcending ourselves, moving through the normally prickly boundaries out into the vast inner spaces of Amiens, is sublimely pleasing. We ourselves become lighter, less earthbound; in the new estates that we for the moment call our own we have the power of angels. It is in part a return to the very first days of childhood, when the boundaries of self were vague, and in our best moments we flowed freely in the emotional space of the vast mother.

At home in Amiens, there is another gain. We are not here utterly dependent on our own physical and psychological defences. We have four walls to hide and protect us from the potentially hostile outside. Within the thick, fortress, stone walls of the cathedral we are cut off even from the elements; we see, smell, and above all hear nothing from outside. Moreover, we have, in entering, accepted the psychological support that this great edifice carries with it, by virtue of what it stands for, its past, the institution of the Church, its God; as with Friedrich's cathedral we have placed ourselves in the arms of a kindly yet omnipotent father. Here we do not need to be as thick-skinned, for we need our skin less. We can almost believe that we have returned to the dark and silent womb, or at least to its first substitute, the house that was home.

But this sense of being at home is precarious. Rilke's Toledo today, Paris tomorrow, means nowhere next week, and the homes are empty. With home as the place where the rhythms of one's being are for the moment in harmony with the environment, if that environment contains people, then they are *friends*, whether or not they have been met before, or will be seen again. Blood, age, sex, class, nationality, culture may all play a role in the homecoming; but they may not. A stranger encountered in Amiens Cathedral, in a like mood, becomes kin; one is perfectly at home with him.

The two poles of the experience of home are the familiar house in the familiar city, of which more will be said below, and Amiens. Why call Amiens a home, rather than an exciting novelty? Because, unlike a novelty, its image lasts; it will call again and again; the return to Amiens will be as the most beautiful dream of homecoming, like in mood to that very different experience of a weary traveller at night on a lonely country way seeing the welcoming light of a village inn. The sense of belonging in Amiens is not fickle, like the pull of a one-night affair. Back in Amiens there will again be the excitement, but that of meeting with an old friend after a long time, the excitement of a shared past, and thoughts of many familiarities to rediscover. Amiens has become a treasured space, because it touched some latent chord in the mind, and gave it life, and a kind of permanency. There is another place now on the earth that one can travel to, and imagine that one is going home. And in this case it will be the imagination, rather than the orthodox definition, that will be true. Amiens is a sublime space; it is not homely, but one nevertheless feels at home.

The most cultivated of all nomads, Tamerlaine, created his own solution to the contempt problem, the problem of living in homes without over-familiarity reducing them to routine spaces. Among his fabulous buildings in Samarkand there was no palace: there were tombs, mosques, and magnificent colleges, the results of his patronage of religion and learning. When at home in Samarkand between campaigns he preferred to live in one of his splendid gardens. To be at home for Tamerlaine was to be camping in his favourite surroundings.

2 Home as familiar space

The scale of the town in which a man grew up, the suburb, the street, their contours, will leave an enduring print upon his imagination. There will be places, parts of cities, later in life where he suddenly and inexplicably feels comfortable, in some strange sense more at ease than elsewhere, and this will be because the proportions are familiar, they echo his fantasy of the scale things ought to be. Scale is a tapestry of the width of streets, the height of buildings, their closeness together, their state of upkeep, their period, the density and placing of trees, of shrubs, of parks, and of water. It is also influenced by light, its intensity, and the sky, whether it is typically a vast blue dome, or a low dour ceiling. The scent of trees, the songs of birds, and the weather contribute to the archetype of what is 'natural', and they thereby influence perception itself – a Scot landing in Singapore at mid-day will gradually lose sight of things, as his body loses vitality in the steamy tropical humidity. In general we depend on messages from our body to stabilize our visual worlds – a man seeing a distorted room as normal learns to see it as it really is by feeling around it with a stick. A child with a crippled arm may well have trouble balancing in certain situations; moreover, his sense of space will be less stable, less reliable. Thus it is not simply that certain spaces are familiar to the eye because they were seen in childhood; streets were walked, stairs climbed, parks crossed, and always the kinaesthetic experience complemented the visual.[5]

Culture, in the general sense of the assembly of images through which we perceive our world as intelligible, and thereby predictable, includes not only customs, manners, rituals, and language, to name some of the more obvious elements; it also includes familiar space. At this level, familiarity could not be further from breeding contempt.

There may, of course, be contempt. A country person may not feel claustrophobia in the metropolis, may rather take like a duck to water to dense urban space with its high tempo of living. And, after all, few grew up within toddling distance of Amiens. For some, for all at times, it will be the novel, the familiar-defying, that excites the imagination, and creates a home out of something ostensibly unexpected and alien. This is the home of one's most extravagant fantasy, like a castle; this home, however, we are unlikely to find comfortable for very long, for as the enchantment of the moment wanes we start to long for the more familiar, the more modest and less challenging, in which to rest our tired spirit, and dwell in recollection of the exhilaration of homes built for the gods, for us in our godlike moments.

At its most tangible, the home is a house, a community of rooms. Proust writes of his attachment to such homes:

Thus my body builds around it room after room: wintry rooms where one loves to hold the outer world at bay, where one keeps the fire going all night and wraps about one's shoulders a cloak of warm air, smoke-coloured, smoke-scented, and shot with ruddy gleams; summer rooms where one loves to be gathered to the breast of nature, rooms where one sleeps, a bedroom I had in Brussels whose proportions were so pleasing, so spacious and yet so cosy, that it seemed a nest to hide in and a world to explore. (*Contre Sainte-Beuve*)

A home extends the private space of the person who lives there; within its walls, behind its curtains, there are rooms in which every object, every surface, every area is known; as familiar as the person's own arm, and safer from unexpected intrusion. In this predictable space, in which mind and body can roam at will, one can relax; the pitch of alertness, of defensive anxiety at the possible unknown, that is necessary outside, may be lowered. This homeliest of homely spaces is filled with treasured objects, a living museum of the inhabitant's own past, used to sustain, deepen, and guide the present; as such this space provides tangible housing for that favoured area of the mind that is populated by treasured memories. It is the person's *territory*, and his attachment to it, as in the case of animals, may have a biological base.

There is one further territory serving as extended privacy: the garden. It is really a preparation for the anarchy of the street, for it usually offers only partial protection: fences can be climbed, looked over or through. But a garden in its arrangements and contours is personal space; when shrubs die the loss is personal, when weeds grow the insult is personal, like dirt or flaking paint inside the kitchen.

Homes in the form of familiar spaces are often in danger from strangers who show unwanted familiarity. If an acquaintance visits the house and strews his belongings around, puts his feet up on the coffee table, the hostess may well be unnerved, taking this as a personal violation, as if some clammy and alien hand had laid itself upon her wrist. In crossing the threshold of another's home for the first time manners rightly insist that one should tread gingerly, one should as much as possible, without becoming awkward, place oneself in the hands of the hostess, as to where to sit, and what to do. A friend is thus the person whom one is at ease having in one's home.

When one's home is scrutinized, one is scrutinized oneself.

Of course, attitudes to the home vary. There are the casual, those who find it cosy to have a crowd of strangers spilling beer on their carpet. Either they are similarly careless about themselves, or homeless. At the other extreme, there are those so nervous about the chastity of their domicile that they never invite anyone inside. When burgled, they are mortified at the thought of some hostile stranger illicitly roaming through their private world – even if nothing is stolen. A person of this type is either so delicate in her sensibility that anything strange threatens violation, or she is a hysteric, not really at home in her own house, or her own skin, fearing the stranger in her rooms because he is so like herself, forcing her to recognize how much at sea she herself is when sitting at her own hearth.

The telephone effected a breach in the fortress sanctity of the home. It both made it safer from the unannounced visit, and more vulnerable. It has provided a surreptitious means of entry into private space – even though it is more difficult to ring someone at home than at work, for everyone shares in part, and respects, the idyll of the idle, carefree Sunday morning, whose harmony can instantly be shattered by the ring, as of a fire bell, at the soft heart of tranquility.

To come up behind someone and tap them on the shoulder, unless they are unusually easy-going, is likely to agitate them, to touch some nerve. As Auden wrote: 'Some thirty inches from my nose, The frontier of my Person goes.' Homes protect from such intrusions. The space between two people is the most basic of all forms of consensus. It is tacit, that is not spelt out verbally, and indicates the degree of intimacy that exists between them, specifically at that moment, and generally if one can read the latent signs. The handshake, the greetings at one pace apart, the withdrawal to three paces, or to the side if it is a cocktail group, carefully define the space one occupies when meeting a stranger, or a slight acquaintance. A little further apart and contact becomes vague, an uneasiness develops as to whether to come closer, or break apart altogether. Closer together than one pace, and another anxiety appears, this time because private space is being intruded upon; physical presence has fallen out of step with psychological presence. The one intruded upon is likely to go cold, avert his eyes, look around or slide backwards, on the defensive. To flirt is to play with this fear, flout it with a series of signs to the other that transform their own similar fears into excitement, that is if they are willing, to the point that toying with the next taboo, that of touch, can build up a most exquisite passion. One could not say that the flirting pair has become 'close'; they have rather become absorbed by the game of deceiving propriety's distance by sneaking up close when its eyes are elsewhere. One only becomes close when the flirting is over, that is when the joust with distance has been won, and it is the distance of indifference rather than propriety (guardian of the physical and erotic unknown) that now threatens. The intense phase of the flirt does not need a home; it is carried by its own momentum, and requires protection only from the most peculiar intrusions, such as a jealous husband.

What is the link between homes and flirtations? Familiar homes are spaces in which distance is at a minimum. Things are known intimately; they are close. But they are often in danger of being taken for granted, making the inhabitant restless. Moreover, the achievement of the most gratifying familiarity, where distance is minimal, is not a passive activity; it depends on a risky tangling with distant things, in order to bring them close. The flirt is such an adventure. It may take place in a home, at a gathering. In fact in its purest form it belongs to this situation, where risks of impropriety are greatest. Inviting a collection of people into the home in itself threatens the everyday familiarity of the space; it is itself an adventure, a play with distance to test whether new elements can be fitted harmoniously into the home atmosphere, or whether one has submerged one's territory in the anarchy of the street. Thus to flirt in such a setting likely puts into question both a familiar, established relationship, or maybe two, and a familiar space. It is driven, however circumscribed the individuals' intentions, by yearnings for the sublime, the hope that an Amiens might be at hand, and its door open. The home as familiar space is always in danger of becoming a 'sterile promontory', especially when it is taken for more than simply a place to return to. The flirt tests its boundaries, and the strength of its hold; it carries the vital challenge that spaces be either warmly, nourishingly familiar or ecstatically sublime.[6]

We have established that the home is not simply a retreat. Its character is dependent on the manner in which it maintains its boundaries, and thereby controls its contact with its external world. It may become too much of a retreat, as in the case of the room in which Chekhov's Three Sisters meet; then it appears as a trap, in which the characters' fear and apathy, the monotony and triviality of their lives, keep them sequestered. For the sisters the outside, Moscow, then plays the role of an ideal, to which they dream of escaping, but never do. In another case, the home as retreat has the special function of providing a distant space from which to view the world, a highroom overlooking the street. Proust liked thus, to restrict his contact with the external world to looking at it through windows. The home, or room, preserves an independence, a lack of involvement. Similarly, Vermeer's young ladies of Delft move alone in their gracefully comfortable bourgeois rooms; they work lace, play musical instruments, loiter meditatively; the most striking pose is of one of their number standing at a casement window, not looking out, but using the light streaming in to read a letter. The letter comes from outside, bringing news into the inner sanctuary of her privacy; it connects her with the outside, but in a strictly controlled way. The insulation here is almost as total as in the later case of Tennyson's Lady of Shalott, who lives in a tower on an island in the middle of a river, and watches in her mirror the world below and at a distance as it goes past.

When under severe strain individuals tend to manifest either agoraphobic or claustrophobic symptoms; some include both in their repertoire. The home is of central significance in the expression of these symptoms. The agoraphobe (literally, terrified by public spaces) under stress retreats into her house, may well take a hot bath, and withdraw further into a warm bed. The home, itself as womb, provides two even more secure, cosy, enclosed spaces in which to curl up safely, and there recoup the energy and the will to be reborn later into the fretful world. The claustrophobe under stress is the opposite; he has to clear out, find air and space, free from all that ties, encloses, depends, possesses, in short all that is familiar. He is the wandering Jew, the flying Dutchman, the explorer, the Don Juan, the merchant. Which leads us into the more dynamic issue in relation to 'homes', that of homecomings and goings.

3 Homecoming

The greatest of the Western myths of homecoming is *The Odyssey*. It is a parable of adult life in its totality. Odysseus wants to get home, after his ten years involved in the Trojan War, back to the familiarities and tendernesses of his wife and son, of his properties, of his native island and its inhabitants. But what precisely is the nature of this 'want'? Odysseus' life is a sequence of adventures, of challenges, in which he must prove his manhood – his cunning, his leadership, his strength, his honour. He wants these adventures, for without them he would not be what he is. As a hero, an ideal man – that is, not tied down by poverty or insecurity of caste or character – he wants to experience everything, and he can. Thus he has to hear the singing of the Sirens, to visit Circe, to outwit the Cyclops, and so on. Home would mean little to him if he didn't spend most of his time in getting there, rather than being there. When he finds himself among the Phaiakians, on his last stop before Ithaca, he entertains, enthralls his hosts with his stories. The stories are not about his home, but about his adventures on the way home. For the Phaiakians, as for us, Odysseus has lived the perfect life – and it now seems that at last he will reach home safely.

After he has reached home, killed the suitors, and been recognized by his wife, he can relax, for the first time in twenty years, in Penelope's arms, in his own bed. At this moment he thinks, not of her, nor of this long-cherished arrival, but of the one trial that remains. The trial is to ensure that:

> Then death will drift upon me
> from seaward, mild as air, mild as your hand,
> in my well-tended weariness of age,
> contented folk around me on our island.

> (FitzGerald translation)

Homecoming, which Odysseus mentions in the same breath, is an image of tranquillity, peaceful prosperity, and it has as its immediate association, death. In Book XIII, as Odysseus, 'the teller of many stories', is restless to start on the last leg of his journey home, Homer provides a metaphor: that of the farmer who grows hungry as he works all day behind his plough and share, then at last at sundown, stiff in the knees from weariness, he turns for home. Again the image is of the adventure over, a man hungry and tired drawn to the comfort of home.

The home that is Ithaca and Penelope is familiar space. The home that is death carries some of the lineaments of sublime space, 'mild as air', or so Odysseus hopes. And is it stretching the home concept too far to suggest that Odysseus in his long journey maps out a space, across the Mediterranean, that is sublime; that he passes through a series of spaces that he succeeds in personalizing, in one way or another depending on the challenge, which are thus rendered sublime for him, in his memories, and for those who hear or read his story? Consider, for instance, that stretch of sea opposite the rocks across which the Sirens sang: has not the image of that space been imprinted on the Western imagination, in association with the haunting song of the beautiful maidens, so exquisite as to tempt him who hears it to his death? Is this not a variation on Amiens Cathedral? Does not the act of homecoming itself, when successful, create a sublime space? Is not Odysseus, in the moment off this beautiful coastline entranced by the song, at home in his homecoming, and again close to a sublime death?[7]

Odysseus lives the myth of return. There is the opposite theme, that of breaking free, of leaving. The best known myth of this type is that of the prodigal son, a tale of what today we would call adolescent rebellion. The prodigal son rebels against his home, not because it is evil, but because it constrains. He is young, meaning naive, enthusiastic, energetic, and curious; he itches to experience the world at large, which he knows only in his own fantasy. He has grown out of total dependency, so he leaves home, and in particular his father, squanders his inheritance on riotous living, learns that friends are sometimes merely parasites, that to fare well away from home one needs to be canny, and finally that the world is tough and full of masters with none of his father's benevolence. So he returns to his father's house, and the parable ends, leaving open the question of whether he will ever break the paternal bond. His first home-going was corrupted by his hostility to his father – expressed in the son's throwing away the gift of his inheritance. The father forgives him completely, which may give him confidence, making him feel worthy, or it may ensure that he never has the courage to leave again.

Just as there are two paths that the prodigal son might take, the benign one of genuinely taking leave of his first home, or the cursed one of remaining a son for ever, Odysseus has his own double, represented by the damned figure of the Flying Dutchman. The Dutchman suffers from such acute guilt that he cannot land. In some versions of the legend a crime is specified, an iconoclasm, a murder. His endless journeying is a curse, and consequently he detests the sea, longing only to find a home on dry land, or, in Wagner's version, to be allowed to die. Because he has no home to look forward to, his voyaging is meaningless, offering none of the gratifications of *The Odyssey*. His sea is restless, formless, unbounded, like his guilt.

Odysseys are possible in any time. The problems of the prodigal son are universal. The same may be true for Flying Dutchmen. However, there does seem something peculiarly modern about their condition, and I shall close this discussion of homecoming by considering some contemporary examples.

It is a commonplace that as distances have contracted in the last century and a half with industrialization, dissimilarities from region to region have been reduced – the acceleration of time has watered down local colours, and imposed a universal hue. At the frontier of this process today lies the massive assault on time, distance, and the exclusiveness of travel, that the Boeing 747 has made possible, complemented by a comforting uniformity of airports, hotels, and guides, to the point that the Hilton Hotel in Vienna provides its own Klimt Room, in which popularized decor reproducing the turn of the century blends a Jugendstil atmosphere into the dim light characteristic of an American bar. Here the threat of the foreign language, the foreign city, the foreign culture is softened; the tourist feels at home, and he is prepared for the adventure of travelling one mile by taxi to view the real Klimt. Eventually that journey itself becomes dispensable, for after all a holiday is for relaxation and where better than in the dim, padded twenty-four-hour Klimt bar. 'Your every need is taken care of', as the travel brochure proclaims. The democratization of travelling has, through catering for a uniformity of tourist, made the destinations and the journeys themselves uniform.

When travelling was an adventure it was the distance between the familiar and the unknown, between the London Club and Samarkand, that determined the thrill. The traveller went in search of sublime spaces. In our remissive age that distance has been so reduced that we may soon expect the outpost of unfamiliarity confronting the tourist to be a new model of seat-reclining button in his supersonic jet.

Rilke's Toledo today, Paris tomorrow, did not depend on railway trains. An hour in Amiens after a two-day coach ride from Paris, and two days to return, might mean more in a year than the same time today populating the mind with the inspiring space of five northern Italian towns. And although Amiens itself has not been spoilt, the very ease with which we can leave it after an hour, in order to save time, and multiply our experiences, is a destructive temptation, augmenting our restlessness. Restlessness damages curiosity, our ability *to linger* with the unfamiliar, and thereby to discover singular homes; it makes us prefer the comforting anonymity of our rented car and of the waiting Hilton, where we can be sure that we shall meet fellow Dutchmen, asking of them nothing but to share their restlessness, amiably, remissly, for a night, before moving on. The modern traveller is in danger, when he leaves home to break the monotony, of finding that his only thought on the journey is of being back home. His ship is prone to rush eternally across the sea, arriving nowhere. Hence the pleasure to be found in the Klimt Bar, a sign of the growing blandness of our modern sense of home.

The blandness is an inevitable concomitant of that being on the move that became the norm in modern life – the shifting between houses, between cities, between countries, and a parallel increased mobility between relationships, whether lovers, friends, or acquaintances. Without the security of stable homes there is less tenacity for the unfamiliar and uncertain. In part the polarity between home and abroad is neutralized, and disappears; in part the entire world becomes familiar, a compromise home in which people travel Dutchmanlike in search of compelling homes, but not insistently, and not really expecting, or even wanting, to find anything much different. As in the parallel case of most relationships, predictability is accepted as a surrogate for the warm, nourishing, gratifying space that is the ideal 'home'. The loss of genuinely familiar space kills the urge to discover sublime spaces. Dutchman restlessness is one of the pathologies of modern life, and usually enforces a need for one form of tranquillization or another, on the slide into depression. One of its causes, and one of its symptoms, is the abandonment of homecoming as an aspiration. A predictable routine is settled for, in fear that another setting sail might bring on inescapably, and unmitigatedly, a Dutchman existence. Again, a parable is contained in *The Odyssey*. The lotus-eaters, the most successful of all remissives, abolish memory, and thereby the past, with their drug; they are freed for the pure indulgence in pleasure. Odysseus warns his men not to eat of the lotus lest 'you lose your hope of home'. To give up entirely on the hope for homecoming is to be dead.

10 The sceptic turns consumer: an outline of Australian culture

A city dweller was driving along a dirt road in the dry outback of Australia, hundreds of miles from the nearest homestead, when he passed an old bushman, his swag over his shoulder, slouching along the track. He stopped and offered a lift. The bushman leant in his passenger's window and snarled: 'Naw, yer can open yer own gates.'
ABC television programme *This Day Tonight*, Sydney, 1976: story chosen as the most typically Australian

There have been three main influences on Australian culture: upper-middle-class Victorian values and institutions, working-class (significantly Irish) egalitarianism, and twentieth-century consumerism.

Australia was colonized by the British and virtually all its institutions — governmental, administrative, judicial, financial, educational, religious, cultural, and trade union — came out of the British mould with at the most minor adaptations.[1]

In the cities, moreover, the middle class settled itself in British-style suburbs, built British houses, planted British trees, sent its children to British-style private schools and whenever possible on to Oxbridge, and its successful males relaxed in London-style clubs. It traded, travelled, dressed, and patronized charities and the arts in a British manner. It valued civility, prosperity, and civic pride. At the same time many Victorian bourgeois attitudes were reinforced by the strong influence of Presbyterian Scots, notably in education.[2]

Working-class attitudes have permeated the more general Australian culture since the middle of the nineteenth century with an egalitarian ethos. The pressure for social equality has carried with it an intolerance of respectability and manners, a hostility to authority, a talent for improvization, and an idealization of male comradeship. Such attitudes were strengthened by a disproportionately strong

Irish influence in the early working class, transporting into Australia a distaste for British middle-class authority. There have been many attempts by the literati to give the egalitarian-mateship theme a greater dignity and mythical weight by locating its origins among the early convicts, and finding it amplified in the lives of the bushmen who took on the harsh conditions of the great outback, in the exploits of the bushrangers, and in particular Ned Kelly, and finally in the experience of the gold rushes.[3] But the same attitudes are deeply rooted in the British working class – especially the preference for male company, gathered in pubs or watching sport. Moreover, Australia has since 1900 been a heavily urbanized society, and it is less and less plausible to look to rural life for the sources of its leading values. Indeed there is no need to search further for an explanation of the Australian mateship ethic: it was imported from Britain and Ireland, and reinforced by an experience of working-class life similar to that in the countries of origin. It is by and large a class product, deriving from a shared experience of economic subordination.

The third influence on Australian culture is consumerism, and as in all Western societies its importance has been growing right through the twentieth century. It constitutes an attitude to life cultivated by the economic needs of advanced industrial societies, their technology, their high levels of production, their material affluence, and their welfare States. These needs are pervasively articulated by the modern mass media. Consumerism is indicative of a process of social change in which progressively higher degrees of uniformity are imposed, both within and between different Western societies.

Consumerism poses a peculiar problem for a relatively new society like modern Australia. Its pressure towards international modes of taste and behaviour, applied across the total spectrum of social life from clothes, houses and motor cars to political styles, music and hero images, threatens the local culture with killing of any of its unique elements before they have had a chance to establish themselves. The first and most important question for any study of national culture is that of what is singular to it. In the Australian case it may be a task of looking for an animal that was always rare, but now shows signs of extinction.

So what is unique to Terra Australis? First and foremost there is the landscape, the light, the flora and fauna, which are all powerfully distinct and represent a force of nature that will always dwarf and humble the humans who inhabit the continent. But culture is the various works of man, and it is those works with which we are concerned here.

In answer to the question 'What is typically Australian?' there has been a remarkable unanimity among the commentators, whether they were visitors or locals: the egalitarian-mateship ethic and its practice.[4] I don't wish to argue against the prominence of the ethic and its practice. However, this prominence is often exaggerated, to the degree of calling Australia the most egalitarian society in the Western world. The commentators have usually either explicitly or implicitly taken Britain as the basis for comparison (most of the visitors came from Britain, and Britain was the society that Australians knew best). It is true that compared to British society there is less social distance in Australia and Australian manners are sometimes more gregarious and easy-going. But British class differences endure in Australia. It is, for example, the norm in a country town for the lower class to gather socially in the pubs while the higher class meets in its own clubs. Accents vary substantially. Generally the attitudes, prejudices, interests and manners of working-class Australia are notably different from those of educated upper-middle-class Australia.

Switzerland is a more genuinely egalitarian society than Australia. It has often been described as a wholly middle-class society. In fact it has its proportion of blue-collar workers, but they are not distinctive culturally. The Protestant ethic remains strong and softens class difference: whilst a man works, whatever his vocation, and does not live ostentatiously, he is respected. It is in no way obvious, moreover, that Australian society is more egalitarian than that of the United States.

The egalitarian-mateship ethic has been prominent in Australian literature, and it remains central to many Australians' perceptions of themselves.[5] It carries with it its own range of attitudes to work and to intimacy. However, the other thing that is typically or singularly Australian about this phenomenon is that it is more widespread than in other Western societies. As I have already suggested, neither its origins nor its essential nature are Australian. Moreover, its prominence is due rather to the weakness of possible alternative philosophies of life than to its own vitality: it has succeeded *faute de mieux*.

The argument might be put that the egalitarian-mateship ethic has been prominent in Australia because of the peculiar nature and strength of the working-class experience. The argument could run two ways. First, it might be suggested that the working class in nineteenth-century Australia was confronted by conditions of peculiar hardship. As a result it was bonded together in the face of common adversity. This argument fails for the simple reason that apart from one or two brief periods the working man was much better off than his British counterpart. Two difficult periods were the late 1850s and early 1860s in Victoria, when large numbers of unsuccessful gold-diggers retired to the towns where opportunities were severely limited; and the 1890s, during the depression that hit Australia with singular severity. However, from early in the twentieth century tariff protection was introduced to ensure comparatively high basic-wage levels. Anthony Trollope concluded his lengthy study, *Australia and New Zealand* (1873), by advising English men and women who were willing to work to emigrate to Australia, for there they would find a paradise: their whole condition of life would be changed in a society that respected labour rather than regarding it as servile.

The second argument for the peculiarity of the Australian working-class experience is one of unrealized expectations. We can assume that the material aspirations of those who migrate are higher than those who stay at home. In the Australian case from the middle of the nineteenth century a majority of immigrants saw themselves as coming to a new land full of promise, offering a prosperous and independent way of life. This was particularly the case for the uncharacteristic population that was attracted to Victoria in the 1850s – a high proportion of educated middle-class people and skilled tradesmen. Many of this group of immigrants found themselves in reduced circumstances in the new country, at least in the short term, making them leading candidates for the role of ideological radicalism – becoming hostile to a social order that had not allowed them to satisfy their own high ambitions. However, before long most newcomers to Victoria improved their living standards, and in the words of one historian of the period, Geoffrey Serle, 'For a large minority . . . the rise in living standards was sufficient to meet all reasonable hopes.'[6] We may assume that the unreasonable were in the minority, and indeed that large sections of the immigrant population in the latter half of the nineteenth century did not suffer from frustrated aspirations to a degree acute enough for them to constitute a significant moral or political factor in the formation of the Australian identity.

A large majority of Australians when asked to name the national hero answer Ned Kelly. This does not mean that they know very much about him, or feel strongly about the issue. What is significant for our purposes here is the confirmation that Australia lacks the pantheon of national heroes normal in other countries. The Cromwells, Nelsons, Napoleons, and Lincolns who save their nation in a moment of great trial or who lead their people on to great deeds do not have a place in Australian mythology. This is not for the lack of potential candidates: Deakin and Monash immediately suggest themselves. Moreover, there is nothing singular about having a Kelly-style hero, the man of humble origins, abused by corrupt authority, who fights ably and courageously against that authority. Robin Hood is partly equivalent, although it is significant that he was fighting for the good king who was away – there is no counter-balancing image of benign authority in the Kelly legend. Even more importantly Ned Kelly is not complemented by heroic figures who unite and integrate the society, who confirm it in its higher purposes. The middle class has failed to incarnate its own values in exemplary figures from the past.

The examination of hero and villain models provides one of the royal roads into the heart of a culture. In the Australian case it immediately supplies the key clue to the prominence of the egalitarian-mateship ethic: that the middle class, or the bourgeoisie, has not been able, from lack of confidence rather than from lack of strength, to enshrine its own values. Whilst it has differed little from its British and American counterparts in terms of occupation, income, styles of living and consuming, and patterns of leisure, it has failed to imprint its own ethos on the nation as a whole. Its manners, for example, have remained the preserve of a small section of its own kind. As a result the values of that part of the working class that has seen itself as under siege, in conflict with the more economically privileged social strata, have had little competition. Their influence has seeped right through the society largely because they met with little resistance.

Thus the vital question about the genealogy of Australian culture has nothing to do with a distinctive egalitarianism, or a particularly assertive working class; it is a question of why it was that the bourgeoisie failed to consolidate its own culture. My own tentative

answer is that the formation of Australian society coincided with a
general development in the West whereby the middle class came
progressively under the influence of an egalitarian bad conscience.
Its British, and, to a lesser extent, American counterparts had an
established tradition to offer them some protection against the
growing self-disgust that they harboured within their own breasts.
At this point Tocqueville's work is peculiarly illuminating: his
predictions about the future path of democracy, and in particular its
pathologies, fit Australia much more acutely than the United States.[7]

Tocqueville argued in his more pessimistic second volume of
Democracy in America that democracies in spite of their many
advantages tended to suppress excellence and individuality; they
stimulated an impatience with constraint and a disdain for
hierarchy; and they made it inevitable that central government
would steadily grow in size and power. Above all their egalitarian
spirit legitimated the envy of difference, and in particular of those
who were better or had more. It is one of the characteristics of the
workings of envy that those who fear that they might be envied set up
disarming strategies: they disguise or underplay whatever is likely to
be coveted. Such a fear of envy has been one of the factors contributing to the modern middle class's bad conscience about its own
privileges, forcing attempts to conceal some of the public signs or
manners of its lifestyle. (There are other sources of this guilt. Middle-
class civility imposes its own strains, sometimes to an intolerable
degree, forcing rebellious identification with the underprivileged.
Again, the goal that most members of this class have today attained,
that of comfortable consumer affluence, does not satisfy them; it
leaves their more important spiritual needs undernourished and
makes them feel in some sense that they have been cheated.)

So far our search for the singular in Australian culture has
discounted the orthodox thesis as spotlighting a theme that is unique
neither in its origins nor in the reasons for its prominence. However,
there is an alternative candidate for our attention, and one that is less
dependent for its existence on general developments that have taken
place in all Western countries. That is the theme of scepticism.
Australian scepticism has two strains, one dark and deeply
pessimistic, without the dignity and idealism of tragedy; the other is
more epicurean, carrying a jocular light-hearted irreverence towards
life.

The dark strain of scepticism is embodied in the theme of failure in

Australian culture. It has no more evocative representation than in what is arguably the finest short story in Australian literature, Henry Lawson's 'Water them Geraniums'.[8] The story is set in a remote bush environment, unyielding to the toil of the pioneer farmer. Nature is persecuting, and even the women, the sole bearers of moral courage for Lawson, finally decline – get 'past carin' as the theme of the second half of the story puts it. The machinery rusts, the horses creak, ten-year-old girls have lined worried faces, and the women are proud but with 'the pride that lies down in the end and turns its face to the wall and dies'. There are the makings of high tragedy here, of man fighting for survival against an inexorably cruel fate as embodied in the harshness of the landscape. But the men are not heroes; Joe Wilson, the narrator and central character, shows little inclination to battle the weight of the elements set against him. He does not have the spine of an Oedipus or a Lear. Rather he and his kind are abject, frightened, pathetic creatures who turn to drink, or 'shoot through' – run off leaving their families to make do on their own. In Lawson's bleak vision these men in the end destroy their women, and therewith virtue itself, and then eventually commit suicide or go mad. There is no triumph over hardship, no dignity won through struggle, simply unmitigated dismal failure. Behind the story runs a bitter scepticism about the human condition.

There have been other significant literary embodiments of the failure theme since Lawson. George Johnston's highly successful middle-brow novel, *My Brother Jack* (1964), traces the failure of the egalitarian-mateship ideal. More recently David Williamson's play, *Don's Party* (1971), examines the sense of failure in two contemporary suburban middle-class couples, and the vicious resentments that it generates. In Johnston's case failure results from the interference of fate in the form of an accident causing physical injury, and from the unavailability of work in the modern city suitable to the aspirations of the egalitarian hero. In Williamson's case there is no explicit cause of failure: it is rather human nastiness and incompatibility, and the vicissitudes and futility of modern aspirations that are to blame.

The more epicurean scepticism has its finest rendition in Jack Hibberd's one-man play, *A Stretch of the Imagination* (1972). Monk O'Neill, the hero, lives the last day of his long life as a wilfully, almost manically anarchic display of self-assertion. He reminisces about the major events in his life: his travels, his three marriages, his romances, the death of his brother, his withdrawal to live as a hermit in the bush, the time he was threatened with a visit, and above all his own physical decline. He entertains himself with a raw, self-caressing monologue, delighting in irreverence towards the ideals of his youth, women, human attachment, and anything that might intrude upon his solitary kingdom. He mocks himself with his own masochism: he cut down the one tree on his hill, although he loves trees and has worked ever since to fertilize a replacement. His last friend was his dog: he shot his dog. His vision is acutely pessimistic; the life he recounts is composed of a sequence of encounters with his fellow humans in which he invariably ends up beaten, abused, or abandoned. Yet he tells his story with such relish, re-enacting each episode then ruminating on it with his own peculiar vernacular philosophizing, that his narcissism is compelling. He is a substantial, likeable figure, and his life gains a sense of fulfilled completion.

One of the richest sources of scepticism was the literature produced during the First World War. The storming, holding, and retreat from Gallipoli in 1915 still carries mythic weight for Australians as the first time in the nation's history that a group of its citizens were on trial, under great duress, a time when the legend has it that the men acted with great courage, inventiveness and solidarity. The mateship ethic gains one of its injections of emotive tonic from Gallipoli: a brotherhood of equals fighting heroically side by side against formidable odds. But what is striking about the literature from the trenches is the light-hearted sceptical wit with which life under the constant threat of death was conducted.[9] *The Anzac Book* (1916), written and illustrated by the soldiers at Gallipoli, has as typical of its style a dialogue that ends: ' "D. . . it. . . shut up, Bill," says his mate. "You're always growling . . . you'll want flowers on your grave next." ' George Johnston repeats a story from the Second World War that struck him as typifying Australian humour: at one bend on the Kokoda Trail in New Guinea the skeletal hand and forearm of some hastily buried Japanese soldier had become exposed and it stuck out of the track over which the Australian infantry were laboriously climbing. Every Australian as he passed would seize the grisly claw and give it a shake, enviously saying 'Good on you sport.'[10]

One of scepticism's offshoots in the Australian case is a talent for satire. The theatre that played the most innovative role in the advance of Australian drama in the late 1960s and early 1970s, the

Pram Factory in Melbourne, created a company whose speciality was a fast, irreverent vaudeville style of clowning. None of the major Australian companies can put on tragedy convincingly. Australia's one internationally recognized one-man performer, Barry Humphries, is the nation's leading sceptic. Moreover, domestically the most able of the television personalities, ones who have created a highly distinctive style of their own, Graham Kennedy and Norman Gunston, both have as their stock-in-trade a buoyant impish irreverence. Kennedy made his name by focusing his variety show, 'In Melbourne Tonight', on the sending up of the products he was meant to be advertising. Gunston's scepticism works through the innocence of a boy from simple origins inadvertently turning the self-importance and ambition of the famous into traits that make them look ridiculous.

Scepticism is not reserved for the exceptional cases such as heroes in literature and television stars. There is a general mood of scepticism that pervades Australian attitudes to religion, politics, and indeed all ultimate values. It contrasts notably with that blend of idealism and sentimentality, of violence and a passion for justice, that has had such a singular influence over American culture.

This generic scepticism has a number of attractive consequences. It means that Australians are less likely to take fanatics seriously, and therefore the nation is unlikely ever to be swept along by extremist politics. It means that the leading political figure is not idealized to the degree that many American presidents have been celebrated as virtue incarnate: it is difficult to imagine an equivalent to the Kennedy cult taking root in Australia. Similarly the momentous evangelical revival in the United States that marked the 1970s had no echo in Australia.

Moreover, to take a more general cultural index, the stock Western with its idealized hero and its happy ending is alien to the mature Australian sensibility. Australian art has been more down-to-earth, readier to confront failure and death, less in need of softening arbitrary or bleak events with sentimental music or glamorized images of compassion and community. There is something much too uncompromising in the harshness of 'Water them Geraniums', the film *Wake in Fright*, or *Don's Party* for them to have been products of America. The darkest themes in American fiction, as in the novels of Hawthorne, Melville and Faulkner, are always offset by the fortitude of the tragic hero, his gains in inner strength, or transcendental recognition.

Australian scepticism equally has its negative consequences. Political idealism has been the exception in Australian history. There is not a convinced belief that mundane institutions and this-worldly activity can be radically transformed for the better, that idealistic passion can be translated into social progress. Australians are more indifferent than Americans to their political institutions; they are less likely to become indignant about injustice or inefficiency. They were quite happy to have the same prime minister for sixteen years as long as he offered them stability and moderation, and didn't become too obviously self-important – indeed Menzies had to retire himself in 1966 to end his reign.

Scepticism means that there are no grand visions of the past, the present, or the future. It means that when there is poetry it draws its rhythms from the struggles and victories of everyday reality, and not from great and exceptional events. In association there is another unattractive consequence: an indifference to excellence. Scepticism reinforces that element in the egalitarian temper that distrusts difference, ambition, and achievement. It was not untypical when Nellie Melba returned to Australia at the height of her international celebrity that rumours should have started circulating about her having become a dypsomaniac.[11]

The roots of Australian scepticism are much more difficult to pinpoint than those of egalitarianism. Traces can be read both of the British capacity for ironical understatement and Irish debunking of worldly pretension and success.[12] But there is at least a prima facie case for finding here a uniquely antipodean species.

My opening proposition was that there have been three main influences on Australian culture. I went on to suggest that if there is a unique element in this culture it is a sceptical attitude towards the human condition. I want to conclude my outline by enquiring into what is left of the three influences and what turn the scepticism might be taking.

The most important enduring British legacy is an extremely stable political system, founded on British political, administrative and judicial organizations and a British sense of liberal compromise. In addition there are some excellent private schools, some fine Victorian buildings and gardens, and a certain British militancy in some of the stronger trade unions. On the other hand the twentieth century has seen the steady decline of British, and especially

Protestant, values. Both the egalitarian tradition and modern consumerism have worked against them.

The egalitarian influence survives best in Australians' own view of themselves, as friendly, easy-going, generous and practical down-to-earth people. The fact, however, is that consumerism has proved a much more potent equalizer than any traditional working-class values, and that the friendliness and so on that one meets in the Australian suburbs (where most Australians live) is not so different to manners prevalent in English or American suburbs.

There is no need to detail the singular dominance of consumerism over the styles and practices of modern living. In this Australia is like anywhere else in the Western world. The new materialism has successfully replaced the patriarchal bias of British cultural forms,[13] and ensured that if the egalitarian-mateship ethic survives it does so amongst families drinking beer and wine around a suburban garden barbecue.

However, in the face of the modern tide surging towards uniformity the native scepticism may have shown some resistance. It is true that Lawson's characters are no more than echoes from the past, the hardship and sombreness of scratching a subsistence living in the wild bush having given way to the comfort of consumer affluence. Moreover, very few take the path of Monk O'Neill, in retreat from humanity. But scepticism did somehow enter the blood, making Australia an extraordinarily secular society, and Australians extremely doubtful about the pursuit of any holy grail, extremely casual in their approach to things.

We should not overemphasize the inheritance from the past. Consumerism breeds its own scepticism, which would have reinforced while somewhat redirecting the generic trait in the local culture. In the first place consumerism's own material values truly command only those in physical need: advanced industrial economies as they have become more successful in satisfying physical need, and providing circuses to counter boredom, have undermined their own ultimate consumer values, of more quantity and more choice. The law of diminishing marginal returns in pleasure applies acutely beyond a certain level of affluence. Consumerism thus creates a scepticism about its own driving values.

In reciprocation the indigenous Australian scepticism has served to accentuate the distance of the average individual from consumer values. Australians have believed less than Americans in the virtues of a successful career and its material rewards, and they have generally been less carried away by the introduction of new appliances on the market.[14] In short they have been less enthused by visions of the materialist utopia, while at the same time remaining largely indifferent to other possible paths to salvation.[15]

Consumerism breeds scepticism at another level. The attainment of relative physical comfort with a high degree of individual mobility and choice seems to lessen the allure of metaphysical goals, whether religious, aesthetic or political. The longing for the infinite is subdued by abundance. The opulent breast of consumerism nourishes a general scepticism about charged beliefs and grand ambitions. At its most dismal the modern mode of scepticism is given voice in the play, *Don's Party*.

The scepticism nourished by a consumer style of life is in danger of becoming lethargic, rather in the manner of the obese man who two hours after his latest feast thinks to himself as he stirs slightly in his deep armchair that over-eating is bad for him, but then recognizes as he sighs with repletion that he will continue in his gluttony, for he has little else to absorb him, and certainly not to the degree of driving him out into the cold on a night like this – eating at least brings him some pleasure. The scepticism of Monk O'Neill and even Joe Wilson is by contrast dynamic, displaying a seriousness about the human predicament: both men keep up the eternal struggle to accommodate the realities of living to the grand expectations fostered by human ideals, consoling themselves with their scepticism for their inability to narrow the distance. When they become resigned there still remains a resistance to how things have turned out. They are not in danger of becoming lethargic; they are not comfortable. It will be a loss if, as seems likely, the typical Australian sheds his bitterly irreverent or Monkish skin and emerges as a full-blooded consumer.

11 Authority and the teacher

Education is the point at which we decide whether we love the world enough to assume responsibility for it and by the same token save it from the ruin which, except for renewal, except for the coming of the new and young, would be inevitable. And education, too, is where we decide whether we love our children enough not to expel them from our world and leave them to their own devices, nor to strike from their hands their chance of undertaking something new, something unforeseen by us, but to prepare them in advance for the task of renewing a common world.

Hannah Arendt, 'The Crisis in Education',
Between Past and Future

To become responsible adults, children must be made familiar with where they live and how that place came into being; with the challenges, the triumphs and the failures of their ancestors; with what is good and worth preserving in the world they inherit. They must come to recognize that they do inherit. They must also learn, as Plato stressed, to discipline their desires, above all to harness their pleasures to what is virtuous (*Law*: Book II). The virtuous will have as its leading command what is good for the society. About education we cannot afford to be sceptical, although we may teach scepticism.

Educational theory in the twentieth century has come increasingly under the influence of the Romantic view that the first task of schooling is to bring out the child's latent personality. More specifically it has seen the child as an autonomous being who needs the teacher more as a solicitous friend than an authoritative father, to give advice rather than instruction. This perspective is founded on a number of fallacies, that there is a dichotomy between being and doing, and virtue resides with those who 'be'; that children are inherently secure in the world and do not need fathers, either to protect them from harm or to inspire their interests; that integration into a community larger than the child at play with itself is fairly unimportant, and in any case readily achieved.

That we can even doubt that education must by its nature be based on authority, the authority of the teacher and of the tradition he passes on, is indicative of the demoralization of our culture. The Western tradition, notably since Plato on one flank and the Old Testament prophets on the other, has taken that authority for granted. As education starts to fail we begin to forget, and one of the first things we forget is the nature and importance of education itself. Any serious discussion of education today must take as its point of departure the problem of authority. In this essay I shall open with an examination of the necessity for authority in education, move on to the sources of that authority, and finish by glancing at why that authority has failed, why our culture is becoming demoralized. This essay aims to clarify the ideal educational relationship, an ideal that it claims has become obscured. There is no assumption here that the ideal, which ought to guide all our thoughts on educational reform, might ever be put into widespread practice.

Authority is necessary in education because students crave it – that is one side of the equation. Authority is equally necessary from the other side, that of the educational process itself: schooling depends on authority. The craving for authority, especially in children and adolescents, is endemic; it must be satisfied if the child is to develop into a relatively sane adult. Whether, on the other side, education is authoritative, whether it is capable of satisfying the craving, depends on the state of the culture, on how the society at large views itself, its past and its future. I shall postpone discussion of the culture's authority and devote attention first of all to the universal longing for authority.

All men to a greater or lesser degree long for authority. In Freud's imagery it is a yearning to recapture the security and tenderness experienced in early childhood under the protection of parental authority. Such longing may of course take a malign form, destructive to the individual and to his society, in the case, for example, of it being attracted to imperial or totalitarian politics. But, by and large, it is a constructive drive whose satisfactory expression is necessary for the development of the mature person. When this drive is success-fully exploited in schools and universities, continuing the experience of family authority, then it is very unlikely to take a pernicious form in adult life.

A student learns best when the classroom is governed by the covert laws of authority, mirroring the early family. Such authority has nothing to do with authoritarianism, which is a rigid outer shell of punitive constraints disguising a lack of inner confidence. Likewise the mechanical discipline that may be appropriate to the army does not provide a model of authority suitable for learning. The class-room must provide the security in which the child can relax, release himself to the influence of the teacher, and through the intensity of this relationship experiment with his own latent potential. He must, that is, cast himself into the stream of his own character develop-ment. The dominant mood of the classroom must be reverence and tenderness rather than competition. For all of this to happen the teacher needs authority, needs a commanding presence; he must become the benevolent father with whom the child is driven to identify.

The master-apprentice model of education is the only viable one. There are roughly four levels at which its advantages demonstrate themselves. First, a child's curiosity, his interest, his enthusiasm for learning is not something that flourishes in a vacuum; it needs arousing. It is the parents who play the major role in infecting their child with interest in the world around him. The teacher takes over this role in the classroom. His enthusiasms, if he has authority, will prove contagious. If he lacks authority the child is left restless and bored. To a large degree what happens psychologically in the ideal classroom is that the child introjects the teacher's passions. Freud, reflecting on his own schooldays, wrote: 'in many of us the path to the sciences led only through our teachers'. The introjection at work here is a type of identification, living off the passion to be like the master.

The second gain in the classroom that is governed by covert authority is that the children do not waste their energy either in hostility or indifference to the teacher and a situation that is potentially constraining. When hostile they will be restless and prickly, when indifferent restless and bored; in either case they are unlikely to learn much. In other words, when the teacher has authority the forces of rebellion and dissent in the student are held in abeyance. Moreover, in the presence of an authoritative teacher students are likely to be less competitive amongst themselves; strong paternal attachment reduces sibling rivalry and envy. Absorbed by the relationship to the father-teacher, involved in the tasks he commands, there is less energy and attention available for worrying about what the next student is doing – that is unless the master unduly favours one son over the others.

The third gain from authoritative teaching relates to method. It is largely through imitating the teacher's method of setting up and approaching problems, his technique of thinking, his style of rigour, that the student himself starts to develop these skills. This process is the more obvious in the teaching of manual skills. For the child to want to imitate there must be identification, he must have vested his teacher in the cloak of authority. More generally, a sense of vocation itself is passed on in such a manner. I shall return below to the other side of the educational relationship, the fact that the type of vocation that attracts the child, the kind of techniques he feels drawn to develop, depend as much on his own character and its unrealized potentials as on the orientation of the authoritative teacher.

Education has a fourth function, which again depends on authority in the classroom for its fulfilment. Certainly in the humanities, knowledge itself is introjected (I leave aside the case of the natural sciences, which is more complicated because of the quite different relationship of the student to its theories). A child learns not only lines from the poems and plays that his teacher recommends. He takes also by impassioned imitation much of his understanding of themes and characters, many of his judgments, associations, images, and ideals. They lodge in his mind as traces of theory, as types of rhythm like a line from Shakespeare, often waiting there in a kind of cold storage until the child's experience of life can catch up and test them out. When the experience is rich enough to meet these introjected traces of explanation many will be rejected, some will be adapted, and some will be integrated into the person's developing view of the world, a view that in the mature adult comes more or less into harmony with how the person experiences the world. The growing child, particularly in adolescence, needs this matrix of intellectual connections and directions to order his experience, experience that otherwise would prove too threateningly chaotic to be faced. The development of the sane adult depends on a vital and sustained interaction between theories about the human condition (including religious, scientific and common-sense theories) and experience of it. The teacher plays a crucial role in contributing theories.

The teacher whose teaching is introjected is taken as an exemplar in the field of understanding. His authority is even more widely based when as often happens in the humanities and social sciences personal knowledge is involved. The class that discusses the great metaphysical questions of how to live and what to do – and all work in the humanities indirectly involves these questions – becomes more personal. It examines not just facts, and the interpretation of facts, but experience. The teacher will inevitably in part become an exemplar in how to live – how to experience and what to make of that experience. Then not only his knowledge but also his style will be introjected by his students.

But what of the critical method, what of rationality, what of independence of mind and judgment, what of objectivity, in this highly personalized relationship of student to teacher? In today's educational climate in particular it must be stressed that the ideal relationship is not personal in the sense of the teacher taking an interest in the individual personality of a student; his concern ought to be with his own discipline, with thought and knowledge, and how to communicate it. Moreover, the critical method is passed on primarily in the same manner as everything else, by introjection on the part of the student. The student imitates it as a style, as a method of thinking. Plato's dialogues make it clear that Socrates passed on his method not primarily because it was effective, but because *he* had authority; his method did turn out to be effective, which was in turn one of the reasons for his authority.

We have talked loosely about introjection. In fact the process of identification has its complexities. Freud outlined in his *Group Psychology* two different types of identification, making a distinction that has some significance for our investigation. The first type of identification involves the subject projecting his ego-ideal onto the figure of authority, that figure then serving as a substitute for some of the individual's unrealized ideals. In this case, Freud suggests, the subject humbles himself and idealizes the authority figure, a situation to be observed in the case of hypnosis, of love in which there is sexual overvaluation, and of mass politics in which the crowd is inspired by a charismatic leader. This form of identification inhibits character development; it is symptomatic of a fear of responsibility and a lack of self-confidence.

The second type of identification involves introjection of the object, and is most strikingly manifest in infancy and early childhood. It is identification of this sort that I have been associating with the ideal classroom. The child, however, does not introject indiscriminately and he does not introject the whole teacher. The child has many latent capacities and he is drawn to adults who have those same capacities in a developed form. He is drawn to mature qualities in the teacher that correspond to undeveloped parts of his own personality. Thus it is only certain aspects of the teacher that are introjected, those that are needed. In choosing what is needed projection is involved. The student projects on to his teacher the potentialities that he yearns to develop, and then takes back into himself as part of his own identity their realized embodiments. The student in effect loves his own potential, in its developed state, in the teacher. A form of narcissism is at work, giving the child confidence for the long and difficult undertaking of growing up, and giving shape to that undertaking. Susan Isaacs, a pioneering psychoanalytical educationist, wrote: 'The teacher cannot do her work well unless she attracts to herself mainly the forces of love.' The decisive love as far as the child's maturing is concerned is love based on selective projection. The identification differs from Freud's first type in that it is not the child's ego-ideal that is projected. What is projected is a net of wishes, or enthusiasms, concerning what the child would like to become, intertwined with his untested abilities, talents, and capacities. The ego-ideal may also be present, but in a subsidiary role, and encouraging the more deeply-rooted elements of character on stage; above all it is not a daunting and impossible ideal that is projected.

We have been discussing the best of all possible educational worlds. In reality there may be identification of the first type, involving projection of an impossible or unrealizable ego-ideal. As much as this happens the educational process will break down. The vital bond between teacher and student, working on the student's embryonic character, becomes inverted producing an idealization of the teacher and a regression by the student to a state of infantile dependency. There is dependency whenever there is authority; but in the case of introjective identification the dependency is a transitional state allowing the student latitude in which to develop to a point at which he no longer needs his teacher's authority. Once he himself has fully developed the qualities of the teacher with which he identified, that identification loses all purpose, and drops away. The weaning from authority, like the other earlier and equally decisive weaning, from the mother's breast, takes place naturally.

We have observed that the longing for authority in the classroom is ideally more than a longing for security. It carries the need for security in order for the child to be at ease enough to let his own embryonic character experiment with asserting itself. It is a longing in the child both for security and to gain the authority himself that he identifies with. The longing to become authoritative includes a range of elements: a desire to be competent, to be able to act decisively and effectively, to control the person's own destiny and the forces that threaten it. It is in part a longing for vocation. A vocation is one of the surest repositories of authority, involving work that commands obedience to its ends, that compels him who is called to it. Moreover, the process of learning a vocation, assuming that the particular student has chosen a type of work appropriate to his talents and interests, is the most secure and well-defined path along which to progress towards maturity. For the path to vocation is protected and invested with purpose by the authoritative master. (The second path to inner authority is that private one of personal intimacy; it is usually a more hazardous path and one over which there are fewer rules.) It should also be noted that the master-apprentice model for the passing on of faith and competence applies not only to academic fields taught in schools and universities; it also applies to the professions, business, and the trades and crafts.

Most of the reform movements in twentieth-century education, and the literature that has influenced them, have unwittingly taken the model of the authoritative classroom as their basis, and at the same time claimed that they were doing away with authority and replacing it with a democratic relationship between teacher and child. The ideal has been of the teacher serving as an aid and companion in a community of equals. The example of A. S. Neill and his school, Summerhill, stands as sufficient demonstration of the hypocrisy of modern progressive education. The freedom that children experienced at Summerhill was a direct consequence of the security they felt in a school run by a man whom they regarded as a great father. It is hard to imagine a headmaster with more authority. Neill's own presence made his children feel so much at home that they could dare to be adventurous in their school life. Such a teaching situation cannot be replicated without charismatic teachers. Moreover, without authoritative teachers the child's longing for authority will be frustrated, producing aimlessness, depression, rebellion, and perhaps malign identifications with authoritarian figures.

We have considered the necessity for authority in education. The next logical consideration is the sources of that authority, and where they might lie. The question poses itself, where can a teacher draw his authority from today? The answer will depend, as always, on what type of a teacher he is. If his style is that of the visionary, inspired by his own morally charged view of the world, then he will be his own source of authority, at least for those who find him compelling. The question about the visionary teacher, in any age, is whether his enthusiasms will help his students to take a meaningful responsibility for the world they inherit, and for its renewal, or whether they will detach them from it by seducing them with mysticism or ideology.

Let us discount as unimportant to the future of our educational institutions those with private religious visions. There remains another type of visionary, he who is inspired by elements within his society, and aspects of its history that he considers worthy, elements that must be preserved and nourished for the sake of the future.

The past is significant for three reasons. The first is one of understanding: to know where a society is and where it is most likely going, it is essential to know the path along which it has travelled. The second reason is more elemental, or cosmological: it is an essential part of the human condition for man to recognize that he is a creature on the earth, subject to the forces of nature, which include the forces of birth, reproduction, and death, that he is a link in a long chain of generations, tied by its blood and its traditions, a key link with a responsibility to continue the chain in a worthy manner.

The third reason for the significance of the past is a specific instance of the second: it concerns foundation. The sense of belonging to the great chain of generations roots man in the general human condition. To be rooted in the specific traditions of his own society and its culture means that he must have a sense of the legitimacy of those traditions; he must believe that they are important and command respect because of the virtuous acts and the noble intentions that they represent. His own society and its foundation must have authority for him.

When the past has authority for the teacher then he will necessarily communicate the weight of that past to his students. His own reverence will be contagious. Thus he fulfils his role, teaching the past and teaching a respect for the human condition itself, a respect for, as Heidegger put it, man's place on the earth, under the heavens, amongst mortals, and before the divine. His teaching will itself be a lesson in responsibility, connecting the child to his society, helping him to gain some distance from the embrace of his own family. However, when the past does not have authority there is no ground for respect, and education loses its sense.

Education, as Hannah Arendt has pointed out, is of its nature conservative. It roots the child in his society, and does this above all by teaching its past and its customs. Even schools in countries that claim to be revolutionary teach the revolutionary *tradition*; the existence of education in itself indicates that the revolution has become established. Education prepares the child for an adulthood in which he may choose to change things, and it may even suggest possible choices. But his preferred changes will be chosen from understanding; his approach to the faults of the existing order will be with Burke's mood of 'pious awe and trembling solicitude'. Plato, in his last work, the *Laws*, defined education as 'the drawing and leading of children to the rule which has been pronounced right by the voice of law, and appeared as truly right by the concordant experience of the best and oldest men'. The definition sounds anachronistic only to those who have become mindless of the importance of order. While we do not today respect our old men as Plato would have hoped, his reference is more generally to the wisdom of the past. We are served in this regard by our books, by for instance the Western classics of social and political theory, including the work of Plato himself. Plato's reference to the best and oldest men does, however, sound a warning to a society that is unsure whom its elders ought to be, whom it ought to refer to for advice. Our problem is exactly the one that Plato addressed in his late comments on education: to select those who have a good sense of what in the past and the present ought to be conserved, and to vest in them the authority to legislate and to teach.

Today in the West there are but a few visionaries whose teaching is grounded in the authority of the past, who are called by a responsibility framed by the virtuous achievements of their forefathers to pass on to the next generation a sense of mission, of obligation, and thereby a sense of belonging. These teachers depend by and large on private inspiration, on enthusiasm drawn from their own private pasts, usually that of their own families. Moreover, they receive little support from the culture in whose schools they teach. They keep education alive in the few good schools that survive, and while this remains the case there is some hope for the future, morally speaking, of our culture.

The contemporary teacher usually finds himself without a strong sense of vocation and consequently without authority in the classroom. To pose now the question of why his authority has failed is to ask the more general question of why the authority of Western culture itself is in doubt, why the teacher finds himself with little enthusiasm for passing on anything. This is not the place to entertain a general theory of Western culture in the twentieth century. However, there may be merit in sketching the outlines of failure in the case of education, and inquiring about its sources.

The leading symptom of the failure is the difficulty the teacher has feeling responsible for the society he ought to be preparing the child to enter. The fact that tradition has lost its weight leaves the majority of teachers either depressive, carrying out a job, or paranoid, seeing nothing but evil in a social order that does not hold their respect.

The teacher's failing sense of purpose is essentially to do with the want of an ultimate public value. Following the secularization of Western society, and the corresponding loss of spiritual salvation as a commanding goal, the humanist and nationalist ideals have also failed to sustain themselves. The humanist ideal was that man through material progress and better education and learning would approach a higher level of civilization; teachers were inspired to work for this end. But the twentieth century has seen a growing disenchantment with the liberal-humanist faith in progress. Similarly the nationalist ideal, that the particular nation and its culture carry with them a great tradition worth preserving above all else, does not look like sustaining itelf in the West. The latest casualty among the upholders of nationalism appears to be the United States.

The folk wisdom that easy living makes men soft is relevant here. In a time of high affluence, with little direct threat of war, men are likely to become careless, absorbed by the daily pursuit of pleasure, indifferent to their community and its traditions. It is difficult to sustain either the humanist or nationalist ideals, let alone religious activity, in times of ease. Affluence is a perverse kind of blessing, bringing with it the disease of impiety. Such different moral teachers as Plato and Buddha both saw man's worst two vices as desire and ignorance. Times of prosperity stimulate desire, and have little need for understanding – that is until their spreading decadence erodes the wealth on which they are founded. When ease continues long enough men stop striving to better themselves spiritually, and eventually materially also. Thus education loses most of its rationale. However, there are cycles in most things, and necessity inevitably returns in one form or another. Necessity sets specific goals and it likely enforces discipline, and the need for differentiating talents and using them efficiently. Or it forces the reluctant individual into religious withdrawal. In either case education regains its importance.

The notable characteristic of modern Western affluence is consumerism, a way of life with its own innate resistance to the foundations of education. The consumer culture fosters a psychology of easy gratification, of treating any anxiety or threat of boredom with the search for a new pleasure. Such a psychology makes it difficult for an individual to develop resources of self-control, of concentration and inner discipline. Students from such a cultural background are likely to resent a teacher who sets them demanding tasks, who requires their patience, their perseverance, their rigour in application to their studies.

Moreover, there is no role for responsibility in consuming: the single reflex is for more. The pressure is on schools to turn into playgrounds. And why not, for the worthy deeds of the founding fathers, of the Cromwells and Lincolns, have no relevance to the consumer style in modern culture. The educator's problem then becomes both for himself and for his students, responsible for what?

The foundations of education have been assaulted from another quarter in modern culture. The tendency towards cultural democracy has generated a bad conscience about stressing differences that exist between talents and between achievements. The cultural democrats have wanted to downplay the singular virtue of those who create things of extraordinary beauty or technical accomplishment. Indeed our own high culture has come into bad odour because its values are ruthlessly discriminating: it respects only talent, and even more restrictively talent that has been demonstrated. One of the tasks of schools is to pass on high culture, and to train some of their more able students for entry into that culture's apprenticeship. In this, schools need to select out those with exceptional gifts. There is another close tie between education and high culture that makes contemporary cultural democrats hostile to its fundamental principles. Schooling is itself medieval in its dependency on hierarchy and the undisputed authority of the teacher. Schooling is of its essence undemocratic. One of the consequences of the democratic bad conscience is that educational reform has come to focus in the end on spending more money; it has evaded the one issue of importance to the improvement of education, that is getting better teachers. Where have been the debates about what is happening within the teachers' colleges, and the means employed for selecting trainee teachers? Such debates would cross the forbidden line into comparative questions, of the competence of different teachers, their authority, and the content of what they are teaching.

Teaching has been a peculiarly testing vocation in any time. The teacher has often had to contend with large and disorderly classes, containing children from backgrounds in which their imagination has received no stimulus, and they have learnt neither patience nor concentration. The teacher has needed many resources to make his classroom more than a child-minding penitentiary. Another universal challenge has been that much of teaching, certainly to younger children, involves rote learning. It takes exceptional skill to make the learning of the rudiments of grammar, for instance, more than drudgery for both teacher and child.

Today the ordinary teacher has not merely the traditional challenges threatening his morale. He has had many of the props that would have supported earlier generations removed. The rules of the classroom, the definiteness of the syllabus, and the authority that a teacher had simply by virtue of his position, are supports that are all under threat. So it is little wonder that recently many teachers have been attracted by radical politics and revolutionary theories of education, and that many of the rest have simply given up. While the educational ideal elaborated in this essay does not favour that sort of traditional classroom in which authority was a milder version of that of the penitentiary, it is probably the case that a strict but dull classroom is a lesser evil than an unruly one.

Early in our discussion we opposed the Romantic view that the task of education is to develop the child's latent personality.

However, we observed through examining the child's longing for authority and how it worked itself out in the ideal classroom that such development was indeed central to the schooling process. There is a decisive difference. Personal development is not a *task* of education; it is an accompaniment whose progress helps the true task of education. Moreover, if schooling is successful then development is also likely to be successful (although there are numerous exceptions, of well-educated but emotionally retarded children, and of those with a bad record at school who turn into dynamic, strong-minded and moral adults). The task of education is learning and its methods, the preparation of the child's mind for his life as an adult. It is only indirectly that it improves the child's character, as a kind of prize that a teacher earns in recognition of his particularly successful work – that prize is of vital importance to the child. The authority of the successful teacher is based on his ability to interest students in his discipline; it does not depend on whether he is a competent therapist or moral guardian.

The teacher is not a moral guardian in the sense of looking after the personal well-being of his individual pupils. He is a moral guardian in the different sense of having the responsibility to teach his students the eternal truths of the human condition, to acquaint them with the beauty, the wisdom and the virtue available to man if he hears their call, and to impress upon them that they belong to a cultural tradition with a worthy past, a tradition whose future will depend on them. This is what Plato meant when he stressed again and again that the task of the teacher is to teach virtue.

12 Confessional sceptical afterthought

Is it possible at one and the same time to take up the doubting pose and remain moralistic? Can the sceptic be a moralist? Moreover, because the sceptic gets much of his pleasure from pointing out the inconsistencies of others, from getting a good laugh out of the contradictions across which his more naive brethren stumble through life, should he not himself be scrupulous in the consistency of his thought and action? He is in a difficult position, for what is his scepticism if not to a large degree his defence against his own moral fervour and his own certitudes, overconfident responses to his world that his reason tells him he ought to be ashamed of? His reason tells him to be sceptical. But his disposition is moral, that is not at all doubting. Thus he either becomes fervid in his scepticism or gains some release from this conflict by telling jokes about the foibles of others and becoming ironical about himself. Whatever his final behaviour he is riddled with inconsistency. What then is left of his dignity?

I have been moralistic, for instance about motor cars, tourism and above all education. I have attempted to lay out a method and apply it. Most importantly my work, like anyone else's, has its own singular moral tone, reflecting the disposition of the writer. On the other hand I have been sceptical about some of sociology's pre-conditioning morals. I have neglected most of the methods that have been standard within the discipline since 1918. I have been irreverent towards intellectuals. I have tried at times to be light-hearted; and I have asserted that our knowledge is a toothless old tramp. Overall I have been motivated out of a disenchantment with sociology rather than a desire to disenchant the world. One might conclude that the scepticism has been at best partial, at worst a hypocritical veneer.

I wish to end with an attack on scepticism, and not in order to be contrary, or sceptical to the last. Scepticism is a disease. Man is a moral animal. His morale keeps him alive. If his morale is high he has everything, whatever might happen to him. Then there is the other side of morality: the best man is the good man. Now if one were in the position of Noah, having to select those who would best contribute to the future of the human species, then one would choose the good man and the man of high morale long before one would choose the wisest sceptic.

The most powerful of modern scepticisms, psychoanalysis, has one glaring weakness, that it provides no basis for morality. It understands virtually everything about human motivation, including the reasons why we become addicted to morality. But it leaves us no commands about what to do and how to live. It has little time for human dignity outside the realm of the intellectual's command, to know thyself. Its blind spot is that human dignity by and large resides with men who are good. It realizes that men do not live by bread alone, yet hints that it would prefer that they did. As Philip Rieff has pointed out, its irreverence towards saints and sinners, heroes and cowards, is in danger of leaving the whole world disenchanted.

In reality intellectual activity has no direct relationship to virtue. Consequently if we wish to improve its style we do not have to concern ourselves about whether we are helping the forces of good. My own ambition in this book has been to sweep a corner of the stables, hoping to clear the air a bit and make the stables a more attractive and interesting place to inhabit. I would not want them too clean, for I am reminded that a serious concern with cleanliness precludes a sense of humour. If good men were finally to walk into my freshened stables I would be overjoyed. But I would be surprised. In the main this has been an aesthetic enterprise, and the fact that moralisms have crept in at times is subsidiary. That is my confession. It is a shameful confession for it is a far more serious problem for us in the West that our morale is low than that our taste is going off. Also aesthetes are effetely narcissistic characters who do not like to dirty their hands, and spend their lives clowning around, juggling their stock of ideas and selecting from their wardrobe of poses.

I opened this book with lots of steam, or so it seemed from the seat of the writer, with lots of criticisms of sociological practice since 1918, and lots of prescriptions for the revolution. In a rough sort of fashion it is true that I have tried to put those commands into practice in the intervening essays. However, it would be more honest to admit that what I have done is to pursue a few subjects that caught my fancy, or that have been on my mind in recent years. And so what: ought not sociology, first and foremost, to be the attempt by each of us to understand the society in which he finds himself?

Let us remember the tourist to the last, those of us who suffer from that agitation of the spirit, the compulsion to know. His lifestyle – what drives him, how he behaves, the assumptions he makes at the end of the day, his hopes and his sense of achievement – is very similar to our own. I am thinking of that smart tourist who in travelling in a foreign country learns a smattering of the local language, and thinks because he knows enough to buy potatoes and cheese that he is fluent.

Notes

6 The soap fetish

1 A sample of thirty separate hours of evening television between 7.30 p.m. and 9.30 p.m. were recorded. Ten hours of afternoon television were sampled.

2 This is a very crude estimate taken from the Australian Consumer Price Index, which does not differentiate enough for accuracy. 5 per cent of consumption expenditure is taken up by two general categories: 'Health and Personal Care' (pharmaceuticals, toiletries, cosmetics) and 'Household Supplies and Services' (cleaning agents and paper products, garden supplies, pet food, travel goods, house insurance, repairs). I have taken one-fifth as an estimate of the soap component.

3 Other related figures for 1977 in Australia are that Colgate spent approximately 6 per cent of its turnover on advertising, and that roughly 5 per cent of the retail price paid for soap is advertising cost.

4 That this is the case was dramatically confirmed by an experiment conducted in Britain following a Monopolies Commission enquiry in 1966. Both the large companies in Britain agreed to market a detergent at 20 per cent reduced price by cutting all promotions and heavily cutting the advertising budget. In both cases the significantly cheaper detergent rapidly lost ground to its advertised equivalents.

5 Valerie Lawson, 'How the Soap Boys Handled the TPC', *Financial Review*, Australia, 8 September 1977, pp. 2–3, 30. Although the Commission conducted its findings *in camera* its report was leaked to the *Financial Review*.

6 Mary Douglas, *Purity and Danger*, Routledge & Kegan Paul, London, 1966.

7 Norman Brown, *Life Against Death*, Routledge & Kegan Paul, London, 1959, ch. 13.

8 Mary Lutyens, *Effie in Venice, Unpublished letters of Mrs John Ruskin written from Venice between 1849–1852*, Murray, London, 1965, pp. 20–1.

9 Vance Packard, *The Hidden Persuaders*, Penguin, Harmondsworth, 1962, p. 79.

10 Quentin Crisp, *How to Have a Life-Style*, Woolf, London, 1975, pp. 138–40.

11 Melanie Klein, *The Psycho-Analysis of Children*, Hogarth, London, 1949, p. 281, n. 1 and p. 287.
12 Anthony Storr, *Sexual Deviation*, Penguin, Harmondsworth, 1964.
13 Here, as elsewhere, there may also be other motives at work. For instance some women buy mild detergents because they believe their clothes are made from delicate fabrics, and are therefore superior to the coarse cloths worn by those of lower social stations.
14 For an extended psychoanalytical discussion of masochism see Theodor Reik, *Masochism in Sex and Society*, Pyramid, New York, 1976.
15 Otto Fenichel, *The Psychoanalytic Theory of Neurosis*, Routledge & Kegan Paul, London, 1946, p. 198.
16 Ibid., p. 200.
17 It was a related discovery of psychoanalysis that obstinate children who refuse to wash are really refusing to give up their pleasurable impulses (ibid., p. 289).
18 Mary Douglas (op. cit.) provides numerous examples of different beliefs about impurity and vice in different religions.
19 Walter E. Houghton, *The Victorian Frame of Mind*, Yale University Press, New Haven, 1957, p. 368.
20 Theodor Reik, *Myth and Guilt*, Grosset & Dunlap, New York, 1970. The linking of guilt with civilization, apart from various hints in earlier theological writings, was originally Nietzsche's.

7 Automobile culture and citizenship

1 Emma Rothschild, *Paradise Lost: the Decline of the Auto-industrial Age*, London, Allen Lane, 1974.
2 For example, Rothschild, op. cit.

8 The tourist

1 'Ferien '78: "Ik bünn all dor!" ', *Der Spiegel*, 33, 1978.
2 Daniel J. Boorstin, *The Image*, Atheneum, New York, 1962.
3 Dean MacCannell, 'Staged Authenticity: Arrangements of Social Space in Tourist Settings', *American Journal of Sociology*, 79, November 1973.

9 On homecoming, or man's tyranny over space

1 Cf. George Simmel, 'The Ruin', included in *Essays on Society, Philosophy and Aesthetics*, ed. Kurt Wolff, Ohio State University Press, 1959.
2 To reach any greater precision in answering the question of how universal, or how culturally relative, the projection of authority fantasies are to cathedrals, would require a study all of its own. Marjorie Hope Nicolson, in her book *Mountain Gloom and Mountain Glory* (Norton, New York, 1963), provides evidence that would help to answer this question in the partly analogous case of mountains. In particular, she illustrates the transformation from the seventeenth to the eighteenth

century of the way in which men looked at mountains. In the earlier period these outstanding natural phenomena were viewed as examples of the degeneration of the earth from the perfect sphere, a degeneration initiated by Adam's sin, and continued by the flood. Poets referred to them as signs of the earth being a garment growing old; Donne described them as warts. By the next century these cankers had become symbols of the eternal and the infinite, of the wild grandeur of nature, incentives to the most sublime of human strivings. In short, mountains were transformed from places noted for their alienness to places where Romantic poets felt more at home than anywhere else. These new homes were sublime. To answer whether or not the Romantic viewing has a universal element requires a lot of further discussion: it does, however, seem that it was a strong cultural factor (theological belief in the progressive degradation of man's earth) that was responsible for the earlier hostility to mountains.

3   Walter Pater, *Miscellaneous Studies, Works*, vol. 8, Macmillan, London, 1901.

4   Incidentally, the building of Amiens, begun in 1220, roughly coincides with the European origins of the myth of Romantic love.

5   Edward T. Hall, *The Hidden Dimension*, Bodley Head, London, 1966, p. 62. This is a fine book in the field of environmental psychology.

6   The territorial limits that surround each individual are defended by the familiar home. The flirt is one means of breaking this cocoon of segregated space. The crowd is another, as Elias Canetti has illustrated at length, in his book *Crowds and Power* (Gollancz, London, 1962).

7   Martin Heidegger, in his 1943 meditation, *Heimkunft*, on Hölderlin's poem of that name, 'Homecoming', writes that 'all the poems of the poet who has entered into his poethood, are poems of homecoming'. Heidegger continues that the poet's principal return home occurs in the writing itself, that is where he finds joy. For the people, there is a homecoming too, in that poem, for as long as its message still sounds.

10   The sceptic turns consumer: an outline of Australian culture

1   One important institution that was not derived from a British precedent was the Conciliation and Arbitration Commission. The obvious case of a significantly adapted institution is Federal Parliament, the establishment of which took elements from the United States example: a written Constitution and a Senate.

2   Nineteenth-century Melbourne, in particular, benefited from the Scottish influence. For instance, it was hardly more than a small town when in 1854 its university was founded – four years earlier Melbourne's population was a mere 23,000.

3   The most systematic and influential modern version was Russel Ward's *The Australian Legend* (Oxford University Press, Melbourne, 1958). Ward in part covers himself by claiming that he has written a history of a legend about Australia, leaving aside whether the legend mirrors the

social reality in Australia. However, his account is full of suggestions and inferences that Australia is like its legend. In any case my objection here is about the legend itself: that the egalitarian-mateship ethic, the core of the legend, has little to do with singularly Australian experiences of convicts, bushmen, gold-diggers, and so on.

4 For an account of its genealogy, and a critique of the empirical research on which it has been based, see R. W. Connell, 'Images of Australia', *Quadrant*, vol. 12, March–April 1968.

5 Early Australian literature was aggressive in its assertion of these values (for example, Lawson, Furphy, Patterson, Steele Rudd, and the poems and stories published in *The Bulletin*). The ethic also recurs, although in a more problematic sense, in recent literature (for example, Kenneth Cook: *Wake in Fright*; Allan Seymour: *The One Day of the Year*; Jack Hibberd: *Stretch of the Imagination*).

6 Geoffrey Serle, *The Golden Age*, Melbourne University Press, 1963, p. 374. Serle provides a detailed discussion of migration to Victoria in this period, and speculates on levels of disillusionment (pp. 372–6).

7 W. K. Hancock in his profoundly influential study, *Australia* (Benn, London, 1930), advised all Australians to read Tocqueville's *Democracy in America* in order to make comparisons (p. 269). However, Hancock himself did not see the crucial relevance of Tocqueville, who knew that democracies would in the end pursue the equality of enjoyment rather than the equality of opportunity (Hancock, pp. 183, 269–70).

8 See Chris Wallace Crabbe, 'Lawson's *Joe Wilson*: A Skeleton Novel', included in *Melbourne or the Bush*, Angus & Robertson, Sydney, 1974.

9 Roger Fair states in his introduction to *A Treasury of Anzac Humour* (Jacaranda, Brisbane, 1965), which he edited, that Gallipoli gave him the happiest days of his life. There were two things above all that he valued, the comradeship and the humour of the soldiers.

10. *Australian Walkabout*, Landsdowne, Melbourne, 1968.

11 Keith Dunstan tells the full story (*Knockers*, Cassell, Melbourne, 1972, pp. 295–301), and he provides many other examples of attempts to cut down the tall poppies.

12 Bill Wannon finds the origins of the main stream of Australian humour in the jests and street ballads of London, Glasgow and Dublin in the latter part of the eighteenth century (*A Treasury of Australian Humour*, Landsdowne, Melbourne, 1960, p. 16).

13 See, for example, Stuart Ewen, *Captains of Consciousness*, McGraw-Hill, New York, 1976.

14 The sense of failure that Studs Terkel found most Americans suffering from in relation to their work would not be mirrored in Australia to nearly the same intensity (*Working*, Pantheon, New York, 1974).

15 It is worth reflecting for a moment on the version of the modernization thesis, prominent in sociology since the nineteenth century, and revitalized in the middle of the twentieth century by Talcott Parsons, that traces a single path of evolution from pre-capitalist community to modern Western society. This evolution is characterized by the secularization of values on the one hand and industrial and technological

progress on the other. Apart from the historical implausibility of the thesis it does not even work for modern societies. Within the Anglo-Saxon countries modernization is a process with a central schism. Australia (like Britain) by comparison with the United States is more modern along one axis, being highly secular and sceptical. Along the other axis, that of technological and economic progress, the United States leads the world. Indeed it is the survival of the Puritan religious influence in the United States that underpins a continuing economic predominance. One attempt, by Lipset, to explore Parsons's modernization thesis in the cases of Australia, Canada, the United Kingdom and the United States, besides its other faults, misses the key difference between Australia and the United States (Seymour Martin Lipset, *The First New Nation: The United States in Historical and Comparative Perspective*, Basic Books, New York, 1963).